It's
Christmas!

Chicken Soup for the Soul: It's Christmas!
101 Joyful Stories about the Love, Fun, and Wonder of the Holidays
Jack Canfield, Mark Victor Hansen, Amy Newmark
Published by Chicken Soup for the Soul Publishing, LLC www.chickensoup.com

The publisher gratefully acknowledges the many publishers and individuals who granted Chicken Soup for the Soul permission to reprint the cited material.

Front cover photo courtesy of iStockPhoto.com/friztin (© friztin). Back cover photo and and interior photos courtesy of Photos.com.

Cover and Interior Design & Layout by Brian Taylor, Pneuma Books, LLC

Distributed to the booktrade by Simon & Schuster. SAN: 200-2442

Publisher's Cataloging-in-Publication Data
(Prepared by The Donohue Group)

Chicken soup for the soul : it's Christmas! : 101 joyful stories about
  the love, fun, and wonder of the holidays / [compiled by] Jack
  Canfield, Mark Victor Hansen, [and] Amy Newmark.

    p. : ill. ; cm.

  ISBN: 978-1-61159-925-1

  1. Christmas--Literary collections. 2. Christmas--Anecdotes. 3. Anecdotes. I.
Canfield, Jack, 1944- II. Hansen, Mark Victor. III. Newmark, Amy. IV. Title: It's
Christmas! : 101 joyful stories about the love, fun, and wonder of the holidays

PN6071.C6 C452 2013
810.8/02/03942663   2013937412

PRINTED IN THE UNITED STATES OF AMERICA
on acid∞free paper

22 21 20 19 18 17 16 15 14 13   01 02 03 04 05 06 07 08 09 10

Chicken Soup for the Soul

for the Soul®

It's Christmas!

101 Joyful Stories about the Love, Fun, and Wonder of the Holidays

Jack Canfield, Mark Victor Hansen and Amy Newmark

Chicken Soup for the Soul Publishing, LLC
Cos Cob, CT

Chicken Soup for the Soul

www.chickensoup.com

Contents

❸

~Santa's Elves~

❹

~From the Mouths of Babes~

5

~Bark! The Herald Angels Sing~

6

~The Naughty List~

7

~A Little Help from My Friends~

❽

~Holiday Hijinks~

❾

~Bittersweet Christmas~

❿

~Making Memories~

A Note from Santa

Mrs. Claus and I are having so much fun reading our advance copies of *Chicken Soup for the Soul: It's Christmas!* We worked closely with Chicken Soup for the Soul's editors to make sure that this book keeps the magic alive for everyone, including young readers or listeners. We're looking forward to delivering a few of these books ourselves on Christmas Eve, to our friends and relatives. I must say these stories make me look forward to the Christmas season, even though I'll be so busy.

By the time you read this, we'll be in full production mode up at the North Pole: the reindeer will be practicing their landing maneuvers in the simulator that we got after so many of you installed satellite dishes on your roofs; the factory will be running at full speed making toys and dolls and those new electronic devices that I don't really understand; and I will be pretending not to listen as Mrs. Claus tells me once again about the cholesterol in those cookies.

I know that you will all be rushing about too. Everyone loves Christmas and we all want to make it perfect. Remember that it doesn't have to be perfect! Your family won't notice if you use paper plates instead of fine china, or don't clean every last corner of your house, or don't make everything from scratch. What's really important is who's around the table, not what's on it. So take a few minutes each day for yourself and read a story. You deserve a break and we don't want you to overdo it—you need to save enough energy to make my cookies on Christmas Eve, don't you?

It's Christmas!

The True Meaning

*Christmas waves a magic wand over this world,
and behold, everything is softer and more beautiful.*

~Norman Vincent Peale

Something to Give

No one has ever become poor by giving.
~Anne Frank

"I t seems colder than last year," my son, Jordan, said with a smile. One Saturday every December, his Sunday School class volunteered to man the Salvation Army kettle in front of our local grocery store. Jordan and I were assigned the early afternoon shift.

"You're right," I said. "It does seem colder this year."

Jordan and I split the duties evenly. He rang the bell while I passed out candy canes to the children who passed by.

Everyone was so kind to us. The lady who worked at the deli counter brought us hot chocolate. People smiled and wished us a Merry Christmas, whether they donated any money or not. And one man, when I thanked him for his donation, said, "No, thank you. I gave a bit of money, but you're giving your time."

Their kindness made the time fly by, despite the cold.

Shortly before our replacements were due to arrive, a young woman and her little boy passed by. I smiled and offered the boy a candy cane. "Merry Christmas," I said.

The woman looked at me, her eyes full of sadness and defeat. "I'm sorry," she said, "but I don't have anything to give."

Her words brought an instant lump to my throat. Just a few

short years ago, I too had uttered those words. And I'm sure I had the same look in my eyes when I said them.

It happened on Christmas Eve in 2005. Just four days before, my husband had asked me for a divorce. His announcement had been devastating in every sense of the word. I tried desperately to maintain a sense of normalcy for my children's sake. So there I was, walking into my local discount store, hoping to snag a few more presents to go under our tree.

I heard the bell long before I spotted the elderly gentleman ringing it. When he saw me, he smiled and wished me a Merry Christmas. He couldn't have known it, but I'd been barely holding onto my composure. His kindness was my undoing. Tears filled my eyes as I said, "I'm sorry, but I don't have anything to give."

At my tears, his smile faded, but he quickly recovered. "Oh, dear, you've got it all wrong," he said. "We all have something to give."

"I really don't," I said. "You see, my husband..."

"Not all of us are called to give money," he interrupted. "Some of us can only offer a smile or a listening ear. Sometimes, a kind word or a hug can go a long way. And praying for someone is always a gift." He smiled. "So, even with empty pockets, you always, always have something to give."

I nodded. "Thank you, Sir. I'll remember that."

"I'll be praying for you," he added, "for whatever troubles you're having."

I smiled through my tears and thanked him again.

Back in the present, I thought about the hot chocolate from the deli lady. I remembered the smiles and the kind words from everyone who passed by. Their thoughtfulness had warmed my heart, despite the near-freezing temperatures.

I looked in that young woman's eyes and repeated those words I'd never forgotten: "Oh, dear, you've got it all wrong. Empty pockets or not, we've all got something to give."

Especially at Christmas.

~Diane Stark

Finding Christmas

Because that's what kindness is. It's not doing something for someone else because they can't, but because you can.
~Andrew Iskander

The sound of my infant daughter's crying burst through the baby monitor. "She can't be awake already," I sighed, glancing at the clock. Only fifteen minutes had passed since I'd put her down for a nap. Caring for her and my six-year-old son, coupled with suffering from a bad case of the baby blues, had turned my days into blurs of diapers, bottles, crying, and whining. To make matters worse, Christmas was approaching. I had no idea how I would finish my shopping and gift-wrapping or bake the three dozen cookies I had promised my son's teacher for his class party.

I was lucky if I managed to take a shower each day. With my mom living only ten minutes away, I desperately wanted to turn to her for support. But she was in another state caring for my grandmother, who was recovering from a heart attack. I battled tears as I gently lifted my daughter, red-faced from crying, out of her crib. I dropped heavily into the rocking chair and cradled her. And as I rocked her back to sleep, I let my tears flow. Without my mom, I was unsure how to quiet the apprehension and worry I felt.

My mother's stay with my grandmother was lasting longer than expected. "I'm not going to get home in time to put up my Christmas tree," she had told me on the phone. "Your dad is still on a business trip so he won't be around to do it either."

"Don't worry about it, Mom," I told her, hoping I sounded reassuring. "You'll get done what you can and the rest won't matter this year."

But I knew better. Mom always made Christmas at her house magical. Every year, the scents of cinnamon, sugar, and chocolate would mingle as she baked her special cookies and fudge. The fresh balsam wreaths she would hang on every door brought a sweet, woodsy scent to each entrance of her home. She'd also make sure the aging, handmade felt Santas and Styrofoam snowmen blended perfectly with the newer ornaments that adorned her tree. She'd spend hours finding the perfect gift for each person on her list and planning the menu for Christmas dinner.

It looked like this year would be different. As I had hung up the phone, I thought, "I should put up her tree this year." I quickly dismissed the idea. Who was I kidding? I could barely drag myself to the coffee pot each morning. I doubted I'd even finish decorating my own tree. But I couldn't get the idea out of my head. I couldn't stop thinking about the weariness I'd heard in my mother's voice. I became ashamed at my self-centeredness. I realized that I wasn't the only person who was tired and overwhelmed this year. My mother had always made Christmas special for me, and now it was time for me to make it special for her.

A few days before Christmas, my husband and I loaded the kids into the car and drove to my parents' home. Amazingly, my daughter fell asleep on the way there. When we arrived, I placed her—still strapped safely in her infant car seat—on the couch. We began to work. My husband brought the much-loved artificial Christmas tree up from the basement, along with box after box of tree ornaments and decorations. While he strung the lights on the tree, my son and I began looking through the boxes. It felt like Christmas morning had arrived early. Each decoration I found transported me to a wonderful childhood memory.

"I remember this! I made this in Girl Scouts," I exclaimed, as I pulled out a round ornament decked out in glitter and fabric scraps.

"And look at this one," I said, holding up a large, blue, hand-blown glass ball. "This was my grandma's ornament. I remember hanging it on her tree when I was a little girl."

"Mom, these are cool," my son said. His blue eyes sparkled as he studied several faded, red-and-white candy canes made of twisted pipe cleaners.

"I made those when I was about your age," I said.

"Can we make some for our tree?" he asked.

"Yes, that will be fun," I answered, smiling. My joy at watching his excitement canceled out any thoughts of my own exhaustion.

Miraculously, nothing went wrong. No knots were in the light strands, and each jewel-toned bulb shined brightly. No ornaments were dropped or broken, and my daughter enjoyed a rare and extended slumber while we worked. I forgot about my fatigue and depression because I was focused on how my mom would react when she saw our handiwork.

We worked for several hours hanging ornaments and arranging other holiday decorations around her house. Then it was time for the finishing touch. My son giggled as he was put on his dad's shoulders. My husband lifted him high above the tree's branches to put the star on the tree. I looked at my daughter, still sleeping, and smiled at her sweet, contented expression. I had to blink away the grateful tears that suddenly filled my eyes.

The next day, we made the three-hour trip to pick up my mother. I could see dark circles under her eyes and the worry lines etched in her forehead as she gazed out the car window.

"I can't believe Christmas is only a couple days away," she sighed. "I am never going to get my tree up. I still have shopping, wrapping and baking to do."

I simply nodded and smiled. My son bounced in his seat the entire way home, talking nonstop, but somehow managing to avoid blurting out our secret. When we arrived at my mom's home, he and I ran into the house ahead of everyone else and turned on the Christmas tree lights.

My mother walked in and he yelled, "Look Grandma!"

Her gaze was drawn to the tree standing regally in the corner. Her eyes grew wide and she gasped, covering her mouth with her hand. She started to cry and then ran to me and held me tight. We laughed and cried at the same time.

"Thank you. I can't believe you did this," she whispered, choking back her tears.

It was one of the best moments of my life. What we did for my mother changed my whole attitude that Christmas. It shifted my focus from my troubles to my blessings and the feeling of pure joy I received by giving to another. I had truly found Christmas.

~Annette McDermott

O Holy Night

I brought children into this dark world because
it needed the light that only a child can bring.
~Liz Armbruster, www.robertbrault.com

After eight years of marriage, I thought my husband knew me better. I was wrong. It all began when our pastor asked everyone in our small congregation to participate in the annual Christmas program. Not being one who enjoys the spotlight, I cringed. But my husband had other ideas.

"You want me to stand up in front of the entire church and sing?" I dropped my knife, splattering red frosting across the table. I was sitting at the kitchen table decorating Christmas cookies with our three-year-old daughter, Emily.

"Not by yourself." He snatched a heavily-sprinkled cookie from our daughter's pile. "I'll sing with you."

"Oh that's comforting," I said, folding my arms. "You know I don't like all those people looking at me."

Curt shrugged and took a bite of the cookie. "It's a small church."

"Not small enough," I mumbled.

I don't know how he did it, but a couple of days later, Curt managed to persuade me. We dug through our collection of Christmas music, looking for the perfect song. Finally we agreed on "O Holy

Night." I ran to the mall, bought the karaoke version and popped it into the cassette player. As the intro began, I felt a twinge of anxiety. I just need to get more familiar with the song, I thought.

So I practiced every time I got in the car. When I ran to the store, I sang along with the lyrics. As I drove to the mall, I flipped the tape over and sang with the accompaniment. When we went out for dinner, Curt and I practiced harmonizing the chorus. Emily always sat buckled in her car seat, happily humming along.

But I was not happy. With each passing day, panic grew inside me. I imagined myself standing up front on program night. Everyone's eyes would be fixed on me. What if I forgot the words? What if I tripped over a poinsettia on the way up the steps? How had I ever let Curt talk me into this?

All too soon, the night I'd been dreading arrived. Curt and I sat in the back of the church waiting our turn. On the platform, a pleasantly plump woman recited her version of *'Twas the Night Before Christmas*. I took a deep breath, trying to calm the butterflies dive-bombing my stomach.

Suddenly, something occurred to me. What would I do with Emily when we went up front? I couldn't leave her sitting by herself. I scanned the church, looking for someone she could sit with. Maybe I could bring her with us. But Emily was pretty shy—what if she got scared in front of all those people? As I wrestled with my decision, the pastor interrupted my thoughts.

"Curt, Sheri, come on up...."

I scooped Emily onto my hip. Then we walked to the front and stood together on the platform.

The congregation sat still, watching and waiting. I nervously switched Emily to my other hip, holding her between Curt and me. I felt the warmth rising in my cheeks. I glanced over at Curt and gave him a subtle, you'll-pay-for-this smile.

Finally the music began. I cleared my throat. "O Holy Night, the stars are brightly shining..."

As Curt and I sang, I was surprised to hear Emily whispering the words along with us. How sweet, I thought. She'd heard the song so many times, she'd also learned the words.

After a couple of verses, Emily grew more confident and sang a bit louder. A few rows back, two gray-haired ladies nodded and smiled at our charming trio. They probably think we planned this, I thought, gazing proudly at Emily. My nervous butterflies began to disappear. Things were going so well—until we reached the chorus.

As the chorus opened, Emily began to sing with such enthusiasm, it startled me. She opened her mouth wide and belted out each sour note with tremendous conviction. I gave her a firm squeeze, but she didn't take the hint. Curt and I stared at one another in shock. Across the pews, men snickered. Women covered their mouths to hide their giggles. Curt and I sang louder, hoping to block her out. But her passionate performance overpowered us both.

Finally we could no longer maintain our composure. Emily's innocent joy was contagious. Curt and I stopped singing and joined the rest of the church in sweet, unreserved laughter. Emily grinned and continued her solo.

Once the applause died down we returned to our seats. Someone else took a turn on the platform, but I couldn't concentrate. I looked down at Emily, her eyes still sparkling as she picked up a crayon and began flipping through a coloring book. Suddenly I realized my three-year-old had taught me a lesson.

During my week of nervous jitters and trivial irritations, I had only been focusing on myself. Christmas wasn't about me. Christmas was about giving to others. I reached down and patted Emily's little knee. She hadn't worried about what others might think. She openly shared the joy in her heart—and didn't hold back.

Mommy missed the point, I thought. But Emily reminded me that true joy comes when bringing happiness to others.

~Sheri Zeck

A Christmas Present, Delayed

Having a sister is like having a best friend you can't get rid of. You know whatever you do, they'll still be there.

~Amy Li

I was ten the summer my dad helped me buy my first ten-speed bicycle from Father Allen. I put up $60 of my grass cutting and snow shoveling money, and my dad put up the other half. I would pay him back in installments over the next six months. Although it was the kind of bike you'd expect a priest to have (dull silver, slightly worn, no baseball cards in the spokes), it was my ticket to the adult world.

I spent that summer and autumn riding as if to put Greg LeMond to shame. My sister Liz, a prisoner of her five-speed and banana seat, never had a chance to keep up. We'd always been stuck with hand-me-downs from our older brothers and sisters, a few of whom had notoriously bad taste in bikes. Now, however, I was able to ride to every corner of town, sometimes even as far as the beach. In those heady days before one acquires a driver's license, a good bike is a magic carpet.

Just before the Christmas deadline to pay my dad back, we were hit with several snowstorms. This allowed me to shovel enough driveways to pay off my debt. I was now officially a bike owner; it was a feeling unlike any other.

It's important to note that while my mom and dad were fantastic parents, they couldn't be trusted with the awesome responsibility of buying appropriate Christmas presents. They were too quick to pass off gloves, sneakers, and shirts as "presents." And while we might say a prayer over the Baby Jesus in the manger on our way to church, He seemed too busy at this time of year to leave presents under the tree. We outsourced our requests for the really good presents to Santa.

For her family of seven kids, my mom developed a system in which she decorated the outside of seven large boxes with different types of wallpaper. We each had our own box that contained six or so presents, and we'd close our eyes and reach in to grab one when it was our turn. This cut down on hours of wrapping and satisfied my dad's Naval sense of order.

The downside was we opened one present at a time so everyone could "appreciate" each other's gifts. Neither Liz nor I "appreciated" this system because we went last. After the obligatory "oohs" and "aahs," each of us held up our present for family review, a process that averaged about five minutes or so. This meant Liz and I had to wait about forty-five minutes between each present, so patience was in short supply—when one of us pulled out a belt or package of underwear, we seethed the entire time.

My dad, a master showman, liked to keep a few of Santa's better presents for the end. On that fateful Christmas morning, he gave me a used portable record player. I was ecstatic—I was finally untethered from the "family stereo" that all of us fought over.

Alas, my elation was short-lived after my dad called my sister to the kitchen. "We have one more gift for you," he said as he opened the door that led to the garage. There, on the steps, stood a brand new ten-speed Schwinn. I didn't hear her screams of joy—all I could hear was the sputtering engine of the lawnmower, the endless scraping of the metal snow shovel on concrete. I'd endured far too many hours of indentured servitude for my used bike; that Santa could give Liz this sparkling machine less than a week later was a sign that he was losing his touch. Could Mrs. Claus be putting something in his food?

I slumped onto the floor. My ten-speed chariot had turned into a pumpkin in the time it took my sister to hop on the gleaming leather seat.

"Let's go for a ride, Rob!" she sang, my dad holding the bike upright as she put her feet on the pedals.

"Too snowy to ride," I muttered, pushing the record player farther away from me. The symbolism seemed lost on my dad.

I seethed for the rest of the day, then the rest of the week. My dad was not someone to whom we complained about presents (not if we ever wanted to see another, anyway). Santa always seemed to lose interest after Christmas, rarely accepting returns or trade-ins. That left the Baby Jesus, but He wasn't answering my prayers—I could tell because Liz's bike had yet to crumble into a pile of rust flakes.

After a few weeks of watching me pout, my dad finally pulled me aside. "Everything okay?"

"It's not fair," I whined. "I worked so hard for my bike, and it's not even new. Then Liz gets a brand new bike as soon as I make the final payment. She didn't have to do anything for it."

My dad smiled. "She didn't have to do anything for it because it's not really for her," he said, and then left the room.

What did that mean? I didn't want her bike—it had the girly bar that sloped down to the ground and a flowery white basket on the handlebars. I could turn it in for a new set of action figures, I figured, but she'd been on it every day since Christmas—no way they'd let me take it back now. I eventually got over it, chalking it up to elf error (the naughty and nice list can be cumbersome).

By spring Liz and I were riding all over town together now that she could keep up. Sure, I'd lose her on the steep slopes, but I always let her catch up when we went downhill. Initially, the youngest children in a large family form a bond out of necessity—older siblings can be taxing, and there are only so many locked doors one can hide behind. Sometimes, you need someone else in the foxhole with you.

As we grew, Liz and I became true friends. We biked down to

swim at the local pool, then put in seven miles to take the free town tennis lessons together. We planned secret parties when my parents went on trips and played a game of "Who can leave less gas in the tank" when we finally got our drivers' licenses. I relied on her to put names to faces when we were at parties, and she treated my best friends as her personal dating service. We ended up at the same college, and even graduated the same year.

Still, I wasn't smart enough to figure out what my dad meant until years later. That brand new bike was not a gift for Liz—it was a gift for me. He'd given me the gift of my sister's company, the ability to stay together rather than drift apart in the face of my ability to travel. He gave me my best friend.

It's a gift I've treasured every day since.

~Robert F. Walsh

A World of Thanks

There are two lasting bequests we can give our children.
One is roots. The other is wings.
~Hodding Carter, Jr.

This past fall semester my daughter, Elizabeth, had the opportunity to study abroad as part of her college experience. She was off to Florence, Italy in August, not to return until mid-December. Like any mom I was worried, stressed, happy, sad, lonely, and broke.

Elizabeth was wonderful about keeping in contact. There were frequent calls and texts and many pictures posted on social media. She introduced me to her blog prior to leaving and taught my husband and me about Skype. I've never been more thankful for technology than I was throughout those long four months.

As I read Elizabeth's blog, including adventures to various sites in Italy and beyond, I could not even imagine what an experience this was for her. I saw her climb Mount Vesuvius, dance on the hills of Ireland's countryside, share beautiful photos of ruins in Rome, and lounge on the beach in Viareggio. There were stories and pictures of incredible museums, paintings, ceilings, sculptures, and even the everyday cafes and shops in Paris and London. Part of the study abroad program was to experience the culture and it was obvious that Elizabeth was doing just that!

My husband, Ted, and I anxiously checked Facebook and

Elizabeth's blog each day. We kept our phones with us at all times. The time difference made it fairly unpredictable when a call or text would come in, often in the wee hours.

Each story we read and each picture that we saw (and there were hundreds!) showed Elizabeth incredibly happy. While we remained worried and concerned each and every second of each and every day, I couldn't help but think that this experience of a lifetime was perfect for my somewhat shy and mild mannered baby. She was blossoming.

As the holidays drew near, Ted and I decked the house as we always had done, knowing Elizabeth's pure love of Christmas. To her, Christmas was never about gifts, but simply about the beauty and joy of the season. We set up the nativity and the Christmas village in our family room, made sure that every special ornament adorned the tree, and ordered a large "Welcome Home Elizabeth" banner to add to the front yard decorations.

On December 14th, we drove to the Cleveland airport, arriving nearly an hour early to greet Elizabeth. Ted made some excuse about wanting to leave early because of traffic but I knew that it was more the anticipation of seeing our daughter. Thankfully, the flight was right on schedule or we would have spent even longer wandering around and looking at a Lego display, albeit quite impressive!

With it being so near Christmas, and Elizabeth having many friends and relatives to connect with after four months away, it was an extremely hectic time. We did manage to sit by the fire, enjoying the Christmas decorations that Ted and I had spent days arranging, listening to stories of Elizabeth's wonderful four-month adventure whenever there was a spare moment.

On Christmas morning, Elizabeth presented us each with rectangular packages beautifully wrapped in sparkly blue paper. She instructed us to open these gifts simultaneously, which, of course, we did. The packages were large frames containing four pictures each. They also had admission passes from art galleries and museums, various mementos, and coins and currency from around Europe.

The pictures were the best part. Elizabeth had her travel

companions take pictures of her throughout her journey. In each photo, she was in a different city or even a different country. In each, she was holding a handmade sign, similar to simple signs held at an airport to pick up travelers, made from paper and a marker. Put together, the pictures spelled out: Thank—You—Mom and Dad—For—Giving—Me—The—World!

As the tears filled my eyes, I glanced at Ted to see his own eyes damp with tears, and as simultaneously as we had opened our rectangular gifts, we both rushed to hug our daughter.

Within a few days we had replaced a drawing of Elizabeth when she was five years old that had been on the wall much too long (that Elizabeth hated!) with our collage of thanks... and the heartfelt spirit of Christmas.

~Lil Blosfield

Christmas in Texas

You can't live a perfect day without doing something for someone who will never be able to repay you.

~John Wooden

Imagine moving your household and family, at a moment's notice, from Florida to Texas—two weeks before Christmas. When my children were young and my husband worked in management for a national hotel chain, the above scenario was not unusual. We received little notice of impending moves to other hotel properties—sometimes no more than a few days—and depended on the moving company hired by the hotel chain to pack our belongings in an organized manner.

One December we were living in Key West, Florida when the call came from the corporate office that my husband was being transferred to Dallas, Texas. A scant week later, a moving van sat in front of our house and we prepared to abandon the beach and relocate to the dusty Southwest.

We arrived in Dallas two weeks before Christmas and settled into the hotel downtown while my husband got to work learning the ins and outs of his new position. I contacted a realtor and started looking at rentals. I felt pressured to find a house to call home before the Christmas holiday; there was all the unpacking to be done, my son was in the first grade and had to be enrolled in school, and we still had to do our Christmas shopping!

We were fortunate to find a great house in a nice suburb north of Dallas. Then began the explosion of activities—setting up bank accounts, new address notifications, and scheduling the delivery of our belongings with the intent of being situated before Christmas.

The holiday came upon us in a rush. We managed to squeeze in time to find a Christmas tree, and the movers had labeled the boxes well enough that we found our decorations. My in-laws traveled to Texas to help us unpack and settle in. They spent time with their grandchildren so my husband and I could shop for gifts. By Christmas Eve, we were happy to have our world as calm as it could be two weeks following such a big move.

After dinner on Christmas Eve my son and daughter completed their evening ritual of baths, bedtime stories, and bedtime songs. The added incentive of knowing Santa wouldn't show until they were asleep had them snuggled in their beds and snoozing by 9:30 p.m. It was then we realized we had yet to wrap a single present.

Out came the gifts in an excited flurry of bags and boxes. We hunted down scissors and tape.

"Where's the wrapping paper?" My husband and I asked each other. Panic followed. Neither of us had seen wrapping paper or remembered unpacking it.

We looked everywhere, poked through unpacked boxes and searched even unlikely places like the trunk of the car and kitchen cabinets. After thirty minutes of scrambling, our fears were realized. It was the night before Christmas and we had nothing with which to wrap gifts for our children.

I made my way through the local phone book, praying with each dialed number that I'd find a store still open which had not run out of Christmas wrap. By now it was almost 10:30 p.m. Every place I phoned was closed. I tried all the department stores and drug stores, all to no avail. Finally, in desperation, I dialed the place least likely to be open or carry Christmas wrap: a gas station with a small convenience store.

"Hi," I said to the woman who answered the phone. "Please tell me you sell wrapping paper."

"Sorry," she said. "If you need milk or snacks you're in luck, but that's about it."

"Our family just moved to Texas," I sighed. "I never thought to buy wrapping paper. Can you think of any place that might still be open?"

"Not this late at night on Christmas Eve," she said.

"Okay. Well, thanks, anyway."

What would I use to wrap my kids' presents? Paper towels? Toilet paper? Aluminum foil?

"Hold on a minute," she said. "I've got a ton of Christmas wrap at my house. My shift is over in a few minutes. Give me an hour to get home and see my kids and then I'll meet you back here at the gas station and let you have what I've got."

"Really?" I said. "I hate for you to go home and then have to turn around and leave your family again. Especially on Christmas Eve."

"I'm doing it because it's Christmas Eve," she said, and I could almost hear her smile through the phone. "See you in an hour."

She was as good as her word. Between 11:30 and midnight she met my husband and father-in-law at the gas station and gave us more wrapping paper than we would ever need. My husband tried to reimburse her, but she wouldn't hear of it.

"Merry Christmas!" she called as she drove off to spend what was left of Christmas Eve with her family. "And welcome to Texas!"

I've thought of that lady many times through the years, of her generosity and wonderful spirit. She blessed us with her time, precious time that belonged to her and her family. And because of her kindness, my little ones awoke on Christmas morning with gaily-wrapped presents under the tree and no idea of what transpired to achieve it.

We returned to the gas station to thank the woman again, but she no longer worked there. I never knew her name, but I will always remember her. She demonstrated the true heart of Christmas, going out of her way for strangers so late on that most special of nights, for something as trivial, but as important, as wrapping paper.

It was a single act of kindness that touched our hearts for a lifetime.

~Lisa Ricard Claro

A Little Peace

The phrase "working mother" is redundant.
~Jane Sellman

When I learned that my third child's due date was December 25th, I tried not to panic. I figured the odds were fairly low that the baby would actually arrive on, or even near, the due date. With two little ones under the age of five, I was determined to keep the sparkle in the holidays despite my constant and overwhelming urge to lie down anywhere and go to sleep.

I carefully weeded out traditions that were just unrealistic (baking seven different types of cookies) and switched to the more practical (having the girls dip pretzel rods in melted chocolate and sprinkles). We visited Santa, but at a local rec center, not the mall. We skipped the holiday zoo festival and opted to expand our variety of Christmas movies, bringing back some classics.

But there was one tradition that I couldn't shake.

Every year we met my mother in downtown Chicago at Marshall Field's where we would look at the decorated windows and have lunch under the giant Christmas tree. This year it would mean navigating crowds while pushing a double stroller ahead of my swollen belly. This baby was so low that with every step I felt it might drop right out.

My mother convinced me to take the train, rationalizing that it was so much easier than driving, parking, and then walking. What neither of us realized was the reality of parking at the train station, lifting a toddler and preschooler onto the train, lugging the stroller behind me, and then repeating upon arrival and departure. By the time I got to Marshall Field's, I was exhausted and irritable.

It seemed that our tradition was also a tradition for half of the greater metropolitan Chicago area. Our wait was almost two hours.

Once we sat down, the magic returned. The girls were darling in their fancy holiday dresses, patent leather shoes, and heavy wool and velvet coats. We ate underneath a giant glittering tree and a fairy visited every table, sprinkling fairy dust on our heads. My girls solemnly closed their eyes, concentrating very hard on their wishes. We ate Frango mint pie, shopped, and went outside to look at the windows.

By the time I reached my car in the lot at home (after the pushing and pulling of the train) I was so exhausted that I could barely stand. When we pulled into the driveway, I almost wept with relief.

Then I opened the door.

Sunlight streamed in the back window, which had lately been blocked by our enormous tree. Our giant, round, take-up-half-the-room tree was now resting on the ground, as if in sympathy with my desire for an afternoon nap.

It was too much. I put my head in my hands and wept. I cried from overwhelming exhaustion, I cried for the broken ornaments, many of them sentimental ones from our wedding or souvenirs carefully chosen on vacations. I cried for the mess that I would have to clean up and the tree I would have to pull to standing and redecorate.

My girls hugged me and wrapped their arms around me as best they could and we all cried. I wondered how I could ever do it all. And then the "all" turned into the universal all, not just the tree and the mess, but how could I raise three children with no money for sitters and a husband who traveled frequently. We stood rooted to the spot holding each other for a while.

And then, like most mothers, I got to work and cleaned it up.

I felt the baby drop on Christmas Eve and went into labor during

Christmas dinner at my in-laws, timing my contractions between bites of beef tenderloin. We made it home, put the girls down, and headed to the hospital. Anna was born shortly after midnight.

Then came the greatest gift given to mothers of Christmas babies: Peace. The presents had been bought, wrapped, and opened. I had been home to see Santa's bounty. The cleaning up of the Christmas morning destruction wasn't my problem. The hospital maternity ward was quiet. I was deeply in love with my new angel.

The day I came home, snow was falling gently. My mother had bathed the older girls and my mother-in-law had baked a cake. I snuggled in front of the (now restored and magisterial) tree and took in the true meaning of the season.

~Laura Amann

The Thanksgiving Christmas

I don't care how poor a man is; if he has family, he's rich.
~Dan Wilcox and Thad Mumford, "Identity Crisis," M*A*S*H

The best Christmas we ever had was on Thanksgiving, without a store-bought present in sight. We were taking our large family—seven children under ten years old—to visit my parents in upstate Minnesota. It was an eight-hour drive from Green Bay, Wisconsin, and a grueling one with that many children in one crowded station wagon.

"She's on my foot, Mom!" "He's looking at me!" "Are we there yet, Dad?" You know the story; it's the same with every family in every car on every long trip. We usually tried to travel during the night when, hopefully, most of the kids would sleep.

With our large family and little expendable cash, making the trip often wasn't an option. We went once each summer for a short vacation, and again at Thanksgiving, when my husband and father could spend some time in the woods bird hunting. Visiting was always bittersweet, a combination of happy times with my parents and not-so-happy times corralling all those kids into makeshift beds and generally trying to keep the mayhem to a minimum. We always stayed home for Christmas. I wanted my children home in their own beds when Santa came.

This year the Thanksgiving weather was mild, not at all winter-like. The kids spent a lot of time outdoors kicking leaves, throwing each other on the ground, coming in grubby and out of breath. They loved going to the woods, loved looking for deer, fishing, and finding what they called "treasures," which were odd-looking stones, bird nests, or anything out of the ordinary that they could take home and show off to their city friends who didn't have rural grandparents to visit.

Thanksgiving dinner was the usual turkey and trimmings. We finished with the dishes at about three in the afternoon, and suddenly it seemed that the holiday was over.

"What can we do now?" asked nine-year-old Julie.

"Just relax," said my father from his nearly prone position in his recliner. He obviously had already started to do just that. My husband, who agreed wholeheartedly, was stretched out on the couch with a paperback.

Ten-year-old Randy looked out the window. "I wish we could have Christmas here," he said.

"Really?" asked my mother, surprised.

"Really." Randy said, "I never get to see you open my present."

"That's true," said Grandma. "I never get to see you open mine, either." She thought for a moment. "So, let's have Christmas today."

That got a reaction from all the kids, who were busy working on a jigsaw puzzle.

"What? We didn't bring presents." Six-year-old Bruce frowned. "And we don't have a tree."

"That's easily remedied," said my mother, a genius at improvisation. She got off her chair and pulled an old butter crock from the corner by the fireplace. "So, let's go get us a tree."

With whoops of acquiescence, everyone except my husband and father, who really had meant "relax" when he said it, piled on jackets and trooped outside.

"Follow me," said Grandma, pulling a small saw down from a hook in the garage. "There's a perfect little pine right back behind the shed, and it needs to be cut down. See?"

She was right. A fluffy tree not even three feet tall was trying to make its way through a bramble patch of blackberry bushes.

"I'll cut it," said Randy, and proceeded to saw its small trunk.

"Let me carry it!" "No, let me!" "I'm bigger!" "I'm older!" Despite all the arguing, in no time we had the tree back in the house and upright in the butter crock, right in the middle of the braided living room rug.

The smell of fresh-cut pine filled the whole house.

"Now we need decorations," said Grandma. "Who knows how to make paper chains?" Hands went up. "Who knows how to make paper snowflakes?" Hands up again. "Who can draw an angel?" No hands this time. "Well, then, I'll do that," she said. An artist, she was never short of project materials. In minutes, construction paper, white typing paper, scissors, glue, glitter, and gold paint were laid out on the kitchen table.

"Better play some Christmas music," said Grandpa. "Looks like the season has begun!" He came up with some Bing Crosby and Perry Como carols.

In no time the little tree was festooned with colored chains and white snowflakes. A glittering, golden angel, slightly askew, topped it all.

"Needs some snow," said Grandma, and whipped some Ivory Flakes into fluffy puffs to tip the branches.

Four-year-old Missy sighed, "It's beautiful!"

Practical Kent, eight, said, "But we need presents."

"So make some," said Grandma. "Put on your thinking caps and find or make something for everyone that you think they'll like. Something that will be so special they'll always remember this extraordinary Christmas."

"Like what?" asked Kent, puzzled.

"Oh, you'll come up with something, I'm sure," said Grandma confidently. "You can make it or find it or even say it out loud. You have," she glanced up at the old clock on the mantle, "one hour. There are newspapers and tape for wrapping. Get busy." She took little Philip's hand. "Come with me, Philip. I'll help you. But we'll have to be quiet." They disappeared into the bedroom.

The four older boys put their jackets back on and went outside. Julie and Missy asked for more paper and colors. My father and my husband looked at each other, sighed, and headed for the garage.

Carols rang through the house as the sun disappeared in a spectacular sunset on that Thanksgiving Day. One by one, oddly shaped, newspaper-wrapped packages piled up under the tree. We each had a present for everyone else.

There were cards that simply said, "I Love You," cards that offered things like, "You can play with my train whenever you want," pictures cut from magazines, paper doll cutouts, bird nests, unusual pieces of wood, sturdy milkweed pods fashioned into tiny boats.

My father made each child a cutout wooden figure that my husband sprayed bright Christmas colors. My mother helped Philip color Santas that she drew. She herself had done a quick ink sketch of each child playing.

And she wrote a poem for me. The words have long been lost, but the feeling of love in them has never been forgotten.

It was nowhere near Christmas. We didn't have a beautiful tree. The gifts cost nothing except time and love. But from start to finish it was the most memorable Christmas my family ever had.

It was a Christmas to be thankful for—on Thanksgiving.

~Nancy Sweetland

The Farewell Gift

What we do for ourselves dies with us. What we do for others and the world remains and is immortal.

~Albert Pine

It was only a backache... or so we thought. It would heal with time and rest, or maybe some pills. When it continued getting in the way of my mother-in-law Dee's favorite pastimes, especially her stitching and quilting projects, we decided more tests should be run. When the results came back, the news seemed impossible. The backache was cancer, and it was advanced.

Dee had always stitched and embroidered. She loved presenting handcrafted gifts to friends and family. Many weddings, births, and birthdays were commemorated with her beautiful pieces. When Kevin and I became engaged, she lovingly embroidered the Prayer of St. Francis on a wall hanging, knowing the prayer was dear to me. Dee's talents gave joy twice: first to her while she stitched and then to those who received.

Ready to try something new, Dee enrolled in quilting classes. She loved seeing the individual pieces come together into a work of art. She started small, making placemats, table runners, and tote bags. With the news of my pregnancy—Dee's first grandchild—came the excitement of creating a baby quilt. We didn't know whether it was a girl or boy, so the quilt would use a combination of blues and yellows, plaids and flowers, and the bumblebee theme we had selected for the nursery. She worked on it covertly, not even allowing us to see the fabrics. And then the back pain had begun, worsened, and finally became the devastating diagnosis of cancer.

As summer turned to fall, Dee's activity became more limited. Staying in one position too long was excruciating, and she needed to be on oxygen around the clock. Our world was turning upside down. Then one bright September morning, our daughter Elizabeth was born, healthy and happy and filling our lives with hope once again. Dee was too weak to come to the hospital, but heroically visited our home just a few days later. She oohed and aahed, cooed and sang, and welcomed our daughter to the world.

A few days later, she convinced my father-in-law to take her shopping. Prior to becoming sick, Dee loved outlet malls and bargain hunting almost as much as stitching. I picture my father-in-law wheeling her through every aisle of the baby superstore, oxygen tank in tow. She selected any baby outfit she liked, knowing she'd probably never see Elizabeth wear them all, and returned home exhausted but happy. Somehow she found the perfect costume for Halloween—a baby bumblebee outfit—and laughed with delight on Halloween afternoon when her granddaughter came to trick or treat.

Soon afterward, she entered the hospital for the final time. Dee, the one who everyone had set their compass by, left us. Though she had only held her grandchild a handful of times, she enjoyed every moment that she could.

Christmas came quickly on the heels of her funeral. My husband and I were still lost in the fog that new babies and nighttime feedings bring, and adrift in a sea of grief. We planned to host everyone on Christmas day as we always had, but this year felt so drastically different. In one year's time we had lost a mother and become parents ourselves.

When my father-in-law arrived Christmas morning, he warned us that we might need a few tissue boxes. While taking out Christmas decorations, he discovered gifts Dee had purchased and hidden months earlier. She'd even labeled the boxes with our names. The presents were sweet and funny, just like she was, and we laughed and cried as we pictured her selecting them. Something that in the past might have been "just a gift" now held deeper meaning; these would be our last gifts from her.

The final package under the tree that morning was for Elizabeth. My father-in-law shifted a little in his seat. His normally strong, baritone voice cracked when he threw the tissue box our way and said, "You're going to need this." We unwrapped the package and gasped. It was the quilt. The baby quilt Dee had started and I had long forgotten.

"Your mom couldn't finish it," he said. "So we asked the lady who was teaching Mom quilting if she wouldn't mind finishing it for us. I got it in the mail last week."

It seemed impossible, but there it was. The quilt that had been born out of expectation and excitement, created for the new life entering our family, was there. All of those pieces that had been left loose were now stitched together: blues and yellows, plaids and flowers, hopes and dreams, beginnings and endings—creating a new work of art.

So much more than a gift, it was a farewell hug. We could wrap the quilt around us and still feel her love.

~Katie O'Connell

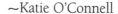

Wanted:
A Christmas Tree

I realized when you look at your mother, you are looking at the purest love
you will ever know.
~Mitch Albom, For One More Day

I t was getting close to Christmas, and my brothers and sister and I had a feeling it was going to be a spare one. My mother was working hard, getting in as much overtime as she could at her job, but even then we were just managing to pay the bills and put food on the table. An extravagance like a Christmas tree seemed out of the question.

Still, we could dream, and we could look at the beautiful, green, scented trees that filled the lot of the grocery store down the block, or walk through the rows of them that stood in the back of the nursery just a few blocks from our apartment. I loved to touch the branches of the firs and Scotch pines, to breathe in the scent of the sap and pine needles that stayed on my hands long after we'd left the forest of Christmas trees behind.

At night my brother and I would lie in the dark in our room and whisper the hopes we had for Christmas. Usually I had a long list of things I wanted Santa to bring, and my dreams would be filled with visions of wonderful gifts. That year all I could think about was having a Christmas tree. It had become an important symbol of the season's magic, something that was out of the ordinary in our tiny apartment.

"I want a toy truck and a toy rocket that you can use to zoom to the moon," my brother Larry said. "And a toy cowboy and a horse for him to ride on, to catch stray cows."

That sounded great to me, too, but then I turned to where he lay on his bed and asked, "What about a Christmas tree?"

"What about a Christmas tree?" he said back to me.

"That's what I want for Christmas; a Christmas tree."

My brother must have seen the serious look on my face. "It's a week before Christmas. Don't you think if Mom had the money to buy a Christmas tree we would have one by now?"

I thought about it, staring up at the dark ceiling, and I knew he was right. We always got our Christmas tree at the beginning of December, because we loved to see it decorated for as long as we could. Here it was a week before Christmas and no tree. I knew all of Mom's pay was spoken for already, with nothing left for something as expensive as a tree.

"I don't think we're having a tree this year," my brother repeated through the darkness.

I closed my eyes, seeing a beautiful, fully decorated tree standing in our living room. Its branches were strung with garland and lights, and handmade decorations covered the tree. There was even a gold star at the top. "That's okay," I said, snuggling down to sleep. "It probably would have dried out and died after a few days anyway."

I tried not to think about having a tree and busied myself making Christmas cards for my family. Our Mom baked cookies and made Christmas candy, and the smell of divinity candy, popcorn balls, and freshly cooked toffee filled the house. We sang Christmas carols, told Christmas stories and talked about all the wonderful Christmases we'd had in the past.

On Christmas Eve we stayed up as late as we could, but eventually I nodded off. At one point I woke up because I heard a noise in the living room. I got up and saw my mom sitting in her chair singing to herself. She sang in a soft voice, and I stood and listened to her sing "Silent Night." She looked up, saw me, and smiled.

"Hey, sleepy head," she said as she got up and gave me a hug. "You should be asleep. You don't want to peek at what Santa is bringing."

I looked at the spot where we usually put the Christmas tree. "How can Santa put presents out if there's no tree?" I asked. Tears began to form in my eyes. "We need a tree."

My mom held me tight and smiled. "Don't worry. Santa will know where to put his gifts. Now you go back to bed and have sweet dreams."

I tossed and turned the rest of the night, and when my brother and I finally woke to the sound of my mom's voice calling to say that Santa had come, I got out of bed and followed after him, not really wanting to see just a pile of gifts on the table.

My eyes opened wide when I walked into the living room. I couldn't believe what I saw. Sometime during the night my mom had taken the Christmas lights and formed the outline of a Christmas tree on the wall where the tree normally stood. She had stuck garland across it, and hung the strands of popcorn and cranberries we had made. Then she had hung all the homemade and treasured ornaments we'd saved over the years on the garland. She'd even taken a length of gold garland and shaped it into a star on the top.

I stood there staring at the most beautiful Christmas tree I'd ever seen, and the smile on my face was about as big as the joy I felt in my heart. I ran up to my mom and hugged her with every ounce of my strength.

"See," she whispered as we stood looking at the wonderful tree, "I told you Santa would figure out where to put the presents."

I nodded, feeling the spirit of Christmas deep in my soul, and held onto her like she was the most precious gift in the world.

~John P. Buentello

11

Wreath Rivalry

Mother's love is peace. It need not be acquired, it need not be deserved.
~Erich Fromm

I t was a wreath only a mother could love. The program promised "100 holiday ideas for a total of $100." As with virtually every designer show on cable, I was completely sold at the first airy wave of the hostess. Beautifully dressed interior designers frolicked through their demonstrations of ideas, many of which required a master's degree in glue guns and access to esoteric waxes from India. But then a handsome, delicate man in a black turtleneck with an air of bored superiority showed how anyone could make a wreath with drycleaner bags. By tying shredded strips of the plastic bags around a disassembled coat hanger, you could create a shiny, ecologically friendly wreath.

We rarely went to the dry cleaner, but our mountain of un-recycled grocery bags looked like decent substitutes. So I started cutting and tying strips around a wire circle of an old coat hanger. A few hours later, I was astonished. It looked pretty good.

This is what cable does to you. You actually come to believe that plastic bags tied around a coat hanger look pretty good.

I added a few ribbons and ornaments and decided I'd give this to my mother to add to the huge number of decorations around her house. She loved to decorate, would set a beautiful table at the holidays, and I thought this would be a fun addition to a window somewhere.

When I delivered it on one of our family visits early in December, it was fourth grade all over again. She loved it and promptly displayed it on the mantle. I was a little embarrassed, but also ridiculously proud.

As the holidays reached their fever pitch, we returned to her house for the big dinner. Everyone was there, and we were a bit late, having had a few meltdowns with the kids along the way. After we finished hugging and getting rid of coats and shoes, I walked into the formal dining room.

On the mantle was a huge wreath, practically encompassing the fireplace, filled with glimmering ribbons, bells, and ornaments. It was gorgeous, the greenery absolutely perfect, the colors flowing in a holiday harmony that would have silenced any decent choir. I was in awe.

And there, on the little music stand next to the mantle, was my recycled bag wreath.

"Oh! Did you see the wreath Christy sent me?" my mother said, walking into the room behind me.

Of course. My sister. From across the Midwest she had reached into our open-ended game of sibling rivalry blackjack and tossed down a big, fat ace right here, in my mother's house. Like a typical little sister, I didn't even see it coming.

"Wow. It's amazing," I said, hoping there was as little animosity in my voice as was possible under the circumstances.

"And see? I put yours right there. I wanted everyone to see the wreaths my daughters gave me."

There had to be a dagger somewhere. Something sharp I could pluck out my eyes with before I saw the look on everyone's face. I was mortified.

I turned to look at my mother, to try and apologize for my sad little homemade wreath. But one look at her brought me up short. She had no idea. She had no idea of the vast gulf that lay between my wreath with the ripped grocery bags and the epic salute to the spirits of yuletide through the ages on the mantle. In her eyes, they were somehow THE SAME.

I was floored. First and foremost, I realized I'd have no chance to ditch my plastic ring of Christmas in the closet, sparing myself from the inevitable comparisons that would race across the faces of every relative at the table. Then, it dawned on me.

My mother is incredible.

For her there was no difference. Forget the white shredded plastic versus glossy greenery and silk ribbons. Never mind the cheap ornaments versus hand-painted porcelain from Europe. So what that one was small and insignificant versus the other, large enough to rival the tree itself. None of that mattered. In her heart, in her eyes, they were from her daughters. They were our love shaped into circles and she cherished them both.

I looked at my own daughters, who were busy running from room to room at my mother's house, squealing with energy. My eyes burned with love and I hoped when the day came, they would see this beautiful blindness in me.

As a daughter, I'm still completely mortified by the memory of the wreath rivalry where I was so completely left in the dust. Yet I take considerable comfort in knowing that to my mother, there was no contest — and there never has been.

~Winter Prosapio

It's Christmas!

Miracles Happen

Miracles happen to those who believe in them.

~Bernhard Berenson

By This Time
Next Year

Faith works miracles. At least it allows time for them.
~George Meredith

The Christmas hubbub had finally died down, and my family members were lying around my parents' living room, basking in the wrapping paper remnants and the piles of shiny new presents. Everyone was full of eggnog, ham, and joy. Well, everyone was happy except me. The living room was crowded with the people I loved most, and yet in my mind, someone was missing—someone I had never met. My baby, the child I could not conceive, was not there, and that baby's absence spoke louder than all the words of Christmas cheer.

Christmas is about children, but there were no children in our family anymore. My three siblings and I had grown up, and now that I had been married to my college sweetheart for five years, a baby was long overdue. But we couldn't get pregnant, and no one knew why. As the lonely months stretched into years—two childless Christmases came and went, and our refrigerator was covered with photos of our friends' babies wearing Santa hats—I sank into a deep sadness. I began to question everything, even my lifelong faith in God. Did he hear our prayers at all? How could he stand by silently while my husband and I suffered?

Even so, as we faced that Christmas, I had vowed not to let my aching emptiness ruin our family festivities... and yet the loss cast a pall over the whole day.

As night fell, my father, who had been a preacher for more than forty years, gathered the family together, and we began to recount the blessings we'd been given over the past year. The talk then turned to the future. What did we hope to see next year? What were our dreams? Every family member wished for the same thing: For my husband and me to have a baby by the following Christmas. We shed tears, and as the hour grew late, Dad ended our Christmas by asking us all to pray for the coming year. Around the circle we went, each of us asking God the same thing: "Please give us a baby by this time next year." We had prayed for a baby before—pleaded, cajoled, bargained—but never like this, never as a family, united in the same plea: "By this time next year..."

The next month, I began to see a new doctor, who had some fresh ideas for my treatment. And that spring, we received the news: I was pregnant! I embraced the months of exhaustion and nausea with ecstatic gratitude—every time I hung my head over the trashcan, I was singing inside.

The baby was due December 18. All through my pregnancy, people teased me: "A Christmas baby, how terrible!" But I, in my first-pregnancy naiveté, was convinced that the baby would come early, so that I could recover from the delivery in plenty of time for Christmas. We had waited so long to get pregnant, surely we wouldn't have to wait past our due date to meet our child!

But December 18 came and went, and the baby only seemed to settle deeper into my womb. December 19, December 20, December 21... nothing. Not a single contraction. As Christmas day loomed, I began to despair. I was never going to have this baby. I had prayed for so long to get pregnant, now I'd be the only pregnant woman who stayed that way forever.

When my husband and I first awoke on the morning of Christmas Eve, we called just to check in with our doctor. Minutes later, we were throwing suitcases into our car, rushing to the hospital to have labor induced. On the way to the hospital, we laughed and cried, terrified and giddy in equal measure, sure that our baby would arrive by that night—a Christmas Eve baby. Wouldn't that be delightful?

But labor dragged on into the early hours of Christmas morning. Our families drifted in and out of the hospital's waiting room all Christmas day, rushing through the morning gift-opening without us, eating Christmas dinner with cell phones by their plates, waiting for news. But the baby wouldn't come, wouldn't even move into the birth canal. Finally that night, it was clear that our baby was not coming without help. I would need a C-section.

That first wail—the cry I thought I'd never hear—was a foreign but familiar sound, the song my heart had been singing all those years. And what lungs she had! The baby cried angrily—after all, it hadn't been her idea to come out—but the moment my husband spoke to her, saying, "Daddy's here," she quieted, calmed by the voice she had come to know from inside my womb. And when the doctor held up a tiny head with black eyes and a scrunchy nose, my brain tried to reconcile sight with faith. That squirming bundle was our baby!

Cassidy Joy Thompson entered the world—seven pounds, five ounces of answered prayer—on Christmas night at 9:46 p.m.

But we didn't get it right away.

It was several weeks before my mother suddenly turned to me, tears filling her eyes, and breathed, "Do you remember our prayer last Christmas night?"

And we realized that Cassidy Joy had been born, to the minute, one year after my family had begged God, "By this time next year, please give us a child.... "

Now, whenever I am tempted to wonder if God remembers us, if he hears our prayers, I look at my daughter—our family's Christmas miracle—and I know that he does.

~Elizabeth Laing Thompson

Annie's Little Christmas Miracle

Be realistic: Plan for a miracle.
~Osho Rajneesh

One Christmas, when a friend of mine was down on her luck, an anonymous stranger rang her doorbell. She answered the door and was amazed to find a Christmas tree deposited on her doorstep. I was thinking about that one year as I baked cookies for my four children. We were struggling and broke and there wasn't any Christmas tree at our house. I wondered if any one would remember us, like they had remembered my friend. I was hoping for a miracle.

It was mid December, and already snow glistened on all the lawns. The front door slammed and seven-year-old Annie came in, her brown ponytail swinging. She was bubbling over with excitement.

"Mom, they're having a coloring contest and I'm entering it."

"That's wonderful, Annie." I placed a tray of cookies in the oven.

"The garden center in town is sponsoring it."

Annie was our third child, our family artist, who spent hours cheerfully coloring with crayons and markers as she filled sketchbooks with her original creations. "I hope I win the prize."

"What's the prize?"

"I think it's money. When I win the contest, we'll go to the craft store so I can buy supplies to make Billy, Michelle, and Krista awesome Christmas presents."

"That would be nice," I thought. It was so like Annie to think of everyone else before herself. But I knew there wouldn't be much of a Christmas that year. Frankly, I was tired of worrying where our next dollar was coming from.

Annie grabbed a pack of markers from her backpack and started coloring the contest entry at the kitchen table, as the aroma of cinnamon sugar warmed the room. She went the extra mile, adding all kinds of special effects to her picture. When she finished, the result was beautiful. The outline was a plain Christmas tree with packages around it, but Annie's creativity had brought the tree to life and the effect was magical. She decorated all the packages in bright colors and interesting designs.

"You did a great job," I said.

"It looks just like my friend Katie's tree," Annie said. "She has a real tree just like that in her house with ornaments in every color of the rainbow. It has a golden garland on it and an angel on top. It's so beautiful. Oh, I wish we could have a tree like that at our house."

I turned away, feeling an ache inside, not wanting her to see my sadness.

"I hope I win." She clapped her hands in excitement, wishing with all of her heart.

"So do I," I thought. "Let something good happen to this family." I was so tired of saying no to trips to the store and movies. And my children barely knew what a mall was, they visited so infrequently. Even if it were just a little money, enough for Annie to buy her craft materials—it would give us all some hope.

Days flew by and our financial situation was worse. Christmas was coming and we paid the bills, but there wasn't any money left for gifts. My parents offered to help out. They bought Billy a collector truck that he wanted. They purchased some pretty clothes for the girls and the stuffed lion Krista wanted. But I was still discouraged because there was an empty corner in the living room where a Christmas tree should have been.

Soon Annie learned that people were voting for the contest entries. "Mom, you and Dad should go to the garden center where the entries are hanging up and vote. Other parents are voting for their kids and my picture needs votes."

"Sure Annie, why not?"

Early that evening, our entire family headed to the garden center to see Annie's picture hanging on the wall. There were so many imaginative entries to choose from, I wondered how any judge could choose a favorite. Annie raced to hers with a huge smile on her face. Her picture really stood out. We cast our votes.

Billy tugged on my arm. "Hey Mom, look."

I looked out the window of the store and saw them. Rows and rows of regal Christmas trees were lined up outside. Families were loading them into vehicles and driving away. "Can we get one?"

I looked over at my husband. He looked as uncomfortable as I did. He shook his head sadly.

"Not today. We'll get the tree another day."

Fortunately, that answer seemed to satisfy Billy. We could not tell the children the cold reality. There would be no more paychecks until after Christmas. After shopping for the essentials and paying the bills, there wouldn't be enough left for a tree.

It was three days before Christmas and the children were all looking sadly at the lonely spot by the window in the living room—the empty spot where there was supposed to be a tree.

"How come there's no tree?" asked Michelle, who was two years older than Annie. "Aren't we going to get one this year?"

"How will Santa know where to leave the presents if there is no tree?" Krista looked worried.

"When I win the contest I'll buy us a tree," said Annie. Her childhood faith astounded me.

The next morning I watched as the children left for school. I questioned my decision to stay home and raise them. I hated disappointing them, especially at Christmas. Maybe there was a job somewhere with cheap enough daycare that I could afford to work and help out with the finances.

That afternoon, as I searched through want ads, the children came dashing in, Billy leading the way.

"Guess what, Mom!" Billy said, looking happier than I had ever seen him. "Annie won the coloring contest!"

"Wow! Did she win first prize?"

"No, she came in third."

"Oh well, that's good," I said. "Third is good."

"Annie, tell her what you won. You're not going to believe it, Mom!"

Annie had a big smile on her face, and her dark brown eyes sparkled with joy. "A Christmas tree, Mom. I won a Christmas tree! We have to go to the garden center to pick it up."

Never had I seen a more grateful group of people.

That evening we piled in the old van and drove to the garden center to see Annie's winning entry once again. Billy helped his father load the majestic Blue Spruce into the van and carry it into the house. The tall tree brightened the room, while the refreshing scent of pine filled the house, invigorating us all. We had new hope for the future. The children hung lights and sparkling ornaments, laughing and singing in joyful excitement. Annie climbed a ladder to place a golden star at the top of the tree.

There wouldn't be many presents under the tree that year, but we didn't care. The tree was an answer to a young girl's prayer, and Annie's Christmas miracle was enough to warm our hearts and give us hope for years to come.

~L.A. Strucke

When No One Else Will Do

When prayers go up, blessings come down.
~Author Unknown

"Mom, can I have some money for the Santa Shop at school?" my seven-year-old son Jordan asked. I sighed. As a single mom, money for non-essentials was pretty much non-existent.

"Please, Mom? The Santa Shop is where all the kids go to buy Christmas presents for their families," Jordan added hopefully. "And there's something I really want to get for you."

"Honey, I don't need anything," I said.

But he nodded. "You need this, Mom."

I sighed again and reached for my purse. "I'll give you three dollars, Bud. I know it's not much, but it's what we can swing right now."

Jordan grinned. "That's exactly how much I need, Mom. Thanks!"

On Christmas morning, Jordan was beyond excited about the present he'd bought for me. "Open it, Mom, open it," he said, jumping up and down.

I ripped off the wrapping paper and inside was a small, plastic plaque. It read, "Mom is the person you need when absolutely no one else will do."

Tears filled my eyes. "This is what you wanted to buy for me?"

Jordan nodded. "Do you like it?"

"Oh, Honey, it's the best present I've ever gotten."

"I just wanted to show you how much I love you," Jordan said.

I hugged him close and thanked him for the gift. "It really is the best present anyone has ever given me," I told him.

That Christmas night, after Jordan and his sister were asleep, I held that plaque in my hands and thought about the meaning behind its words.

Mom is the person you need when absolutely no one else will do.

My children needed me. As a single parent, I was pretty much all they had. They counted on me for everything. If I weren't there for them, no one else would be. It was a lonely, overwhelming realization, and the responsibility of it weighed on me heavily.

I loved the plaque, I really did. And I would live up to it. I'd be the person my kids needed me to be.

But who would be there for me? Who was my "when no one else would do" person?

I had my parents, but I was in my thirties, a little old to be relying on Mommy and Daddy. My siblings and I are a close-knit bunch in our hearts, but geographically, we're spread out across the country. I had wonderful friends too, but they all had families and other responsibilities, and I didn't want to be a burden or a drag.

For me, life as a single parent was lonely, and scary, and not at all how I'd dreamed my life would turn out. But here I was, both alone and scared, and on Christmas, no less.

And in moments like this one, there are only two viable options: cry or pray. I did the former until my eyes were red and my nose was stuffy, but I didn't feel any better. So I prayed.

I told God about my fear and loneliness. I told Him that I was worried about being enough for my kids. "I'm all they have," I reminded God, "and it wasn't supposed to be this way."

In that lonely, scary moment, I remembered Bible verses I'd memorized as a child. I remembered that God promised that He would never leave me. He loved me and He always would. No matter what.

The loneliness faded as I realized that I wasn't really alone. Maybe God could be my "when no one else would do" person.

The thought was comforting, although I couldn't help wishing for someone special here on earth. "I know You're here with me, God," I prayed, "and I thank You for it, but maybe someday, if it's not too much trouble…"

God heard my prayer that Christmas night and His answer was better than I ever dreamed.

That February, I met a single dad named Eric. He was raising a couple of kids on his own, and he didn't like it any better than I did. The more time we spent together, the surer I became that Eric was truly the answer to my prayers. We got married that summer, and began raising our four children together. I no longer had time to be lonely, and I was happier than I'd ever been in my life.

That first Christmas as a new family was really special. Eric and I had shopped for the children's gifts together. We'd bought matching pajamas for his daughter and mine. The girls loved them. I smiled through my tears when I heard them say that all sisters should have matching pajamas.

It was a wonderful day, but God had one more surprise for us. I hadn't been feeling well, so on a whim I took a pregnancy test. It was positive. Yet another blessing.

At bedtime, I spotted the plaque Jordan had given me the previous Christmas. My eyes filled with tears as I thought about all of the changes over the past year. "Thank you, God," I said. "Thank you for hearing those desperate words from a lonely single mom. And thank you that I'm not that person anymore."

That Christmas, I learned that God really is there when no one else will do, but sometimes, if we're especially blessed, He gives us people who also fit that description.

~Diane Stark

Catch

We do not remember days; we remember moments.
~Cesare Pavese, The Burning Brand

Following Christmas dinner, my family was relaxing around the kitchen table. We had all enjoyed traditional turkey, sweet potatoes lightly glazed with brown sugar, and a final wedge of pumpkin pie topped with a dollop of ice cream. The good cooking smells still lingered; the oven remained warm. My sister, our chef, was basking in the compliments—"Fabulous meal," "I really couldn't eat another bite," "Everything was wonderful." Dad had risen from his chair and was contentedly standing nearby.

My nephew, never one to sit still for too long, began dribbling his new basketball around the table and throughout the kitchen. Upon nearing Dad, he stopped—almost uncertainly. With shaking, wrinkled hands, Dad had reached out for the ball. He did not speak, and the boy, confused, looked up and over at us. It took some convincing, but the ball was gingerly passed over.

I watched my father closely to see what he would do. A playful smile appeared on his face. The twinkle in his eyes shone brighter than any Christmas lights. Holding the ball and reaching forward, Dad bounced it on the floor then caught it.

This action was repeated. Nodding approvingly, he then turned towards our assembled group. Gently tossing the ball away, Dad began a game of catch.

The ball continued to be passed through eager pairs of outstretched hands. Cries of "Over here!" rang through the warm kitchen. Dad's active participation in this game was remarkable to me, since he had advanced Alzheimer's disease. This dementia had robbed him of many memories and the recognition of people, places and points in time. Despite this, Dad clearly recognized the ball and what you could do with it.

In my younger years, playing with Dad was rare. To his credit, Dad worked hard and provided for us. He was very private and never showed nor shared much emotion; his game of choice was chess, which he did eventually teach me how to play. As an adult, I had become a caregiver and watched helplessly as Dad declined. Connecting moments between father and son had been few and far between before he took the basketball.

I'm not sure how long we played catch. Watching the clock was not important. Dad gleefully led us until he began to tire. What I do know is that our game ended all too soon, and it was time to face the reality of dirty dishes piled high on countertops. The moment, though, will certainly last forever. On this Christmas, Dad gave me a special memory — one that I will always treasure.

~Rick Lauber

Dreamhouse

Thorough preparation makes its own luck.

~Joe Poyer

"Stacy, you're going to love what Dad and I got you for Christmas," my mom said with eager anticipation.

My ten-year-old heart filled with excitement and I counted the days until I could open the thing my parents had been alluding to for weeks. My parents weren't known for picking exceptional gifts. In fact, my mom normally took me to the store to select my own presents.

"Mom, can you give me a clue?"

"Nope! You'll just have to wait."

I started daydreaming of the perfect present my parents conjured up for me. Visions of the Barbie Pink World 3-Story Dream Townhouse filled my head. I'd been asking for it for years, but my parents always dismissed that request. Were they finally going to get it for me?

"Barbie, just think. Pretty soon you'll have a beautiful house to live in," I said to my favorite doll. "No more pretending old Kleenex boxes are houses. Before you know it, you'll have your very own home!" Barbie, Ken, and I celebrated its pending arrival.

The days dragged on, but finally it was Christmas Eve. My sister and I were allowed to open one present. I tore into the red paper, hoping I had picked the right one. Before I even got all the paper off, my fingers felt flannel. Pajamas. Bummer.

Presents tumbled out from under the tree Christmas morning. I eyed them all, trying to figure out which one held the coveted gift.

At long last, after the carpet was long lost under scraps of torn wrapping paper, only one present remained. "Here, Stacy," my dad said. "You can open it now." He handed me a rectangular package just slightly larger than a shoebox. Sorry, Barbie.

"Can you guess what it is?" my mom asked.

I tore into the Barbie wrapping paper, scraping my fingers on a cardboard box. I looked at it for clues, but only saw a picture of a fire extinguisher.

It wasn't uncommon for my parents to wrap something in a box originally intended for another object, yet the huge grin on my dad's face was cause for alarm. Slowly, I pried open the flap on the box... and pulled out the very thing pictured on the label. The prized present I'd heard about for weeks was a fire extinguisher? Confusion and disappointment flooded my face.

My parents beamed with pride.

"We always figured if there was a fire, you could get out your window, but after Mom got stuck in the window well when she was cleaning, we knew you needed something to keep you safe in your basement bedroom." Months earlier, my mom had tried cleaning the window well, but in the process the pin slipped and locked the window shut. She tried pushing up the plastic bubble over the well, but the weight of the landscaping rocks outside weighed it down too much.

"Oh. Um, thanks."

"Stacy, after breakfast we'll go outside and practice using it," my dad said.

"Uh, sure, Dad."

And that's exactly what we did. As my neighbor walked her new Christmas puppy, I practiced proper fire repelling techniques.

The fire extinguisher went behind my bedroom door, hidden from sight so I wouldn't have to remember the anguish and disappointment it caused. It sat there for a few years, collecting dust. But one day while my parents were out of town, my best friend and I made sopapillas for Spanish class. As we dropped the batter into the pot of bubbling oil, flames erupted, stretching from the stove to ceiling. As the cabinet began smoking, I envisioned my parents returning to a pile of rubble. I knew I had to do something, but couldn't remember how to fight an oil fire.

"Hang on," I yelled as I ran downstairs. Flying back up the steps, I pulled the ring on the extinguisher and began spraying like a veteran firefighter. A yellow residue coated all the surfaces and the once-white ceiling was black, but the house was intact.

The present I least wanted was the very thing that saved us.

If I'd received Barbie's Pink World 3-Story Dream Townhouse all those years ago instead of the fire extinguisher, it would have gone up in flames along with the rest of the house. I didn't get the gift I wanted, but it was ultimately what I needed. If only fire extinguishers came in Barbie pink.

~Stacy Voss

Christmas Vision

It is hard to wait and press and pray, and hear no voice,
but stay till God answers.
~E.M. Bounds

Two months before my family sat around a Christmas tree, we were sitting around a hospital waiting room hoping for good news. My sister Jessica, thirteen at the time, had just been diagnosed with a brain arteriovenous malformation, an AVM. The doctors were relatively shocked and they told us it was a miracle she hadn't dropped dead after one of the aneurysms in her brain burst the previous year. The details of her condition were somewhat complicated but the simple diagnosis was this—she needed another miracle. Her rare condition had doctors unsure of how to proceed and had us anxiously waiting for them to decide on a plan of action. They told our mother that her chances weren't exactly good and tried to prepare us for a worst-case scenario.

She was sedated heavily in order to help with her pain and was made to go through numerous procedures so the doctors could get a better idea of what they were up against. Speaking to her on the phone was comforting but difficult, since she sounded so far away because of the morphine and seemed to be in so much pain. It seemed so unfair that such a young girl could be facing so much. I passed through my teenage years without so much as a broken bone and here was my young sister who had barely made it to adolescence and was now fighting for her life.

Our family did what we always did; we turned to prayer. We prayed constantly for her recovery and our church, extended family, and friends all did the same. Prayer groups from one end of the country to the other prayed that we would, in fact, get our miracle.

And remarkably, we did. After a surgery to stop the bleeding and repair some of the damage, the doctors told us she could go home. We were overjoyed, but it wasn't the end of her struggles. When she arrived home she was still recovering from a stroke, a consequence of the surgery they had done on her brain. She had to be in a wheelchair and had partial hearing loss in one ear. She also had double vision and, to avoid vertigo, needed to wear an eye patch every waking moment. It was a devastating blow to see her like that and to hear how weak she sounded, but we had to focus on the positive; she was alive. We were so thankful to have her with us that we felt we'd never have to ask God for anything else. He had given us our miracle and that was all we needed.

That Christmas we were happy to be celebrating as an entire family again. No matter the bumps in the road we faced that holiday season, our mantra was this: it could have been so much worse.

It seemed, however, that we were in for one more holiday surprise. On Christmas Eve Jessica woke up and she could see. Her vision had somehow corrected itself and she no longer needed her eye patch in order to function. It was our very own Christmas miracle. That night at our Christmas mass, we all stood a little taller, prayed a little harder, and sang a little louder.

Even though there were piles of presents under the tree that Christmas the unspoken feeling in the air was unmistakable. Jessica's regained eyesight was the best gift by far and the one nobody had even thought to ask for.

~Melissa Pearn

Peaches in Winter

Home is not where you live but where they understand you.
~Christian Morgenstern

I was fourteen years old and sure the Christmas holidays would make my miserable life even worse. Mother and my little sister Rosa were busy decorating the Christmas tree but I stayed in my room, listening to Los Huasos Quincheros, my country's most famous singers. "Chile lindo," they sang and strummed their guitars. I joined in, remembering my beautiful country and thinking about all the things I didn't like about my life in America. No, I didn't like it here, not one little bit, and I really hated my mother for taking me away from my family. But my misery didn't end there, oh no. Things got worse when Mother called me into the kitchen.

"Now that school is out," she said, "I'm going to teach you how to cook."

"But Mom," I said and slumped into a chair. The metal rim around the kitchen table felt cold against my arms. "I don't want to be the cook."

Mother didn't even hear me. She poured water into a pot and went on with her lesson. "All you need to know," she said, "is how to boil water. Now you can cook rice, spaghetti, hard boiled eggs, everything." She smiled brightly as if she had given me the secret to eternal happiness.

"I don't like hard boiled eggs."

How could she be so mean? Back home, Dominguita was the cook and she served us delicious empanadas and we sat at a long, mahogany table set with china and silverware. Here we ate on paper plates. Everything changed in my life after my father died. First of all, we had to move in with my grandmother. I liked it but Mother grumbled every day that she got bossed around and treated like a child.

"I need a job," Mother said over and over. Grandmother told her decent women didn't work outside the home. Mother ran out of the room and slammed the door. I could hear her crying in her room so I went in to see her.

"I have to go to America," she told me. She held a box of tissues in her hands. "I know I can get a job there. I'll be independent and you'll grow up in a country where women make their own destiny." I didn't know what she meant. But I knew I didn't want to leave. Then one day she came home very happy, waving our airline tickets for America in the air. My stomach sank. All too soon, with my nose pressed against the window of the airplane, I waved goodbye to all the people I loved. Tears ran down my cheeks all the way to Washington, D.C.

America, where I spoke with an accent and felt miserable at school. Oh, joy.

"How do you pronounce your name?" the teachers asked. "Is it eczema?"

I wanted to scream. "I'm not a disease!"

"Ximena," I heard my Mother say, "could you pay attention?"

I glared at her.

"In the spirit of Christmas, could you smile a little and be nice to your sister?"

I stared at The Brat, who sat on the sofa. Mother said The Brat looked like an angel, with her blond hair and short bangs. She didn't look cute to me.

"Will the spirit of Christmas help me like her?"

"Yes. If you let your heart accept it."

"I don't understand."

Mother turned away from the stove and came over to me. She stroked my hair.

"The spirit of Christmas is really the love of God being born into our world," she said.

"I thought Christmas was about the birth of Jesus."

"It is. But remember, Jesus also represents the love of God coming to us."

I liked that Mom was talking to me like a grown-up.

"You see," Mom continued, "God needs us. He comes into the world through us."

"He does?"

"Especially so when we open our hearts to love another person, even if they irritate us."

That sounded really nice but I didn't think it was going to happen to me. The Brat really irritated me, not like my ten zillion cousins who kept me from ever, ever getting lonely. Here, lonely was all I knew. Lonely and cold. Why did people want a white Christmas anyway? Snow made my nose red and earmuffs looked silly. In Chile, Christmas marked the start of summer. I loved to spend the summer with my cousins, swimming, horseback riding, and best of all, eating peaches right off the tree. No peaches for me this year. Mother said they were too expensive. I was going to have to be happy with canned ones. This is what I had to look forward to this Christmas: lonely, cold and eating canned peaches.

When the dreaded day arrived, Mother plugged in the red and green lights on the Christmas tree and we began to pass out our presents. I was surprised when The Brat came over to where I sat and snuggled in next to me. She gave me a card made of beige construction paper. Across the top, she had carefully printed my name in pink crayon. I stared at the card. A big yellow sun rose over snow covered mountains and at the bottom of the page, she had drawn a row of peach trees.

"I told the kids at school how to pronounce your name," she said. "Pretend the 'X' is an 'H' I told them."

I felt a funny feeling in my nose and for a weird moment I thought I was going to cry.

"That was really nice, Rosa." I could hardly believe I said that. The Brat smiled at me and I tried real hard not to smile back.

I opened Mother's gifts—socks and underwear. Oh, joy. When they handed me a large box, it felt so heavy I guessed it was a pair of shoes, probably something waterproof and ugly. I put it down next to me on the floor. Maybe I could go to my room now.

"Go on, open it," Mother said and put the box on my lap.

I pried it open and gasped. Inside there were oranges, figs, grapes, and six yellow peaches, all marked "Product of Chile."

"Maybe now you won't be so sad," Mother said. I couldn't believe it. When she kissed me on the forehead, I reached out and threw my arms around her.

"Gracias, mamacita," I said, "Gracias."

Mother hugged me tight. The Brat put her arms around my neck and I was surprised at how nice her soft cheek felt against mine. She gave me a big, sloppy kiss that I had to wipe off my face. She looked at me, her big, brown eyes half hidden under her golden bangs. I had to admit, Mother was right. The Brat did look like an angel. I reached over and kissed her.

"I... I... I love you," I whispered.

"I love you too," she said and took off dancing around the room. "Feliz Navidad," she sang, "Feliz Navidad!"

~Ximena Tagle Ames

Christmas Ornaments

The message of Christmas is that
the visible material world is bound to the invisible spiritual world.
~Author Unknown

At the beginning of December we begin the ritual of hauling boxes upstairs from their yearlong resting place in the basement. The boxes are filled with treasures that will make our Christmas tree sparkle, adorn our fireplace mantle and leave every surface with some sort of holiday jewels, glitz and glamour. Some of the ornaments were from my childhood, and my parents' and grandparents' childhoods. Every time I see them, I am reminded of days gone by, filled with warm, happy memories. One year, unpacking the ornaments made me realize I needed to make a few new memories with my children.

When I was adopting Juliana and Andrea from Romania, I looked for Christmas ornaments while we were there, but could not find anything to hang on our tree. I bought a few miniature plastic Romanian dolls that I thought the girls might like on the tree, but I felt they needed something more in comparison to the many items Pat and I had from our families. It was unrealistic to fly back to Romania to shop for Christmas ornaments in a store, so the next best thing was to make some.

The girls did not enjoy crafts the way I did, so the handmade versions looked pathetic. The art teacher at the elementary school conducted art projects where the children brought home delightful ornaments they made, but none of it related to their Romanian heritage. I was adamant that I would find something Romanian for them to hang on our family Christmas tree.

My sister knew someone who would be traveling to Romania on business right around the holidays. I called him and explained how important it was that my daughters have something from their birth country on our Christmas tree. He understood and promised to buy something for each of them. I was thrilled.

As the days ticked by, I was getting more worried that he would not be successful with his quest to buy the girls ornaments. I remembered how barren the store shelves were in Romania when we were there, and I couldn't imagine the economy had improved much. I knew it would be hard for my sister's friend to find anything. Yet, I couldn't stop myself from dreaming about some gorgeous shiny orb that he might find and deliver to my daughters for Christmas.

A few days before Christmas he called to say he found something "small" and we should look for it in the mail. He also warned that it was not a typical ornament. He said the stores didn't offer much and he was hard pressed to find something to hang on a tree. He refused to give up until he found something for the girls. I was impressed with his devotion. He was a total stranger offering to do a kind gesture, and I assured him that whatever he found would be cherished.

We were all excited when the package arrived. We huddled around the kitchen table and waited patiently as Patrick opened the package with a knife. He gingerly folded the top flaps back and let the girls carefully look through the tissue paper that filled the box. The moment Andrea felt something she retracted her hand and whimpered. "I'm too excited," she said. "I can't do it."

Juliana giggled. "Oh, Andrea. I'll do it."

Andrea bent down close while Juliana slowly and carefully

unfurled the object. A brown ceramic pig tumbled onto the kitchen table with a thunk. The girls looked at each other, expressionless.

Andrea picked it up and examined it closely. "What is that?" she asked in a high-pitched, squeaky voice.

"Andrea, it's a pig," Juliana said matter-of-factly.

Andrea's mouth dropped open. "Why in the world would he give us a pig?" She looked at me through her tiny glasses. "When I think of the baby Jesus being born in a stable I think of sheep, cows and donkeys. Not a pig. Was a pig there?"

Juliana laughed so hard she fell off the chair and rolled around on the kitchen floor.

I sighed deeply as I watched Pat pick up the pig and examine it, figuring out how to hang it on the tree. To him, this was the essence of their culture and it did not matter what the object was. Pat would rig it up with wire and duct tape and I would camouflage it in ribbon. Together we would hang it on our Christmas tree and be grateful.

Two weeks after Christmas the girls were sick with ear infections. Following a trip to the doctor's office, Pat waited in the car while I ran into a pharmacy to get their prescriptions filled. As I waited for the medications, I wandered through the store. A "90% off" sale sign caught my eye. That might be a great deal! That's when I saw a box of ornaments, and my heart skipped a beat. I quickly checked the small print on the side of the package to see where the ornaments were made. When I saw "Made in Romania" tears filled my eyes. I ran to the front of the store, grabbed a cart and filled it with every box on the shelf. I was so excited about the ornaments I almost forgot to get the medicine for the girls.

I cannot imagine what Pat thought when he saw me push the cart overflowing with packages to the car.

"What's all of this?" he asked. He got out of the car and opened the trunk. "This can't possibly all be medicine."

I laughed as I told him that I had been dreaming about these shiny glass ornaments with glitter and jewels for the girls. I showed him one of the boxes filled with the sparkling ornaments. "This is exactly what I wanted for the girls. They were made in Romania and I got them on sale for ninety percent off."

"That's unbelievable," he said smiling.

"What's unbelievable is that I asked if they would be getting more next year and they said no. They had never seen these ornaments before and would probably never get them again."

That was fifteen years ago. Every year I look for them, but always come up empty handed. It only makes the day that I found them that much sweeter.

~Barbara S. Canale

Santa Fell Off the Roof

It is good to be children sometimes, and never better than at Christmas,
when its mighty Founder was a child Himself.
~Charles Dickens

The room, toasty from the fire and glittering with Christmas lights, smelled of pine from our freshly cut tree. Footsteps on the roof disrupted our peaceful Christmas Eve.

Vincent, my oldest, gave me a grin and sprang to his feet. "Santa!"

Joseph, my youngest, leapt from the couch. "Santa?" He looked at the ceiling. "Really?"

"Shhh. You two should get to bed before he finds out you're awake."

The footfalls came closer and evolved into stomping. "Ho, ho, ho!" a deep voice boomed from above.

Putting his hands together like a prayer, Joseph stuck his bottom lip out so far it reached his chin. "No, Mommy! Please let me stay up and see him."

I put my finger to my lips. "You don't want to startle..."

"Agh!"

From outside, we heard a loud thud.

Vincent raced to the window. "Oh no! Santa fell off the roof!"

The rest of us hurried to look. Seeing the backside of a man in a red suit sprawled in the snow, I rushed outside and fell to my knees. "Santa! Are you okay?"

The big-bellied man rolled over and moaned, then sat up and adjusted his cap. "I think so." Chuckling, he said, "Good thing for the soft snow." He wrapped his arms around his protruding belly. "And all this extra padding I have."

Taking his hand, Vincent helped him up.

"Goodness." The big man let out a belly laugh. "That's never happened before." Bells jingled as he brushed off the snow.

Spellbound, Joseph stood with his hands on his cheeks, mouth agape, eyes huge with disbelief.

Vincent picked up the bulky bag and handed it to Santa. "Hey, my mom's a nurse. You should come in so she can make sure you're okay."

"Well..." Santa put his gloved hand to his cherry-red nose. "That sounds like a great idea." He limped inside and plopped into a chair.

I turned back and saw my son in the snow, standing as motionless as an ice sculpture. "Joseph?"

Startled, he turned his head and looked at me.

Holding out my hand, I said, "Come inside, Sweet Pea."

He drifted toward the door and then tugged on my sleeve. "Is... is that really Santa?"

Smiling, I cupped his face in my hands. "Yes, and we need to get inside so I can examine him." Before he could protest, I pulled him into the room. He sat far away and stared at the magical man from across the room with unblinking eyes.

A thorough examination found no injuries. "Nothing cookies and cocoa can't fix," I said.

When my husband entered the room, I sent him for the goodies. A few moments later, he handed them to the jolly man, who thanked him and took a bite of a cookie.

Santa's put his face over the mug and breathed in, steam wetting his white beard and coating his glasses. "Mmm. I love hot cocoa even more than milk. And these sugar cookies are my favorite."

I smiled and pointed at my petrified son in the corner. "Joseph helped me make them."

Santa waved the cookie at him. "Great job, son! Best cookie I've ever had."

Huddled in a corner, my child didn't move or speak.

Santa's white eyebrows furrowed. "What's the matter, little one?"

Everyone looked at Joseph and waited for an answer.

After a moment of silence, Santa put down the cocoa and cookies. "Are you afraid of me?"

No answer.

"Well..." Santa picked up his toy bag. "I might as well give you boys your presents while I'm here." Stuffing his head and hands in the bag, he searched. "Let's see... ah yes, here we go." When he looked up, he had three Xbox games. "I believe Vincent asked me for these."

In the blink of an eye, Vincent was at Santa's knee. "Awesome!" Excitement all over his face, he hugged the games. "Thank you. They're just what I wanted."

Santa fumbled in his bag again, then looked up at Joseph. "Come over here so I can give you your presents."

Joseph headed toward Santa at the speed of a turtle, stopping before he got too close.

Out came a tool kit. "I believe you wanted some big boy tools. Is that right?"

Joseph slowly nodded. "Yes," he whispered.

Santa unzipped the kit, pulled out two screwdrivers, a hammer, pliers, and a wrench. "These are real tools for doing real jobs. Are you going to do real jobs?"

Joseph's head bobbed up and down.

He reached into his bag again. "Well, if you're going to do real jobs, you need safety equipment too." Smiling, he held up a bright yellow Bob the Builder hardhat, safety glasses, and a tool belt.

The corners of Joseph's mouth curled up enough to fill a momma with joy. Moving closer, he gingerly took the treasures.

Santa opened the bag again. "Let's see what else I have."

A tilt of the head, a step closer, and a timid voice. "Did you get what I wanted most?"

"Hmmm." Santa again dug in his bag. "I'm sure it's in here..."

Up on his tippy-toes, Joseph leaned forward.

"Ah, here it is."

Tiny hands clasped together. "What is it?"

Santa pulled out the box, pushed his glasses in place, and read. "A sword and gun in one... lights up... makes real sword sounds..." He looked up. "Is this what you wanted?"

Unable to contain himself any longer, my sweet son jumped up and down. "That's it! That's it! Thank you!"

"Well, come and get it, boy."

All traces of fear gone, Joseph skipped the last few feet to Santa and took the box. "Thank you, thank you!" His face beamed with joy. "Look, Mommy!"

Warm elation flooded my heart. "Yes, baby. Very cool."

"Well," Santa said, "I have one more thing."

Curiosity on his face, Joseph looked at him. "What is it?"

With magician-like movements, he displayed a leather belt. "A holster."

"Wow!" He took the belt and admired it, his smile reaching his eyes. He hugged the sword and looked at Santa. "Thank you."

Santa grinned. "You bet." He stood and pointed at my boys. "You two be sure to stay on the nice list, okay?"

"Okay," they responded.

Santa threw his bag over his shoulder. "I best be going." As he left, he turned and said, "Merry Christmas to all, and to all a good night."

And then he was gone.

Joseph ran to my side and wrapped his arms around me. "I can't believe I met Santa!"

Taking him in my arms, I stroked his head. "You're a very lucky boy."

Joseph turned his sword on and swung it around, lights dancing in rhythm with the movements. He gathered his presents together and took a protective stance, slicing the air with his weapon as if guarding his spoils. "Can I play with my new stuff?"

"Just until Uncle Garry gets here. He should be..."

"Hey, everyone." Garry stood in the doorway, stomping snow off his boots. He crinkled his white eyebrows as he asked, "Did I miss anything?"

~Leigh Ann Bryant

Reprinted by permission of Dan Reynolds
CartoonResource.com ©2009

The Best Present

Those blessings are sweetest that are won with prayer and worn with thanks.
~Thomas Goodwin

I t was Christmas Day. Our first child was due in three days and I'd been feeling off all morning. Nothing too drastic, just lower back cramps and a general feeling of edginess.

I bustled about, tidying this and straightening that, trying to keep moving and distract myself. I'd been having Braxton Hicks contractions for several days and had discovered the best way to deal with them was simply to ignore them. The discomfort persisted though, and after another half hour, I realized that the pain was increasing. My face felt hot, my nerves tingled, and I couldn't sit still. My husband JP's brother Scott was stopping by to drop off gifts so I thought I would wait for that before I mentioned to JP that I wanted to go to the hospital. When JP brought everyone into the living room to share their gifts, they stopped dead in their tracks.

"What's up with you?" Scott joked. "Your face is beet red."

"Yeah," I shot back. "I think I'm in labour."

JP's jaw dropped and Scott's face went still. "Seriously?"

"Yup. Just wanted our gifts first," I joked, before a sharp pain sliced through my back. On the drive to the hospital, I thought about the path that had brought us to this place in time—a place we never thought we'd get to.

Eight years earlier, my husband had an appendectomy following a dirt biking mishap. That led to him being diagnosed with advanced testicular cancer. He was twenty-three. The cancer had spread to his lungs and chemotherapy was required to reduce the tumor before he could have surgery. He spent the next several months in and out of the hospital. At the time, testicular cancer was not as curable and his was at an advanced stage. It was a fight for his life. A young oncologist at the Cross Cancer Institute, Dr. Peter Venner, was instrumental in his treatment and recovery. One testicle was removed and JP's chances of fathering a child decreased immensely.

By the time we were thirty, we decided that perhaps we were destined to be childless. We put our name on the University of Calgary Infertility Clinic's waiting list. We wanted to exhaust our options before giving up completely.

Years after JP survived his fight, he and his dad flew to Las Vegas for a week for the Mint 400 desert road race. I hadn't been feeling well and assumed it was the flu that had been going through my office. One evening, after watching a particularly poignant romantic comedy on TV, it occurred to me I might be pregnant. The local drugstore was still open and I purchased a pregnancy test and sped home. While I waited for the results, my heart was pounding, and in spite of previous disappointments, I still held my breath in anticipation. When the blue line appeared, I burst into tears and collapsed on the floor. Oh my God, I was really and truly pregnant!

JP was still in Las Vegas so I had no one to share the news with. It was three whole days until he would be home. I was over the moon but didn't want to tell anyone but him. I am sure that I must have seemed like a crazy woman at work with my smile stretched ear to ear, my continued flu (morning sickness!) and constant babbling.

When JP arrived home, I think he already knew by the look on my face what I was about to tell him. The happiness we shared was like nothing I had ever felt before. At the end of May, when we went to the Cross Cancer Institute for JP's yearly check, Dr. Venner was as happy as we were.

As luck would have it, the Grace Hospital was full when we walked in that Christmas—we were the eighteenth maternity admittance that Christmas Day. The contractions that had been steadily building all day quickly became full labour. By the time I was wheeled into the delivery room half an hour later, I was hollering such gems as, "I've changed my mind," and, "Do you think we're ready for this?" into my poor husband's ear while squeezing the blood out of his hand. I am sure the people at the shopping mall a block away could hear me!

After what felt like days but was in fact less than two hours, I heard the words "You have a daughter" and JP's massive hug came to me as if in a dream. Tears ran down my face and I knew from JP's audible gulp that he felt the same way. The nurse placed our daughter on my chest and I kissed her beautiful face, at peace with God and the world as I looked into her eyes for the first time.

"What's her name?" the nurse asked softly.

"Katie — Katherine Sarah Petra, I mean," I whispered, in awe at this miracle I held.

Wheeled to my room, with Katie in an isolette at the foot of my bed, I napped between feedings. At one point I realized I was starving as I had skipped lunch as well as supper. One of the nurses located a tuna sandwich for me and JP went in search of Christmas dinner in the form of Saran-wrapped turkey on a plate. He still talks about the Christmas dinner he missed!

In honour of the day, an ornament with "Baby's First Christmas" written on it was placed in the isolette, along with a large red stocking that Katie could actually fit into.

"Merry Christmas, love," my husband said to me. "Merry Christmas, husband," I replied softly, as he handed me our healthy little girl.

Two years later, we were blessed with our son Evan, making our family complete. While he was not born on Christmas Day, he is as much a gift as his sister. We are truly grateful for both of them each and every day of our lives. Christmas is indeed a magical time.

~Lynn D. Gale

It's Christmas!

Santa's Elves

The joy of brightening other lives, bearing each others' burdens, easing other's loads and supplanting empty hearts and lives with generous gifts becomes for us the magic of Christmas.

~W. C. Jones

The Christmas Stranger

Wherever there is a human being, there is an opportunity for a kindness.
~Seneca

Our daughter and son were now young adults and I had to think of ways to make our time together memorable—especially since our daughter, Alicia, had moved 3,000 miles away after graduating from college. The days of a living room filled with new toys were past, but having us all together for Christmas was even more precious. It was time to create a new tradition.

That's how the Twelve Days of Christmas began at our house. When the kids came home that year they found twelve slips of paper folded in half, numbered 1-12 and taped to their bedroom doors.

"What's up with the numbers on our doors, Mom?" Joshua asked.

"Twelve Days of Christmas," I said. "Each day, starting today, you and Alicia will open one of the slips of paper and reveal something special. It will be fun!" I could see they were doubtful. Maybe they were thinking about the time I took them to Martha's Vineyard and thought it would be a good idea to ride bikes around the island—before I realized it would be a thirteen-mile trek. Or the time we went to San Francisco and almost killed ourselves riding a bicycle built for ten around Golden Gate Park. Or the time we got hit by a sandstorm that wiped out our tent while we were camping at Jalama Beach. My penchant for making memories took us on some pretty wild rides!

"Don't worry... it will be fun," I reassured my kids. One day was movie night and we all went to the show. One night was game night and we stayed in and played our favorite board games. One night we watched our favorite Christmas movies—*Home Alone* and *Christmas Vacation*. It wasn't that we were doing anything exotic or expensive—we were just making sure to spend time together.

One special thing we did was hire a photographer to take our family photo down at the beach. The whole experience was a blast and the pictures that grace our home are a constant reminder of the fun we had that December day.

One by one the slips of paper were opened, until it was Christmas Eve. I had purchased a gift certificate to try a little restaurant that sits on a charming manmade lake near our home. My plan was to get a bite to eat together and then go to church. The restaurant was quiet. We chatted with the owner and waitress for a few minutes before being seated on the patio so we could take advantage of the lake view. We had the patio to ourselves with the exception of one man, sitting alone, at the table behind us. He lifted his glass and said "hello" as we settled into our seats. We all smiled politely and responded warmly, but then went back to our family conversation.

Our food came and, as is our custom, we gave thanks to God. I vaguely remember the man at the table behind us making a nice comment about us saying grace and we again smiled politely and continued with our family conversation. Sometime during our meal, I gave the waitress our gift certificate and when we were finished she came back with the bill on a tray. I reached for my wallet, knowing there would be a difference to pay beyond what the certificate would cover.

"Don't worry about it," the waitress said, motioning me to stop looking for my money.

"But I know the gift certificate wasn't enough to cover the bill;

there must be a balance," I said, wondering if maybe the owner had decided not to charge us because it was Christmas Eve.

"No, here," she said. "You can have the gift certificate back."

"I don't understand," I said. "Is this on the house?" We all had puzzled looks on our faces.

"No," she said. It was clear from her demeanor that she was a little shook up. "The gentleman who was sitting at the table behind you took care of the bill. In the eight years I have been working here, I've never seen anyone do that before. Here's your gift certificate back."

We were stunned, too shocked to respond. What would cause someone to do something like that? We didn't know him; we hardly even spoke to him.

"Oh," the waitress continued, "he asked me to give this to you." She handed us a handwritten note. It simply said:

God bless you!
God loves you & so do I.
Merry Christmas.

We looked around, frantically trying to see if we could find the kind stranger. My son jogged to the parking lot, hoping he might still be around so we could thank him properly. But at some point while we were engrossed in conversation he had left.

Our eyes filled with tears as we realized what a gracious thing this man had done, how his act of kindness had not only affected us, but also the waitress and owner. Our eyes also filled with tears because we realized we had missed an opportunity to be gracious ourselves—we never thought to reach out and ask him to join us, and for that we were filled with regret.

We knew we couldn't go back and change what was done, but the Christmas stranger had inspired us and we realized that we could at least pay it forward. We now had a new thing to add to our Twelve Days of Christmas. The few days after Christmas that we still had together were spent looking for opportunities to bless someone else with little acts of kindness and generosity. We gave each other bonus points if we were able to surprise someone anonymously. Each day we would come home and share the ways we might have been able to be a blessing to someone that day—paying for goods when a wallet was forgotten in the car, paying for the coffee order for the people behind you, stopping to spend a few minutes in conversation with someone who looked lonely.

The Twelve Days of Christmas became a new family tradition that continues. We now treasure the special times and activities we do together as a family—but we also treasure the chance to be a blessing to others. This year we added a new element to our tradition—to take $100 and use it all up before Christmas to bless those we come in contact with who are in need. It is our way of remembering the Christmas stranger who was a blessing to us.

~Lynne Leite

My Own Life

The excellence of a gift lies in its appropriateness rather than in its value.
~Charles Dudley Warner

Father John was young, handsome, and filled with a desire to change the world. When he joined our parish, everyone was surprised by his energy—he seemed to love life and every challenge it brought. As my parents felt it was their duty to make our parish priests an integral part of the community, Father John often attended our private family functions and shared meals with us almost every week. This regular inclusion made me somewhat of an "insider" amongst my circle of fourth grade friends. Nobody ever got to see the priests out of their robes and collars, but I had actually seen Father John in Bermuda shorts and a golf shirt, having a beer with my dad as they told stories and flipped burgers on the barbeque.

All nine of my brothers and sisters liked Father John. I did too. Besides the obvious fact that he was young and good-looking, it seemed he really liked being with us. He could be sillier than any adult I had ever met—the only time I remember laughing so hard that milk spurted out of my nose was with Father John as he impersonated my dad at the dinner table. As a new priest out of seminary, it had not been that long since he had been one of about a dozen kids in an Irish Catholic family himself, struggling for some sort of individuality in a sea of conformity. I think he recognized that we shared that with him, so he spent time with my siblings and me to get to know each of us. Not just the obvious things, like our favorite sports or subjects in school, but things we weren't comfortable telling anyone else: our secret fears, what we wanted but felt we couldn't, or shouldn't, have.

On the Christmas Eve when I was nine, Father John drove up our driveway in his old rusty Pinto and began to empty the back seat, removing ten extremely large wrapped packages. It reminded me of the circus trick when clown after clown bails out of a tiny Volkswagen bug. He carried each oversized and wildly wrapped box (not Christmas paper—that would be much too conventional for Father John) into the house and placed them under the enormous Christmas tree. By the time he was done delivering his packages, our living room went from a scene in a Dickens novel to unimaginable abundance. The room overflowed. We were even more perplexed upon picking them up—they were light as air—and each shook with a slightly different cadence. Father John just laughed and said he would see us all tomorrow at mass. Speculation as to the contents of those gigantic packages went on for hours, until Dad announced we needed to get to bed or Santa wouldn't come.

Before dawn the next morning, we ran down the slippery wooden stairs, right past the gifts from Santa, to rip open the mysterious boxes from Father John. Inside each package were three giant boxes of our favorite cereal. My boxes said in heavy black magic marker "Bridget's Life—Hands Off!" I often have wondered if his message and its double meaning were intentional.

To fully appreciate the import of these gifts, you must understand that my family was strictly a Cheerios and Rice Krispies clan. And not even Cheerios with a capital "C"—I mean the knock-off generic "O-O's" you find on the bottom shelf of the grocery store aisle, that come in giant re-sealable plastic bags that never really re-seal, so the cereal is stale and tastes like cardboard within hours of opening. Sugar cereal was not allowed. The only time we got to partake of such forbidden fruit was at friends' houses on the occasional sleepover. So this gift was truly a treasure. Cradling my boxes in my arms, I could already taste the satisfying, sugary crunch of eating my Life right out of the box. This gift meant at least several weeks of reprieve from the sawdust that was our standard morning routine.

It took a minute before it dawned on each of us that these selections were not random. They were the single favorite cereal of each recipient. But how did Father John know? Even I was surprised to learn that my brother's favorite was Apple Jacks, and my little sister longed for Cocoa Puffs. How could he have known?

My oldest brother burst out laughing, and shouted his secret with delight: "Not one of you suspected!"

Father John had enlisted Leo as his accomplice. He asked him to pretend he was doing a survey on favorite cereals as a class assignment. Under the guise of a school project, weeks before, Leo had collected the data needed for Father John to surprise each of us on Christmas morning.

I've never forgotten the thrill of receiving the perfect present. It required cunning and forethought to learn what I would want. It was unexpected. The package was mysterious. The present was delicious. But most importantly, it was a gift that would mean absolutely nothing to anybody else, but to me it said that I was special and deserved a unique gift. It's everything a nine-year-old would want in a gift.

No, it's everything anyone, of any age, would want in a gift.

~Bridget McNamara-Fenesy

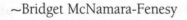

24

Impractically Perfect

We should all be thankful for those people who rekindle the inner spirit.
~Albert Schweitzer

I wasn't looking forward to Christmas. The chronic illness I suffered from took the joy out of what should have been a happy time, I was feeling discouraged and depressed. I didn't have the physical or mental energy to appreciate anything about the holiday season.

A few weeks before Christmas, our neighbor Teri was driving down our street on her way home. When she saw me out in the front yard, she stopped her van in the middle of the road to talk. Teri was a pastor's wife and our young sons were best friends. She was on a tight budget like we were and had just returned from shopping at yard sales.

"I bought you a Christmas present," she announced, with a big grin and twinkling eyes. "It's not new," she warned me. "But it's clean. I found it at my friend's yard sale." It was obvious Teri was pleased with her purchase. "I really couldn't afford to spend the money," she admitted, "but I had to buy it because it's something you've been wanting. I'll bring it over when I get it wrapped."

I was caught off guard by what Teri said. I never expected a present from Teri. And for the life of me I couldn't imagine what it might be. How could she know what I wanted, anyway, when I didn't know myself? With all my health issues, I had become too discouraged to even care about wanting anything.

The next day, Teri came to our front door with the gift. It was wrapped in bright paper, tied with shiny ribbon and topped with a big bow. Teri made me promise to wait until Christmas to open it. As she handed it to me, I felt a twinge of excitement.

When I brought the package in the house, I tried to picture its contents. By the size and weight of the box, I thought it might be a blanket. Did I ever say I wanted a blanket? I didn't think so. What in the world had I told her I wanted?

It's amazing what a little suspense did to my outlook. I couldn't stop thinking about what might be in the box. Sitting there on the floor under the Christmas tree, the package drew me to it like a moth to a light bulb. Every so often, when no one was looking, I would pick it up, shake it back and forth and try to guess what was inside. Why did I keep thinking of a blanket?

Before I knew it, my pessimistic attitude began to change. With something to distract me from my health problems, life didn't seem quite so difficult or dreary. Teri's thoughtful gesture was such an encouragement to me. I felt happier than I had in a very long time.

Christmas morning arrived and with it much anticipation. Even so, I was not convinced that Teri could have known what I wanted. Yet, she seemed so certain, it made me want to believe it was true. The excitement and expectation that had been stirred up in me kept that hope alive.

While we were opening our presents, the phone rang. It was Teri. She wanted to know if I liked her gift. I told Teri she would have to be patient. So important had her gift become to my optimistic state of mind that, weeks before, I made the decision to wait and open it last.

After all the other presents had been unwrapped, I picked up her package. As anxious as I was to know what was in the box, I wanted to savor the moment. I took my time as I removed the bow, loosened the ribbon and pulled off each piece of the tape. I slipped off the wrapping paper, folded it up and set it down next to me on the couch. Then I slowly lifted off the lid and peeled back the tissue paper. What I saw took my breath away! Inside the box was a stunning, snow white, rabbit fur jacket. And when I put it on, it fit me like a glove. Teri was right. It was exactly what I wanted.

Instantly, the picture of a gray rabbit fur jacket I once owned and loved flashed into my mind. A gift from a long forgotten boyfriend, it had been years since I had disposed of it after it wore out. But there was something glamorous about a fur jacket that made me feel like a movie star—young, invincible and fabulous. I longed for the way that jacket made me feel.

Though I did not recall, and usually didn't share such trivial desires with anyone, I must have told Teri about it. That Teri remembered what I told her about my old gray jacket and understood how much it meant to me, made me cherish her friendship more than ever.

The fur jacket Teri gave me was a frivolous thing for someone struggling to make ends meet and totally impractical in the hot desert climate where I live. But sometimes something frivolous is just what you need. Like balm to chapped and weathered hands, it can soothe the soul. It can kindle feelings of hope. Teri knew that. And she was willing to sacrifice so I would experience that magical feeling again.

Years have passed since that Christmas and many things have changed. Teri and her family moved away. Our boys have grown into fine young men. I am at the age when gray hair and wrinkles are my new normal. I will never again be young or feel invincible. But every time I put that jacket on... I feel fabulous!

~RoseAnn Faulkner

25

Past, Present, and Future

May no gift be too small to give, nor too simple to receive,
which is wrapped in thoughtfulness and tied with love.
~L. O. Baird

When my husband asked me what I wanted for Christmas, I'm not sure if he was prepared for my reply: "The Famous Five series." His first response was, "What's that?"

I had to explain. He knew about my life as a missionary kid. He knew there was loss and grief associated with moving so many times and not really being able to go home again. He knew I had lost some material things along the way and would have loved to feel connected to a piece of each homeland I had known and loved. What I hadn't explained quite yet was my desire to connect with my past through the books I had enjoyed as a child.

During our elementary school years in Austria, my older brother and I would frequent the British bookshop in Vienna. During those visits and various book fairs at my heavily British-influenced school we acquired all twenty-one books in the Famous Five series by the British author Enid Blyton.

We were so proud to have the whole series, and enjoyed reading about the adventures of the "Five," which included siblings Julian,

Dick, and Anne as well as their cousin Georgina (George) and her dog Timothy. Their adventures were akin to the Nancy Drew and Hardy Boys series; written in overlapping time periods, albeit set in England, with British perspective and vocabulary. The stories feature outlandish plots revolving around catching smugglers, counterfeiters and kidnappers—quite extraordinary, considering the heroes were mere teenagers! My brother and I loved them, though. The books were our passports to adventures we would never experience in our own lives.

Unfortunately, while my brother and I were at boarding school in Germany, our family had to return to the States quite abruptly from Turkey due to a health emergency. My parents had to make some difficult decisions about what to bring to America. Since books are heavy, my parents were unable to bring most of our books with them, including the Famous Five series. I was heartbroken when I found out, but with so many other adjustments to distract me, my loss was tucked in the back of my mind.

Fast forward to seven years into my marriage, some seventeen years after I'd left my treasured Famous Five series behind, and the Christmas I decided I wanted to acquire my books. I had been searching the Internet for the series and getting frustrated, because no American book publishers or websites had the books. We could have bought them on a foreign website, but we were nervous about using our credit card that way and having them shipped from overseas.

With all the distractions of the approaching holidays, I once again tucked the loss of my beloved books in the back of my mind, and focused on making the holiday memorable for my little girl. Christmas Eve arrived and my husband, daughter, and I sat around the decorated Christmas tree, which sparkled in the darkened living room. We traditionally opened one present on Christmas Eve and each of us picked a gift. My daughter opened hers first, then my husband. I eyed my chosen present, a colorfully wrapped box, and guessed what it might be. "An elephant?" my daughter giggled. "Oh, let's end the suspense!" I said, and began ripping off the wrapping.

It was a brown box, taped shut with clear packing tape. Could it be? I thought to myself. No way! As I picked at and pulled off the tape, my disbelief gave way to amazed joy as I beheld the title for the first book of the Famous Five series... and realized all twenty-one books in the series were nestled in the opened box! I looked up at my husband, with tears spilling over and dripping down my cheeks. "Thank you," I whispered, setting the box down and throwing my arms around his neck as he sat on the floor. "But," I stammered, "What American publisher was selling them? Where did you get them?"

My husband looked at me rather sheepishly and said, "India."

Apparently, he had scoured the Internet and found a British publisher that was reprinting the entire series in India, and paid the amount in British pounds. Never mind he had to break his rule and use our credit card in far-off India; my happiness was apparently more important. This gift did not just replace some of the many cherished items I had lost from my childhood, it signified the incredible love and devotion of my husband. His thoughtfulness gave me courage to believe I could heal, a little bit at a time, and reminded me that I was worth the effort.

Being a teacher, I had the entire Christmas break to read through all the books. It was wonderful. So many memories resurfaced as I read; my mother reading the suspenseful plots from the series to me and my brother, and times I had read by myself, treasuring my solitude in my cozy apartment bedroom. I laughed at how cheesy some of the plots seemed from the perspective of an adult. Throughout my marathon of reading, I felt like I was returning home.

Whether a gift revives the past, celebrates the present or looks toward the future, the way it makes you feel treasured as an individual is paramount. My husband gave me back a piece of my lost childhood, but I am even more grateful for what he did for my future.

~Kristina J. Adams

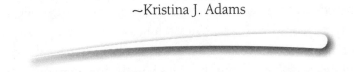

26

The Best Christmas Ever

Keep your Christmas-heart open all the year round.
~Jessica Archmint

The Christmas holiday was approaching, and I was working in a dental office. One day, the dental assistant and I were cleaning the teeth of two little girls — sisters. I asked my tiny patient, "Are you excited for Christmas to get here?" With my hands in her mouth she nodded. Next I asked, "What do you want for Christmas?" She pushed my hands out of her mouth.

"My dad had a talk with us. He told us that Santa won't be bringing presents this year because we don't have any money." She continued, "He feels really bad but it's okay. I went shopping with my aunt and got my mom and dad socks for Christmas." I could hear her older sister "shushing" her from the adjoining operatory.

Tears were burning my eyes. "Well, I'm sure that it will be fun with your family." Next, she said, "My grandma will cook food but we don't have a Christmas tree or anything either."

The other dental assistant and I looked at each other. She was obviously as moved as I was. With a lump in my throat, I said, "I am sure that it will be a good Christmas." My heart was breaking as I watched this adorable little girl head back to the waiting room to join her mother.

I met with her mom to explain the outcome of the day's check-up and in that moment I noticed the office Christmas tree.

At lunchtime the office staff was buzzing as I told them the story of the sisters. I then asked my boss if we could give them the office tree. He wanted to but was cautious because he didn't want to offend the family. He thought out loud, "We have to find a way to give them the tree without being hurtful."

"What if we told them they somehow won it?" I asked. This was getting exciting now. Everyone was chipping in money, presents and food. Another patient overheard us and asked if she could write us a check for $100 so that we could buy the girls and their parents Christmas presents.

The next day, I called the patients' home. I told the mother that we drew the name of her daughter and that they won our office Christmas tree decorations and all... that is, if they didn't have one yet. She replied, "No, we don't have one... yet." Her voice cracked as she answered.

"Great!" I almost shouted, "Can we deliver it tonight?"

We loaded up the tree in my boss's truck and headed to... well... let's just say not the nicest part of town. The excited girls met us at the door and asked us to come in. As we dragged the tree through the door my heart sank. I knew that it was going to be rough; I just didn't expect it to be this hard. It was obvious that the family was struggling to make ends meet and that presents and a tree were not even a slight possibility.

We pulled out the decorations and they asked us to stay and help. When we were finished we plugged in the lights. We all just stood there in silence. I mean, the kind of silence that gets heavy and still. Again I could feel the tears well up. Finally, our little patient exclaimed, "This tree is beautiful. This is going to be the best Christmas ever!"

The next day was Christmas Eve. I shopped, wrapped and bagged the gifts. I boxed a turkey and all of the trimmings carefully. Late that night my husband and I drove with our car lights off down the street with bags and boxes. We carried our first load to the front of the yard.

"The gate's locked," my husband whispered to me.

"Then climb over the fence," I told him.

"Lori, you don't climb over fences at midnight in this neighborhood unless you want to get shot," he replied.

"I bet Santa would," I laughed.

We ended up tossing the bags over the fence and hurrying off to call the family and alert them that their yard was full of surprises.

"Hello," a sleepy voice answered.

"Go look in your front yard, man," Bob said.

"Who is this? What are you talking about? I think you have the wrong number," was the reply.

"No, I have the right number. Go look in your front yard. There are bags of gifts for you and your family. Have a wonderful Christmas!" Bob hung up.

We wondered how the family enjoyed their gifts the next day. I could almost hear my tiny patient shout, "I told you that this would be the best Christmas ever!"

~Lori Bryant

27

Not Alone

Kind words can be short and easy to speak but their echoes are truly endless.
~Mother Teresa

Christmas had always been a big deal in my family. Somewhere deep inside, I believed that I would never spend Christmas away from my loved ones. All through college and a couple of years post-college, I always made it home, even if I arrived, like Santa, on Christmas Eve.

Then came the year I was twenty-four. My family home was in Colorado, but I was working as a waitress in Indiana. I assumed that I would get time off to go home for Christmas. Didn't everyone get a Christmas break? Imagine my horror when the schedule was posted, and being the most recent hire, everyone else's holiday requests trumped mine. I was scheduled to work until closing at 5 p.m. on Christmas Eve and be back to open at 10 a.m. on the 26th. There was no way I was going home.

I tried consoling myself. It was just another day. No big deal. I would be fine spending Christmas alone in my one-bedroom apartment. But my heart was breaking. I went to work the next morning with a heavy sadness engulfing me. I slumped down at the bar with another waitress, telling her about my plight, paying little to no attention to the eighteen-year-old busboy setting up tables behind us. I didn't even know his name.

"I couldn't help overhearing your conversation," he said walking over to where we sat. "I just started here four weeks ago and got the same lousy schedule that you did."

"I'm sorry." I replied with sympathy in my voice.

"It's not so bad for me, I'm from a little town in southern Michigan, only a two-hour drive from here, I will just head up there as soon as we close on Christmas Eve. You could come with me."

"Thanks," I said, and laughed, not taking him seriously. "I will be fine at my apartment."

The following morning, December 23rd, the boy ran over to me as soon as I walked through the door to the restaurant.

"I talked to my mom," he said enthusiastically. "She agrees you should not spend Christmas alone. She is getting the guest room made up for you. It will be fun."

I didn't know what to say. Did I really want to spend Christmas with total strangers? I thought about my tiny apartment and the prospect of eating a turkey TV dinner, alone, and I decided what the heck! "Okay, if you're sure I won't be an intrusion."

He beamed at me. "Not at all. My family is great. Just bring your clothes with you to work tomorrow and we can leave from here as soon as our shift ends."

As he walked away, I asked, "Just one question. What is your name?"

"It's Robert, but my friends call me Robbie."

Christmas Eve found the two us heading north in Robbie's ancient car. As the miles sped by, I learned he had moved down to the city to attend community college in the fall, and he missed his small hometown where he believed he was related to most of the 1,000 residents.

We pulled into a tiny town around seven that evening, with several inches of snow on the ground and a light snow still falling. I felt like we had entered a Currier and Ives Christmas card. First stop was the VFW hall. His extended family, nearly 100 people of all ages, was gathered there to celebrate Christmas Eve. I was warmly greeted by so many nice people that the names and faces became a blur.

After partaking in the huge potluck spread, consisting of every holiday food imaginable, everyone lined the room with folding chairs for their annual White Elephant gift exchange. Robbie's mom had purchased gifts for her son and myself so we could participate. The next hour was spent laughing and joking and stealing the best presents from the others in the room. I had so much fun that I forgot I was not a member of the family.

Later we headed to his family's old farmhouse, and I settled into their quaint guest room for the night. I woke Christmas morning to the excited squeals of his two younger sisters and made my way down to their living room to watch the family open presents. Another twinge of sadness stabbed me. I was an outsider. How I longed to be home opening presents with my family. Much to my surprise, there was a stack of six presents with my name on them.

"Everyone needs presents on Christmas," his mom explained. "I didn't know what you needed, so I hope you will like them."

Tears welled up in my eyes at her kindness. I was truly delighted by the small kitchen items and homemade presents she had assembled for me. When all the presents were unwrapped, Robbie's mom asked if I would like to use their telephone to call my family.

"I would love to," I exclaimed. "But are you sure it's not too expensive?" In those days it was not cheap to make long distance calls, and we all did it sparingly.

"It's Christmas. Of course you should call them."

The conversation with my mom was interesting as I tried to explain where I was and who I was with. Soon Robbie's grandparents arrived and we all enjoyed a huge turkey dinner, followed by many laughter-filled rounds of card and board games.

We turned in early that night, knowing that we had to get up at the crack of dawn and head back to the city to work. Leaving in the morning, there were hugs all around. I truly felt that in a few short hours, I had become part of their family. I was urged to come back and visit anytime and I promised that I would. Even then I sadly doubted it would ever happen.

The next few days flew by and I didn't see my new friend. About a week later, Robbie walked into the bar at the beginning of my shift.

"I have news," he said. "I've decided to move back home and start school nearby this semester. This is my last shift here."

"Good luck. I really enjoyed your family. Let's keep in touch."

Had there been e-mail or Facebook in those days it might have happened, but the truth is I never heard from him again. Later that year, I too left Indiana, moving back home to Colorado.

That was the only Christmas I ever spent away from my family. Since then, so many wonderful Christmases have been celebrated with my parents, and later with my children, and now, my grandchildren. All of them were filled with precious memories. And yet, whenever I am asked the question, "What is your favorite Christmas memory?" my mind always goes back to that long ago Christmas and the kindness of strangers.

~Jill Haymaker

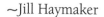

28

Big Brother

Siblings are the people we practice on, the people who teach us about fairness
and cooperation and kindness and caring — quite often the hard way.
~Pamela Dugdale

My brother and I hurried down the steps in bare feet and raced to the tree. "Santa came!" I squealed, spotting several neatly wrapped presents tucked under the branches. We plopped to our knees and began inspecting every package.

"This one's for you." Steve slid a red and green present across the carpet toward me. "And this one's for me." He smiled, placing it on top of his growing stack of gifts.

I studied Steve's pile, and marveled at how he always managed to make Santa's list. He wasn't a horrible brother. Sometimes he was my best friend. But other times, his naughty outweighed his nice. Especially when it came to his little sister. He particularly liked destroying my toys. Like the year Santa gave me a Mrs. Beasley doll.

I remembered Mrs. Beasley's big blue eyes greeting me as I slid her out of the box. I'd never owned a doll that could talk before, and I was eager to hear her speak. I positioned her in my lap, straightened the blue, polka-dotted apron around her waist and pulled the string.

"I do think you're the nicest little friend I ever had."

Mrs. Beasley and I became good friends. We spent hours playing together. Through good times and bad, she always greeted me with a warm smile and pleasant conversation.

Until that tragic day when she stopped talking.

I'm not sure I'll ever know my brother's motive for such a heinous crime. Maybe it was curiosity, like the time he hacked into his Stretch Armstrong to see what was inside, releasing a thick, jelly-like slime. Maybe he just wanted to see what makes a doll speak. Maybe it was payback to an annoying little sister. Or maybe he was just having a bad day. Whatever the reason, poor Mrs. Beasley met an awful fate the day Steve ripped out her voice box. She never spoke another word.

Looking back, I'll admit I wasn't the perfect sister. Steve probably got tired of me following him around and badgering him to play. I suppose he didn't appreciate me snooping through his room, or tattling to Mom when he beheaded my Barbies. But through all our fights I had a sneaking suspicion. He would never admit it, but I suspected that somewhere, deep down in his heart, Steve had a soft spot for his little sister.

However, my brother wasn't into mushy stuff. Even when he did something nice, he'd shrug it off in his "no big deal" kind of way. Like the time he came home from school with a bag full of Christmas candy.

I took one look at that candy and wished I could go to school. Why did I have to stay home with Mom? I wanted a Christmas party!

"Go ahead. Take it," he said, tossing me the bag.

I studied his innocent expression. Was he serious? Why would he give it to me? Maybe he had dropped it on the bus floor. I finally decided to trust him.

"Thanks!" I dug my hand deep into the bag.

"Whatever," he said, making a face.

It's been thirty-five years since my brother and I raced down the stairs on Christmas morning. Eventually, we grew up and forgot our petty sibling rivalries. Now our yearly tradition is to gather at Mom's, now referred to as "Grandma's house," every Christmas Eve. We no longer dig through the presents under Mom's tree. Only the kids get presents at Grandma's. Except one year when a surprise waited for me.

"Hey Mom, there's a present with your name on it." My oldest daughter held up a shiny red box.

"A present for me? Who's it from?" I glanced around the room. No one else seemed particularly interested.

"Doesn't say." She handed me the gift. My three girls circled around me.

I ripped back the paper and immediately spotted the words "Collectible Doll" printed across the box.

"How about that?" I said, pulling the doll out of the box. Her warm, familiar smile greeted me, and I propped her on my lap. "I've got a brand new Mrs. Beasley doll!" She was perfect. Apron neatly pressed. Miniature glasses centered squarely on her nose. Blond hair curled in place.

A puzzled look settled across my daughters' faces as if to say, "What's so special about a blue, polka-dotted doll?" But I knew why she was special. Mrs. Beasley confirmed the suspicions I'd had all along. After all these years, my big brother still had a soft spot for his little sis.

Across the room, Steve glanced up from his pie... and shrugged.

~Sheri Zeck

29

'Tis Better to Give

A mother is a person who, seeing there are only four pieces of pie for five people, promptly announces she never did care for pie.

~Tenneva Jordan

I knew I was not supposed to be quite so excited. I was too old for that. At age eleven, the oldest and my mom's "grown up" girl, I had to keep my cool. I was in middle school after all. But every chance I got, when I was alone, I checked each present under the tree. I read every tag and felt every package, guessing at the contents within. I had examined each gift so often that I could tell which present went to which person without even looking at the tags.

It had been a tough year for my family. Whenever my mom looked over at the tree and scattered presents, she would sigh and warn us, "There won't be as much for Christmas this year. Try not to be disappointed." Christmas had traditionally been a time for my parents to spoil us. In years past, the presents would pile up and spill out from under the tree, taking over the living room. I had heard the phrase "giving is better than receiving," but thought that whoever had said that must have been out of their mind. Getting presents was the whole point! It was the reason I couldn't get to sleep on Christmas Eve.

On Christmas morning, we eagerly waited in the hallway until Dad told us everything was ready. We rushed into the living room and let the wrapping paper fly. We made weak attempts to wait and watch while other family members opened their presents, but as the time passed we lost our self-control.

"Here's another one for you," said Mom as she handed me a package. I looked at it, confused. Having spent so much time examining the presents before Christmas, I recognized this one. But it had not been mine. It was my mom's. A new label had been put on it, with my name written in my mother's handwriting.

"Mom, I can't…"

I was stopped by my mother's eager, joyful look—a look I could not really understand. "Let's see what it is, honey. Hurry and open it."

It was a blow dryer. Though this may seem but a simple gift, to me it was so much more. Being an eleven-year-old girl, I was stunned. In my world, where receiving outweighed giving by light years, my mom's act of selflessness was incomprehensible. It was a huge act. Tears filled my eyes and I thought in disbelief about how much my mom must love me to give up her Christmas so I could have a few more presents.

I have always remembered that Christmas fondly. It had such an impact on me. As an adult with children in my life whom I adore, I can now understand my mom's actions. I see how she was not "giving up her Christmas" as I had thought, but was finding an even greater joy in her Christmas because giving truly is better than receiving. My mom's simple act meant the world to me.

~Jennifer Yardley Barney

30

Sharing a Legacy of Love

Compromise, if not the spice of life, is its solidity.
It is what makes nations great and marriages happy.
~Phyllis McGinley

When my mother died at the age of eighty-four, my four sisters and I were heartbroken. How could we ever get over the loss of this warm and loving woman, a talented artist who enjoyed life in spite of its challenges and always doted on her husband, daughters and grandchildren?

For weeks after, my sisters and I would meet for dinner, laughing and crying over old memories. When it came time to sell the home my mother loved, we spent many days in disbelief, clearing out her belongings. I remembered reading an Ann Landers column years earlier that discussed how many siblings fight bitterly over the possessions left by their deceased parents. I thought, "How lucky we are that will never happen to us." Somehow, we easily and peacefully divided Mom's belongings—furniture, jewelry and household items—among ourselves and a few charities. Although I expected there might be a tug of war over her paintings, that never happened. Pretty good considering there were five daughters and four grandchildren. No conflicts, squabbles or disputes at all. Until we discovered the old nativity set in a box in Mom's closet.

I remembered Mom telling the story of how she acquired the manger. An old friend who did carpentry work gave it to my mom and dad as a Christmas gift when they were first married. My sister, Eileen, however, remembers it differently. Mom told her she found the crèche in a garbage can belonging to Mrs. Bingham, the elderly lady who lived across the street from us.

Unlike some of the ornate versions found in today's stores, this manger was crafted from dark wood and completely unadorned—just a roof, a floor and a railing surrounding it. Though beautifully crafted, there was one flaw: one side of the double gate in front was lopsided. Mom filled it with three figurines to start—Mary, Joseph and the Baby Jesus. For many years after, she continued to add others—the Wise Men, shepherds, angels, and animals. As kids, we loved the annual rites of the Christmas season, especially taking the nativity set and decorations down from the attic and carefully putting them in place. When the sisters all married and grandchildren came along, they added new characters of their own to the stable, including a set of the three little pigs.

After Mom's death, when the nativity set emerged, no one was prepared for the battle that would follow. My sister Joanne was the first to claim the manger, insisting it was the only one of Mom's possessions that she really wanted. Her wish was granted. But when my niece Mandy found out, she called from her apartment in California to voice her objection. She was clearly emotional as she repeated a decades-old promise made to her by my mother: "Nanny promised me that I could have the nativity set when she was gone," she cried. "The nativity set belongs to me." Joanne felt strongly that as Mom's daughter, she had first dibs. Neither she nor Mandy would budge.

When the disagreement showed signs of becoming a full-blown family feud, we realized something had to be done. Enter the family arbitrator, my sister Eileen, who somehow saw through the fog. But as Mandy's mother and Joanne's sister, could Eileen handle this dilemma fairly? Temporarily, she set aside the emotion of the dispute, and thought logically. The nativity set was just a wooden stable, not an irreplaceable masterpiece of art. The beauty was in the eye of the beholders, the perception of two people who coveted a simple item owned by someone they loved. Couldn't a copy be created? Of course! She would order the wood from the lumberyard and get someone to build a second manger.

The following day, Eileen went to Centre Millwork and stood in line behind several contractors ordering lumber from a young man with a crewcut. He was wearing a tag with his name, Brett, written in green magic marker. When Eileen's turn came, she had to shout over the sound of buzzing saws. She pointed to the nativity set in her arms and told him the story, explaining that it was causing a major rift between her sister Joanne and her daughter Mandy. Brett took the stable from her, held it up with one hand and laughed, "They're fighting over this?"

"Yes," Eileen explained. "I know it seems crazy, but it was my mother's and they both loved her very much. Is there any way you could measure and cut some wood so we could have a duplicate built?

Brett said, "Leave it here. I'll see what I can do." Eileen left, hoping he could come up with a minor miracle. That's what it would take to satisfy the two women in her life that were squabbling.

A few days later, she received a phone message saying that her order was ready. When Eileen arrived at the hardware store to pick up the wood, she couldn't believe what she saw—two identical stables sitting side by side. Brett had not only cut and measured the wood, he had built a second manger. "I know you wanted them to look the same, so I added a couple of dings and flaws that were in the original. Hope that's okay."

Sure enough, the new stable had the same lopsided front gate. "Okay?" Eileen said in tears. "You have no idea what this will mean to my sister and my daughter. To the entire family. I don't care what this costs. Your work has saved the day."

"That will be $3.75 for the materials," Brett said. When Eileen insisted on paying him more, he said, "I didn't do it on company time. I built it at home so I won't charge you for the labor." He pointed to the new manger. "I hope this helps your family have a merrier Christmas."

Eileen left Brett with a large tip and a big hug of thanks. When she got home and called Joanne and Mandy about her creative solution, they were very happy and extremely relieved that the problem was resolved. One phone call later, Joanne and Mandy had agreed that Joanne would take possession of the new stable as well as some of the old figurines—including Mary, Joseph and the infant. Mandy would get to keep the original—just as Nanny promised.

~Kathy Melia Levine

Just Passing By

Love and kindness are never wasted. They always make a difference.
They bless the one who receives them, and they bless you, the giver.
~Barbara De Angelis

Spending Christmas at a motel in a small town sounds like the plot of a holiday blockbuster, but for our family, this was no movie. Through unforeseen circumstances, we were called away from our home and friends in Minnesota to a new job in southern Kansas.

To make matters worse, the start-up date for the job was three weeks before Christmas and we were forced to make the move in the winter. We decided to do most of our eleven-hour drive at night. That way, our ten-year-old son Jeff and his five-year old brother Jamie would sleep through much of the tedious trip.

I was fearful that our old brown station wagon wouldn't make the trip because two of the tires were threadbare. I mentioned it to no one, but somebody must have noticed. An anonymous envelope of money was given to us with a note to buy four new tires before we left Minnesota.

That was just like our little community. Most of the love and outreach was a reflection of our Pastor Jim. Everybody loved him. Everybody had a personal story of his kindness and care. He was never too busy to go out of his way to let you know how special you were. The hardest part of our move was leaving him.

At the tail end of our trip, we heard a little, "Are we there yet?" from a groggy Jamie, stirring thanks to the sunrise. I was thankful both boys had slept for most of the trip. Jamie's question woke his older brother.

"Yes, honey, we just got to our new town. Daddy is looking for the motel where we'll be staying tonight," I answered, hoping they would not realize how unsettled I felt.

My husband's new employer had made arrangements for us to stay at one of the local motels until we found permanent lodging ourselves.

"Let's all play a game," I suggested. "Whoever spots the Townsmen Motel first gets to choose where we'll eat tonight. It's somewhere along this main street."

"There it is!" Jeff shouted. "On my side of the street."

We pulled off the street in front of the office. There were fourteen rooms at the Townsman Motel, all on the same level, all accessible from the outside, all in that L-shaped layout that every builder from 1972 motels seemed to use.

No one spoke. Our silence was broken only by the sound of boots sloshing through the snow as we made our way past the front entrance picture window into the office area. There was a tiny plastic tree on the registration desk, which was framed with colored blinking lights. It was a painful reminder that this year, Christmas would be about making the best of it.

"Hello," a cheery voice greeted us from behind the desk. "How can I help you?"

Her name was Evelyn. Plump and jolly, doting and nurturing. She was the perfect agent of hospitality for the new strangers in town.

"I've been expecting you," she continued. "The motel season is relatively quiet right now. You will have the place mostly to yourselves. You can park anywhere."

She quickly checked us in, chatting unceasingly with the boys, and then directed us to our temporary home. Jeff and Jamie, full of adventure, were the first to enter the room.

Two double beds were lined up on one side of the room. An antique dresser with a companion television sitting on top faced them on the opposite wall. A small table with two kitchen-like chairs, a sofa, and an over-stuffed recliner were scattered throughout the rest of the room. Layers of pine green paint with lime green trim were on every wall.

"Okay everybody, let's start unloading the car," I quickly instructed, hoping that filling the room with personal things would somehow "brighten" the room. It began to snow lightly as we carried our few belongings into our room.

Day after day, the boys and I passed time in the room. Sometimes we would draw pictures of Christmas and hang them around the room. Sometimes we would play games or watch television. Christmas shopping and house hunting had to be done at night or on the weekends. Three weeks had passed with no housing available.

Three days before Christmas, I made my way through the snow to the motel vending machine. When I returned to the motel room, loneliness seeped through me. The parking lot was still empty, and the motel room with its two double beds reminded me once again that I was miles away from family and friends.

Sitting on the edge of the bed, I felt the frigid draft that somehow made its way around the closed front door. I held out a bag of chips to the boys.

"Sorry, this is all they had in the vending machine."

Jeff shook his head and wrapped a blanket around his shoulders, "It's okay, Mom," Jeff replied, suddenly appearing many years older. "They look good."

It wasn't quite the Christmas we had planned: an older brother too kind to complain, the younger brother worried that Santa's kid-tracking device wouldn't find him, and parents too tired and stressed to offer more than superficial comfort.

To top it all off, we knew no one. I tried to stay in good spirits for the sake of the boys, but I was miserable.

"Oh, Lord, I miss Pastor Jim and our friends in Minnesota," I whispered to myself.

That night after we were all settled in bed, we heard a loud knock on our door. Who would be knocking on our door this late?

My husband and I peered out the window but we couldn't see through the frost. But then a familiar voice rang out.

Was it possible?

"Open up! It's Pastor Jim!"

I flung open the door.

"Merry Christmas!" he said. His smile seemed warmer than a fireplace at Christmas.

Tears brimmed in my eyes and I couldn't find my voice.

There he stood, the best Christmas gift ever; all wrapped up in a military green parka, laced up snow boots, with a red stocking cap covering his ears and a scarf tied like a bow!

Our pastor explained that he had attended a Christian conference in a city nearby and "just happened" to be passing through our town on his way home. Although it was late, he felt the need to stop by our motel to check on us.

We knew the best Christmas gift we got that year wasn't under a tree. We found it at the Townsman Motel in the caring heart of a pastor named Jim.

~Patti Ann Thompson

It's Christmas!

From the Mouths of Babes

*In the eyes of children we find the joy of Christmas.
In their hearts we find its meaning.*

~Leland Thomas

32

The Heart of a Boy

There are no seven wonders of the world in the eyes of a child.
There are seven million.
~Walt Streightiff

Our son, Denver, was three, and like most children that age, he wanted everything he saw advertised on television. One of the toys he wanted the most that year was a He-Man Power Sword. Robert and I had seen the commercial for the toy numerous times. It was a large, yellow, plastic sword offering a variety of electronic battle sounds accompanied by an array of flashing lights. We decided to get it for him, despite the cost.

On Christmas morning, Denver eagerly tore into the colorful wrapping, shredding miniature snowmen as he went. The moment had arrived. We were ready to photograph his joy. Denver looked at the sword, his face perfectly blank, and then unbelievably, he set it aside. He was ready for his next gift.

I lowered the camera. Robert and I looked at each other. What? No happy surprise? No unadulterated joy? What happened?

We were confused and more than a little disappointed. This was the gift of all gifts. The Holy Grail of Christmas presents.

We tried coaxing Denver into playing with the once desired and now discarded toy, all to no avail. He wanted nothing to do with the legendary He-Man sword.

The day waned, sadly lacking in flashing lights, electronic crashes, and anticipated battle cries of "I am the power!"

The mystery of the He-Man Power Sword would remain unsolved for the next several months. When the solution finally did come, it came via the television.

Denver and I were engrossed in the usual Saturday morning fare of cartoons when the commercial for the He-Man sword aired again. I watched the boy in the commercial grab the plastic weapon. I saw He-Man's archenemy, Skeletor, materialize out of the sword, and I watched the commercial kid battle and naturally vanquish the villain.

And I thought nothing of it.

Not until my son asked, "Does that really happen?" Suddenly, I understood.

"Is that it?" I asked him. "Do you think Skeletor's going to come out of the sword?"

His answer was a hesitant nod. He was not sure, but he obviously had not been willing to risk it.

I hugged him then, stifling my laughter and marveling over the literal world of children that we, as adults, tend to forget. I assured my very frightened little boy that with the exception of a little light and a lot of noise, nothing and no one would ever come out of the sword. I also took the time then that I should have taken before to explain about television and its world of exaggeration and make-believe.

The day is a distant memory now, as are the hours of migraine-inducing fun Denver enjoyed wielding that He-Man Power Sword.

~JéAnne Leites

33

Wishful Thinking

What a bargain grandchildren are! I give them my loose change,
and they give me a million dollars worth of pleasure.
~Gene Perret

I t was Christmas Eve, and the last order from my custom embroidery and apparel decorating shop had been delivered. Numerous fabric scraps and tails of thread still clung to my pants as I flipped the door sign to read "CLOSED." I scanned my workroom with a feeling of satisfaction. This was where I often provided daycare for my grandchildren. They had spent many hours with me, watching as I made clothing for my customers. Their play area shared space with bolts of fabrics, cones of thread, and boxes of garments awaiting decoration.

Now I was joining them for Christmas. My oldest son Eric and his family had invited my husband Rick, my daughter Kathy, son Adam and me to join him for what I hoped would be a new family tradition. We donned our warm jackets and drove the short distance to their home.

The air was thick with excitement when we arrived. Kile, age five, and Cavanaugh, age two, dashed through the house. They squealed with delight as each family member walked through the door. We removed our coats and the grandchildren grabbed my hands to hurry me into the front room. I exclaimed over each special ornament that hung on the glistening tree.

The table had been transformed to a Christmas wonderland. It sparkled with heirloom dishes, crystal goblets, and golden cutlery. Oyster and sage colored linens adorned all the surfaces while festive glass bulbs hung from the chandelier. Kile and Cavanaugh's special place settings were appropriately decorated with snowmen and penguins.

Eric and his wife Trela had outdone themselves. We had home-made lasagna, bread, salad, wine, and, of course, Trela's family ritual of "British crackers." When we finished eating, still wearing our colorful tissue paper crowns, we cleared away the bits and pieces from the crackers.

Kile bounced up to me.

"Grammie, I know what you are giving me for Christmas tomorrow."

"You do? What do you think I am giving you tomorrow for Christmas?"

"You're giving me pajammies or something like that."

"Why do you think I am giving you pajammies or something like that?"

"Because you make things and you always give me something you make."

A pregnant pause followed, and then a wistful sigh.

"Grammie, I wish you were a toymaker."

~Mona Rottinghaus

34

The Christmas Kidnapping

You can learn many things from children.
How much patience you have, for instance.
~Franklin P. Jones

It was Christmas Eve and we were in the back of church with the rest of the well-dressed, slightly depressed parents whose offspring were in various states of unholy discontent. My youngest, an eighteen-month-old terror in pink tights, was slowly sucking the Christmas spirit right out of me. Around and around the poinsettias I chased her, dodging the other kids, blocking the exits and praying for patience.

Eventually she stopped in front of the life-size nativity scene.

"Baby!" she exclaimed.

"Yes, baby," I answered wearily.

As she stared at the statues, I wondered why we bothered coming. Church was a challenge on a regular Sunday and this holiday hoopla was impossible. I didn't hear a word of the sermon, my husband had that frown line in his forehead and my older children kept asking when they could open presents. I felt lousy.

Then, I heard a squeal.

Turning, I saw my youngest running full tilt with the Baby Jesus statue wrapped in her arms. I looked at the empty manger. I looked at my daughter—a golden halo peeking over her shoulder, delicate toes mere inches from the ground. My kid just kidnapped Jesus!

"Baby! Baby! Baby!"

Now when one's toddler is scampering across the room with a fragile ceramic statue of the infant savior you do not simply yell for her to stop. I didn't want her to drop it, nor did I want her to trip and fall on it. So I scurried after, politely pleading for her to give me the baby.

It was a holy hostage negotiation.

Parents parted to let us pass. My face was thirty shades of Christmas red. Finally I cornered her and safely recovered the Baby Jesus.

"Mama! Baby!"

I looked at the statue now cradled in my arms, then I looked at the other parents. Most were smiling; a few chuckled. Suddenly it dawned on me. Wasn't that the reason I was there? To gather the Baby Jesus into my heart and take off running?

I may not have heard the sermon but thanks to my Christmas kidnapper, I got the message.

~Nicole L.V. Mullis

35

Better than Disney World

It is no small thing, when they, who are so fresh from God, love us.
~Charles Dickens, Master Humphrey's Clock

"I want money for a trip to Disney World," my nephew said confidently, as if there were no other logical answer. Excitement filled his brown eyes, and the long dark hair that usually covered some of his face did not hide his enthusiasm. We were sitting in a hotel room in Oklahoma City, where my sister and her family had met up with my parents and me to celebrate Thanksgiving. Mom had just asked Nicholas what he wanted for Christmas.

Nicholas is a great kid. Smart and articulate, his glasses only add to that effect, and he has a passion for all things science. His intelligence was apparent very early. I still smile when I remember him, after his fifth birthday, requesting that people call him "Nicholas" instead of "Nicky" because he thought "Nicky" was for babies and he had outgrown it. He loves video games, charades, and putting things together. He has an impressive ability to remember all the details about the things that interest him. Nicholas was diagnosed with Asperger's syndrome a few years back.

Because I have been affected by cerebral palsy and have been a wheelchair user all of my life, Nicholas has a special place in my heart. I know what it is like to feel different sometimes, and I know the struggle of not always being understood because of something that is beyond your control. I have witnessed Nicholas explode in anger and then go outside and walk the same pattern repeatedly in order to rein in his emotions. And every once in a while, I wish his life were a little more simple.

He continued to chatter about Disney World, and his gestures became more animated as he envisioned riding Space Mountain and chatting with Mickey over breakfast.

The Christmas season was drawing closer—the temperature dropped and colored lights went up all over town. Both eleven-year-old Nicholas and his nine-year-old sister Magee were energized and eager to see what Santa would bring them. Had they been good all year? Sure. But that was irrelevant to them as they made their lists. Typically, they wanted lots and lots of stuff, and I briefly wondered if the true meaning of Christmas might have gotten lost in the shuffle somewhat. But hey, that was okay. They are kids. And to practically all kids, presents are a priority.

On Christmas Eve, we gathered at my parents' house. Around the dinner table, the conversation turned serious.

"Some people don't have enough food." Magee said. Her golden brown eyes were somber with the thought.

"And some people don't have enough money to buy toys for their kids at Christmas." I added gently. The disheartened look on both of their young faces indicated that they both knew peers who were in these situations.

On what seemed like a whim, my brother-in-law asked his son a question.

"Nicholas, if you could give any present to anybody, what would you give?"

Without skipping a beat, he looked across the table at me sitting in my wheelchair. His gaze held mine for a long moment. "I would give Aunt Lorraine the ability to walk."

I was stunned. Nicholas had so many issues of his own to deal with, and yet his first spontaneous wish was to give me something I didn't have. He wanted my life to be more simple too.

The next morning, while most of us slept, Nicholas and Magee made a mountainous mess tearing open brightly wrapped boxes that contained their requested treasures. They found a letter from Santa Claus reminding them not to fight, and letting them know they were going to Disney World after all. Their whoops and hollers made for a pleasant family wake-up call.

If I were to pose the question to Nicholas, he would probably say that he got the best present that Christmas, because it was exactly what he wanted.

But I think he would be mistaken. For me, the most precious gift didn't come in a box at all, but instead from this boy who showed me the place I have in his heart. That gift is better than any material thing that I could ever receive.

Even better than a trip to Disney World!

~Lorraine Cannistra

It's Much

Take full account of the excellencies which you possess, and in gratitude remember how you would hanker after them, if you had them not.
~Marcus Aurelius

Annie didn't own Crocs, those trendy plastic shoes that most of my fourth grade students wore. She wore white tennis shoes that the school counselor bought and jeans that she had chosen from a box of donated clothes.

Every day, Annie came to school smelling like cigarettes. Her hair wasn't brushed. She ate state-provided free breakfasts and lunches and didn't understand why she couldn't take home the food that her classmates nonchalantly threw away.

On the last school day before Christmas vacation, twenty excited students crowded around my desk. They were anxious for me to open their gifts.

"Open mine next!"

"Mine has the biggest red bow."

"Mama paid a lot for that fancy candle. She said you'd better like it."

"It's homemade candy. And I helped make it."

Annie sidled close to me and moved the discarded Christmas paper and ribbon from the floor to the trashcan. But she clutched a crumpled piece of shiny red foil paper and a big gold bow tightly in her hands.

While I continued to open gifts, Annie asked to use the Scotch tape on my desk. She took the paper, bow, and tape to a corner in our classroom. Then she ran back to her desk and shoved something under her shirt.

The other students didn't notice Annie. In fact, they rarely noticed Annie.

I put on every gift of jewelry. I marveled over a hand-crocheted Santa Claus, a glittery angel, and a Christmas sweatshirt that was decorated with sequined snowmen. I stashed gifts of food—honey, banana bread, chocolate—in a basket. These were my family's favorite teacher presents.

As the party ended, the children ate cupcakes with red and green sprinkles on chocolate icing. They drank red fruit punch. The girls clustered in groups of twos and threes. The boys sat in one big group on the floor.

Annie wandered toward me as I set a cup of punch on my desk. "Mrs. Ray," she said. "I've got something for you." She held a small wrapped box tightly in her hands.

"Do you want me to open it now?" I asked.

She laid her gift, wrapped in wrinkled foil paper and the gold bow bigger than the box, on my lap. "Yes, but don't let anybody else see."

As I tore away the many strips of tape, Annie stood so close that her small body leaned against mine. "It's not much," she said.

A button lay inside a well-worn Avon box. A plastic gold coat button with tiny glistening rhinestones.

"Read the note," Annie said.

To: Mrs. Ray
I'm sorry, but the present isn't that much it's all I had. I hope you enjoy it.
Merry Christmas

Annie was wrong. It was much.

It was so much that every Christmas I pin that gold button on my coat lapel. It was so much that it reminds me that giving a Christmas gift isn't about the gift. It was so much that it reminds me every year why I celebrate Christmas.

~Susan R. Ray

37

The Faith of a Child

I would thank you from the bottom of my heart,
but for you my heart has no bottom.
~Author Unknown

My jaw dropped when I saw the prices of playground equipment at the local discount store. How could I buy these items for the kids at the shelter? I had recently become a volunteer at a domestic violence shelter and was spending a couple of hours there on Tuesday nights, playing with the children.

I had first volunteered there in mid-July, and I still remember feeling like I had stepped into a Third World country. A dozen or more motel units housed mothers with anywhere from one to four kids. No indoor facility existed, so I played with the kids outside. But, as I looked around on that first visit, I was dismayed. There was no playground equipment of any kind. An old gazebo with a couple of broken picnic benches served as a play area. Un-mowed grass and tall weeds choked a green space and a tottery basketball hoop stood on one end of an asphalt parking lot full of potholes. A few bicycles with flat tires and bent frames leaned against the privacy fence that hid the area from outside eyes.

Somehow, this shelter had slipped through the cracks of a system that had seen far too many budget cuts. At the suggestion of a friend, I wrote one of the local Sertoma Club chapters a letter describing the shelter's needs, and what happened next was nothing short of divine.

A former Sertoma Club member had recently passed away, leaving a bequest to be used for a "worthy children's organization." The chapter approved the shelter project and within a few short weeks, the shelter received a modern playground set, a graveled play area, four basketball hoops permanently set in concrete, a hopscotch game painted on new asphalt, and shiny new bikes.

With Christmas approaching, my thoughts returned to the nineteen kids who called the shelter home. I realized I could not afford to buy them Christmas presents, so I resigned myself to getting some candy and maybe a few cheap toys from the dollar store.

One Saturday I made a lunch date with a friend, and her nine-year old granddaughter, Sierra, accompanied us. After lunch, Sierra approached me and pressed a small, white envelope into my hand. I asked her what it was and she answered "money to buy toys for kids at the shelter." With tears in my eyes I opened the envelope and found $17.50. She told me she draws pictures and sells them and gives half the money to charities.

I knew God was at work again. I was reminded of the story in the Bible where a boy offers up five loaves of bread and two fishes to feed a crowd of 5,000. Everyone was fed that day and leftovers filled twelve baskets! I knew then that if this nine-year-old girl had faith that $17.50 was enough to buy Christmas toys for the kids at the shelter I should believe it too.

At my next church choir practice, I told the story of the kids at the shelter and my desire to buy them Christmas presents. I also told them about Sierra. I was not ready for their overwhelming response. Choir members donated nearly $600—enough to buy each shelter child a very nice Christmas toy. My Sunday school class held a wrapping party and my car was loaded with presents to deliver to the kids at the shelter the week of Christmas.

I will never forget the smiles on the kids' faces and the tears of their mothers. As I was leaving, one woman ran after me and hugged me very hard. She said she had called a friend to tell her that an

"angel had visited her that night." I told her I was certainly no angel...
but I knew they existed.

~Katie A. Mitchell

38

Lauren's Lesson

We worry about what a child will become tomorrow,
yet we forget that he is someone today.
~Stacia Tauscher

Lauren is just a few days away from her eighth birthday. I don't know why eight seems so much older than seven. Maybe it's just because I've gotten used to seven. Seven is still dirty hands and spilled juice, Cabbage Patch dolls and Junie B. Jones books. Eight-year-old girls are still an enigma. Chances are, eight will still be dirty hands and Cabbage Patch dolls... but I don't know that for sure yet.

Seven means she is still invested in the magic of Santa. She knows that a jolly man in a red suit climbs down her chimney and leaves a present or two behind because she's a sweet little girl who tries her very best not to be naughty all year long.

A few days ago, a crumpled note showed up on my refrigerator. I didn't pay it much attention at first because with Lauren this is a daily occurrence. She's a creator. An artist. She likes to leave notes and cards and paintings and crafts all over the house for the rest of the family to discover. It took me a few days to notice that this note was different. It wasn't adorned with sequins or any other "bling." No pipe cleaners glued to the edges. No carefully cut snowflakes framing the words. It was, simply, a note to Santa Claus.

Dear Santa,

These are the things I would like for Christmas this year.

1. NO MORE WAR! PEACE PLEASE!
2. A goldfish
3. A Furby
4. A nice day with my family
5. A stocking for the dogs
6. A tablet for my brother Ryan. He really really wants one.

Love Always,
Lauren Bietz

At first I thought, "Aw, she wrote her note to Santa this year. That's nice." And then I took the note down and brought it to "the box." You know "the box"—the black hole where Mom puts the things she wants to keep forever. On my way up the stairs, I read it again. And then I sat down in the middle of the staircase and read it again.

My seven-year-old girl has six things on her Christmas list. And four of them are not gifts for herself.

It was at that moment that I realized I really needed to reframe my thoughts about Christmas. It's not about making things perfect. It's not about parties and wrapping paper and shiny gold bows. It's about the gifts you already have right in front of you. Honor those gifts. Give thanks for all the days you've spent with those gifts and ask, humbly, for more days. Have compassion for those around you who are missing some of their gifts. Invite other gifts into your life every day.

If I can learn these things from one tiny seven-year-old cherub with dirty hands and juice stains on her T-shirt, I wonder what she'll teach me when she's eight.

~Kara M. Bietz

What Would You Like for Christmas, Santa?

Children don't need much advice but they really do need to be listened to and not just with half an ear.

~Emma Thompson

Years ago when I was a young man in my twenties, I was one of Santa's helpers. While he was busy getting his sleigh and reindeer ready for the big trip on Christmas Eve, I helped him by dressing in Santa clothes and listening while little children told me what they wanted for Christmas. I felt honored to fill in for Santa, for he doesn't want any child to be disappointed. I never knew how he did it, but he always seemed to know the names of all the children who sat on my lap, and what toys each youngster wanted Santa to bring them on Christmas morning.

My routine was to dress up in Santa clothes, then head to a little mom and pop grocery store in Alloway, a hamlet in upstate New York. Each time someone came through the door I would shout, "Merry Christmas!" and children would wander over and look at me. I would help them climb onto my lap, then I'd ask, "What would you like for Christmas little boy/little girl?" After they told me I would give each one an orange and a candy cane, help them down and send them on their way with a loud, "Ho, ho, ho! Merry Christmas!" It was a job I loved and always looked forward to doing, until one night when I almost decided to hang up my Santa suit for good.

It was the worst night I'd ever had playing Santa. It seemed all the children wanted Santa to bring them more and more presents, rudely issuing orders. Nobody was asking nicely. And when I handed one child an orange and a candy cane, he said incredulously, "Is that all we get?" Later, another child voiced his displeasure too. It was rare for even one child to display such bad manners, let alone two on the same night.

Finally, feeling dejected, my holiday joy and goodwill having taken a direct hit, I glanced at the time and stood up, locking eyes with the woman who owned the store. I let out a long sigh and muttered, "Boy, am I ever glad this night is over!" I started packing up when suddenly a young mother came running through the door.

"Santa, would you please take a moment for my little girl?"

I am sure my lack of enthusiasm must have showed as I mumbled, "Sure," managing only a half-hearted smile. Silently I couldn't help thinking, "Oh well, she will be the last one this year."

Once again I plopped down in my chair and waited, watching as her daughter shuffled slowly towards me. It was obvious that it took great effort for her to place one foot in front of the other, but it wasn't until I looked up that I saw, with surprise, a dazzling smile on her face. She was young, about six or seven, with pretty brown hair.

She came close and said, "Hi Santa," and when I reached down to help her sit upon my lap I felt two hard leg braces pressing against my Santa legs.

I looked into those beautiful beaming eyes, and thus our Santa session began in the usual way. "Hi little girl, what would you like Santa to bring you for Christmas?"

Expecting her answer to be a doll or maybe a stuffed animal, both popular requests I heard all the time, I was totally unprepared when she said, "Anything you have left over Santa." I gave her two more opportunities to change her answer, but she stood her ground and said again, "Anything you have left over Santa." Finally I told her that Santa would bring her something she would like. Answering with a smile she said, "Thank you Santa." I returned her smile. Not a half-hearted one either, but with a grin as wide as the one she'd had—an all-the-way, across-the-face, ear-to-ear grin! I was about to help her down when suddenly she stopped me, looked me square in the eye and said, "What would *you* like for Christmas, Santa?"

Once more I was taken by surprise, so touched was I by the aura of happiness and joy that surrounded her; seemingly unaware of the humbling impact she was having on others and on me. She was a picker-upper, an encourager, a lifter of sprits, with an unselfish penchant for putting others before herself. I experienced a cauldron of mixed emotions as I struggled to keep my composure, but a few renegade tears leaked out anyway.

Her unanswered question was left hanging in the air—"What would you like for Christmas, Santa?" How could it be that I did not have the answer for a question that I myself had asked every child that had ever sat upon my lap, over and over, night after night, year after year?

Finally I blurted out, "Santa would like a hug," and she wrapped her tiny arms around my neck and hugged me for what felt like an eternity. Finally she lowered her arms and I helped her down from my lap, but as she walked away, shuffling along as she had before, she would turn around every few steps, look my way and smile, saying "Merry Christmas, Santa, Merry Christmas."

"What would you like for Christmas, Santa?" In her childlike innocence she couldn't possibly have known—and how could I ever have explained—she had already given Santa his Christmas gift.

~Ed Marriott

The Nutcracker Ballet

While we try to teach our children all about life,
our children teach us what life is all about.
~Angela Schwindt

I took my four grandchildren to see *The Nutcracker* ballet for their first time—three little boys, ages thirteen, ten, and eight, and my granddaughter, who had just turned sixteen. We attended the Grand Rapids Ballet Company's first ever performance of Tchaikovsky's evergreen dance spectacle, at the Detroit Opera House.

My granddaughter wants to be an attorney and someday hopes to win a congressional seat. She's not into dancing or the theater or classical music. The boys are into hockey and baseball and flag football and soccer and basketball and swimming and Lord knows what else that involves physical prowess. They all are fans of their Wii and a variety of video games and stuff to do with iPods and video players and rap music.

The downside of our ballet outing was that none of the three boys had ever expressed the teeniest interest in attending a ballet performance. For that matter, none has ever been keen to participate in dancing of any ilk.

On the upside, the four cousins love doing things together. They get along famously and they all have a sense of adventure. The ballet, for them, was definitely an adventure.

I briefed them on what to expect before we left: the performance would have no talking, and minimal singing (only a children's chorus), and would consist of performers dancing to a rather trite, dorky story. But the music would be beautiful. The full orchestra would be live. The costumes and sets and choreography and lighting and such would be colorful and fantastic.

I outlined the story before we left: At her family's Christmas Eve party, a little girl named Clara gets a nutcracker shaped like a toy soldier from her eccentric uncle. It's her favorite gift. At the end of the evening, party guests go home and the children go upstairs to bed. Clara creeps down the steps to find her beloved nutcracker and falls asleep under the Christmas tree. The tree grows, the toys come alive, an army of toy soldiers fights an army of mice. Clara saves the day by throwing her shoe at the mouse king. The nutcracker turns into a prince, takes Clara to a fantasyland of life-sized dancing dolls, fabulous sweets, dancing snowflakes and flowers, the sugar plum fairy, etc.

They didn't pay much attention.

We arrived early and had to wait about fifteen minutes in our seats until the ballet began. They played "I Spy" with the theater décor while we waited for the show to begin.

"I spy a lion's head."

"I see it."

"I saw it first."

"I saw it first."

"No, I did."

"I spy a candlestick."

"I see it."

"I saw it first."

And so on.

The music began. They were fascinated. Earlier, I had decided not to push the ballet experience as I had with my three daughters.

They remember *The Nutcracker* as something they had to go to every year because I insisted.

I noticed, however, that my daughters now talk up the whole Nutcracker experience to their children. "You'll love it," they said.

Did the grandchildren love it? Maybe.

Maybe they just enjoyed a new experience. Maybe they were humoring me.

Either way, one grandson sat on the edge of his chair, eyes glued to the dancers for the entire first act.

During what they called "halftime," the boys made cootie-catchers out of the program inserts.

I was still determined not to push theatrical performances on this new generation. That's what's so neat about being a grandmother. Occasionally, you get a chance to correct some mistakes you made the first time around.

All four grandchildren were to spend the night at my house. When we got home, they held contests to see who could leap the highest, who could fling one leg the highest without falling, and who could jump in the air and touch the toes on both feet at the same time. They all demonstrated the art of gliding off stage, head held high, one arm flung forward while the other trailed gracefully behind.

So, I think they liked it.

The next day, one especially observant grandson told his mother and father about the costumes. He commented on the unusual clinginess of the men's tights. And now, with apologies to those of you who don't like this kind of humor, I must tell you what he said about those tights.

"They were really, really tight," he observed. "That must be why they call it *The Nutcracker*."

~Margie Reins Smith

Reprinted by permission of
Off the Mark ©1999

A Little Help for Santa

When I approach a child, he inspires in me two sentiments; tenderness for what he is, and respect for what he may become.

~Louis Pasteur

It was Christmas Eve, and we'd just returned from the late church service with a couple of very tired little boys. My husband Tim and I tucked ten-year-old Sean and four-year-old Drew into their beds and smiled at their excited chatter about what might be under the tree in the morning.

"It won't be long now!" Sean assured his brother.

"I just know Santa will bring lots of fun stuff!" Drew beamed.

Soon, though, their sleepiness triumphed, and yawns gave way to peaceful deep breathing as they drifted off to sleep.

As Tim began to put together a bike, I surveyed the house. The tree was beautiful, twinkling with a thousand white lights and filled with the colorful ornaments our sons had made through the years. I was so sentimental I couldn't bear to part with a single one. Every room held decorations—some new, most handed down from both sides of the family, each one with its own story and memory. The carols played on the stereo, the scent of the sugar cookies the boys and I had made earlier in the day still lingered, and the moonlight shining through the windows showed me that snow was beginning to fall. I thought about how blessed we were. The whole scene was picture perfect—truly like a Norman Rockwell painting.

It was time to make sure the stockings were ready. On Christmas morning the boys always woke so early, popping out of bed like toast from a toaster. They were allowed to rush downstairs and look in their stockings right away. As they read books, sorted through the treats and played with the small toys Santa always left there, Tim and I would get up and make our way downstairs after we heard the commotion. It allowed for a more leisurely start to Christmas morning for us and some brotherly bonding time for the boys. And it made it easier for the boys to wait to open the gifts under the tree until after we had breakfast.

As I laid my stocking aside so I could fix its hook on the mantel, I heard Tim call for my help. I rushed to lend him a hand in the living room.

"Lots of assembly required," he groaned. "Will you hold this for me, Deb, while I tighten this thing and try to figure out that thing?"

"Gladly," I smiled.

Together we figured out the directions, and he put the finishing touches on the bike. Exhausted, we headed off to bed.

The sounds of happy kids woke us at six, and we joined the boys in the family room. They had emptied their stockings, and the floor was already covered with the surprises.

"Mommy, look what Santa brought me!" Drew was thrilled with the latest book in the series he enjoyed so much.

"I love this game, Mom and Dad," Sean smiled.

"Let's see what you got, Dad," Sean said as he handed Tim his stocking.

I sat there taking it all in, thoroughly enjoying the laughter and excitement.

"Okay, Mommy, it's your turn!" Drew said.

Suddenly, it hit me. I had left my stocking on the bookcase beside the fireplace when Tim had called me to help with the bike. I had meant to return, but was so tired I had forgotten. My stocking would be empty, since it had not been hung. Sean was older and would understand what happened, but Drew would be so disappointed that Santa had missed my stocking.

"Oh, that's okay," I said hurriedly. "I'll just wait and open my stocking after breakfast."

"No, Mommy, now," Drew insisted.

I looked at Tim in dismay. He was just perplexed at my expression.

Drew plopped the stocking into my hands, and I was surprised to feel that it was heavy. Oh, good, I thought, my stocking hadn't been missed. I glanced at Tim with a look of relief on my face. But he just shook his head, still not understanding my reaction.

I reached into the stocking and pulled out the contents. It was a box of candy, Drew's favorite kind, the box from Santa to Drew that had been in his stocking. My little boy had discovered and peeked into my stocking that morning, and, finding it empty, didn't want me to be disappointed. He had given up his favorite treat, slipping it instead into my stocking.

"Wow, Mommy, you got a great gift!" Drew exclaimed.

Tears filled my eyes as I pulled both of my sweet sons to me for a big hug. "I sure did," I said. "I got the best gift there is."

~Deborah Agler

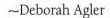

Clay Baby
Christmas

Children see magic because they look for it.
~Christopher Moore

We sat at the dining room table, my five sons and me, pressing holiday cutouts from bright, soft sculpting clay. My three youngest sons peppered theirs with tiny faux gemstones. My two oldest, both teenagers, were a bit more conservative. Their ornaments reflected more time and more patience.

I should have been in the holiday spirit. White lights twinkled on the deep green Douglas fir my husband had trudged over hills to cut the week before. A cinnamon candle flickered on the buffet. Soft, sweet music from our favorite instrumental Christmas CD drifted through our century-old home. Even the weather shared undeniable Christmas charm. Lacy, thick snowflakes swirled and swept past the wavy, antiquated glass of our dining room windows.

But I wasn't feeling festive. And no matter how I tried, thrusting myself into activity and tradition and family and friends, I couldn't feel the holiday spirit.

It had been a hard autumn. Logan, the firstborn of our sons, had gone to public school after eight years of being homeschooled. He was in ninth grade. The transition had been anticipated with excitement and joy, but it was proving to be difficult. Our son had met up with a bully on the first day of school. It didn't help that we were new to our small Mississippi River town, and the other students seemed leery of someone new.

"Hey, Mom, what do you think of my Christmas star?" one of my little sons asked. His question refocused me on our project.

"I think it's perfect," I said. "Let's put it on the tray and we'll bake it with the others. Then you can hang it on the tree."

My little guy smiled a wide, toothless grin. He was content. Pleased. If only all of life could be filled with such simple pleasures. A clay star that would hang amid popcorn strands and Popsicle stick angels could save the day.

Logan's voice now broke my thoughts. "Hey, Mom. When we're finished, can I have the extra clay?"

"Sure," I said. "But why?" Logan had deep artistic abilities. He was always crafting something.

"I have some ideas for ornaments," he said. "I'll use whatever's left when the little boys are done."

I smiled and tried to rescue a clay tree from my little son's exuberant spatula. When I'd successfully placed the tree on the tray, I glanced at Logan. I wished, for him, that Christmas break would last forever.

Prior to Christmas vacation, our evenings all looked the same. Logan, my husband, and I would sit, each night, after the little brothers were in bed, and talk about what had happened that day.

"It's hard to break in," Logan would say as my husband and I perched on the edge of our long, leather sofa. Logan was open and communicative. His tender and gentle spirit, which made him a target for the high school ruffian, was a blessing when it came to our evening conversations. He shared honestly and from the heart.

"Do we need to pull you from the school?" I'd ask every night. We'd already talked with school personnel. They were certain that Logan was not in physical danger. It was his emotion, though, that weighed on my heart. But his reassurance was, every evening, just the same.

"No," Logan said. "I need to work through this. To persevere. I know, in time, things will get better."

I envied his strength and optimism. I also hoped that "in time" would come soon. Watching a child work through hurt is a serious kind of struggle.

The full, festive days of Christmas break seemed to fly past. Soon it was Christmas Eve. The shopping was complete. There were candles in the widows. Stacks of holiday cookies shone proudly under cake domes of clear glass. And my family assembled around our Christmas tree. It was tradition that we'd exchange a few gifts, one for each person. Something special that couldn't wait until Christmas morning. But even in the midst of such sweet, true joy, Logan's struggle weighed on my own shoulders.

"Hey, Mom, don't you just want to open this one?" one of my little guys asked. "You can use it tomorrow morning for your coffee."

"Shhhh," another little guy said, fingers now pressed over his brother's open lips. "You'll wreck the surprise."

I opened the mug and received a barrage of hugs. We continued, for an hour or more, each person taking the time to admire and appreciate the gift that had been shared. When the clock struck nine, it was time for bed. My husband scooted our bevy of boys up our long, curved staircase while I gathered discarded holiday paper and strings.

I was headed into the kitchen with an armload of wrappings when I noticed a gift, in a shiny red box, on the dining room table. I dropped the papers on a nearby chair and lifted the handwritten tag: TO MOM. WITH LOVE, LOGAN.

I didn't stop to wonder if the gift was to be opened then or saved for Christmas morning. My hands lifted the lid from the box. I couldn't imagine what could be inside.

And my heart swelled for what I found.

Inside the box was a Popsicle stick stable. Stained. Assembled. Round edges precisely cut square.

Inside the stable were wise men. They wore tiny, intricate crowns. Their tiny hands held gold boxes and bottles. There were also two angels. On their wings were carvings of delicate scroll. There were also two sheep, white with black faces, and a cow, brown and bent in rest.

I was drawn to the Holy family. Joseph, bearded and strong. Mary, draped in soft blue, face flushed with rosy spots of pink. Her outstretched arms held the Baby Jesus. He was wrapped in white, tiny, with round face and eyes closed in slumber.

I was amazed at the craftsmanship. The detail. The thoughtfulness. But what made my heart beat fast was the message of hope.

Logan was going through a tough time. Without a doubt, the toughest time he had ever seen. But he was solid, anchored, and willing to persevere. And I knew that as he crafted this sweet crèche from clay, the hope of Christmas was in his heart. The strength and promise of the little babe.

"Do you like it, Mom?" Logan's voice startled me.

I couldn't seem to reply. How had my son gotten so strong, so wise? I held Logan close and didn't want to let go. But when I eventually did, I let go of some of the sadness, too.

"Thank you, Logan," I said. "For the gift. And for reminding me how to hope."

That Christmas was a few years ago. Logan did persevere until he achieved happy, healthy high school years. He was right. Things did work out. He's at college now. Still growing. Still striving. Still amazing me and making me proud.

The manger stays, year round, on our old, marble mantle. It's a reminder of something I never want to forget — the promise of hope, and our clay baby Christmas.

~Shawnelle Eliasen

It's Christmas!

Bark!
The Herald Angels Sing

Ever consider what pets must think of us?
I mean, here we come back from a grocery store
with the most amazing haul — chicken, pork, half a cow.
They must think we're the greatest hunters on earth!

~*Anne Tyler,* The Accidental Tourist

Pepper's Last Gift

Dogs' lives are too short. Their only fault, really.
~Agnes Sligh Turnbull

Whatever life threw at us each year, come Christmas our family had one constant tradition: our dog Pepper opened our presents for us. When our beloved Black Lab mix had been a gangly adolescent puppy, we had only given her unbreakable gifts to unwrap—things like pajamas and steering wheel covers. She proved to be so careful that we soon gave her any gift that wasn't edible. Every time, Pepper found the seam in the wrapping paper with her snout and held the present down gingerly with her forepaws. Her front teeth pried up the lip of paper with the utmost care. Then she removed every inch of wrapping paper before stepping back to lie in the midst of our gathering. She never bit or scratched the gifts themselves.

Friends and relatives who joined our family celebrations never believed Pepper could be so delicate until they witnessed her talents. Watching our sweet dog unwrap gifts always warmed the holiday, which was often a little bittersweet because college, studying abroad, or work commitments often kept my two sisters and me away.

One year, everyone made it home for a Christmas together. I was back from Ireland, Kaci flew in from Arizona, and Kara visited from college. Mom's jubilance kept her busy baking cookies for us all. Our Christmas season should have been perfect.

It couldn't feel perfect, though, because Pepper's health was deteriorating. Her life had already been longer than we expected—she was fourteen—and yet her mind was still sharp. Her enthusiasm for life made us feel better. But her body could not keep up with her spirit. She'd already shown the usual signs of deafness and stiffness. That year, her hips and back legs started giving out on her. We knew we would soon have to make a difficult decision.

It was likely Pepper's last Christmas, so we decided to make sure she enjoyed it. On Christmas Eve, we gathered around the tree to open an early present. We each took a turn and then called Pepper to open one more. But her tangled legs could not navigate the boxes and shredded wrapping paper on the floor. She stumbled over the obstacles, and soon she disappeared into the next room. She crumpled back to the floor, as out of the way as she could get.

We were heartbroken. Could Pepper even participate in her last Christmas?

Pepper stayed on the periphery of all our holiday activities. Throughout the day, we gave gifts but did not feel very giving. We shared stories over cinnamon rolls that tasted bland. We played games by the tree whose twinkles had dimmed.

That evening, Kaci said what we'd all been thinking: "I wish Pepper could have helped open presents this year."

We all put down our mugs of spiced tea. "Maybe she still could," Kara said.

"But there's none left," Mom reminded her.

Kara jumped up and left the room. We heard her opening drawers and cabinets in the kitchen. She returned with a box of dog biscuits, scissors, and a roll of tape.

"Hand me that green paper," Kara told me, pointing at a large sheet at my feet. She cut a small section from the paper and wrapped a single dog treat in it. She held it up as if she had just struck gold. "Now there's a present for her!"

I knelt on the floor next to Kara and wrapped another dog treat. Kaci and Mom joined in, too. Soon, we had four elegantly wrapped dog biscuits in a row on the floor. We cleared the floor of discarded wrapping paper. We tucked our legs under us as we perched out of the way on the furniture.

"Go get Pepper," we urged Mom. We all bounced like eager children.

Mom went into the next room. "You want to open a present, girl?" she coaxed. In a moment, Pepper stuck her head into the room. Her ears were fully perked with anticipation and curiosity.

She skidded on stilted legs to the row of presents. She sniffed all four in order, and looked back and forth between them. She'd never had such a wide choice of gifts before.

Soon, Pepper selected her first Christmas gift. She nimbly turned the present with her forepaw, just like she was a spry young dog once more. She tugged every last scrap of paper off the dog treat before she chewed it with her customary grace.

Our family swelled with glee.

Pepper licked the last crumb from the floor. She eyed the remaining three presents, then turned to Mom as if asking, "May I please open another?"

"Go ahead, girl!" Mom encouraged.

For the next few minutes, Pepper opened each of her Christmas presents. While she did, she reminded us of the sheer joy of being together. Our family felt whole—not because we were in the same room, city, or country, but because our love bonded us together.

In the new year, Pepper let us know it was time to call the veterinarian. Her passing, while tearful, was peaceful. In its own way, her passing was also a celebration of life, because she gave my family so much love and laughter.

Long after I forgot each of my presents, I still cherish Pepper's final Christmas gift. She taught me that no matter where we each spend the holidays, and no matter what the passing year brings, the smallest act of heartfelt giving can unite our family through our love. For me, that knowledge is the longest-lasting gift of all.

~Zach Hively

The Catmas Tree

I had been told that the training procedure with cats was difficult.
It's not. Mine had me trained in two days.

~Bill Dana

When we first got a housecat, our concern was that he would chew on the cords of the Christmas tree lights. We need not have worried about that particular issue, as the aptly named Stinker had other ways of aggravating the bipeds. He had no interest in the electrical cords circling the tree.

He wanted to eat the tree itself. And climb it.

December became the month when small piles of regurgitated pine needles would appear around the house. When we acquired a second housecat, Mr. Z, he also showed no interest in the electrical cords, but the quantity of regurgitated needles increased.

Verbal admonishments have no effect on cats, so we needed a different approach to deter them from nibbling on the conifer. When winter rolled around, our very creative Mom would carefully brush hot habanero sauce onto the needles of the Christmas tree, at least on the lower branches. She also cut small habanero chilies into thin slices and hung the small rings of orange and red pepper around the lower branches of the tree like tiny ornaments. The idea was that a tree that rated 100,000 to 350,000 on the Scoville heat scale would be unappetizing to our fuzzy housemates. It seemed to work to some extent—there were fewer piles of barfed up needles scattered around the house. However, perhaps in retaliation, the felines began chewing on the edges of any gifts placed beneath the tree, and trying to eat the wrapping paper. In response, Mom dusted the Christmas presents with a fine layer of powdered cayenne pepper.

The spicy odor that emanated from the Christmas tree seemed to keep the cats away but also made the area somewhat unpleasant for people. An alternative solution that had occurred to several of us was to replace the real tree with a fake one, in the (vain) belief that the cats would find synthetic needles unappealing. It took a while to convince Dad that this was the course to take, as he is a man of habit who prefers dragging a dead tree into the house every December.

At first there was joy in the house that the tree-shaped decoration would not have to be drenched in capsaicin juice. The joy subsided when a small pile of regurgitated silk needles was found near the front door.

These days, we have a kind of truce during the Christmas season. The housecats haven't completely given up on chewing the tree, but they do seem to find synthetic needles less appetizing. As for us humans? Well, at least the presents don't make us sneeze anymore.

~E. Sutton

Operation
Christmas Puppy

The dog was created specially for children. He is the god of frolic.
~Henry Ward Beecher

Mom and I bumped into each other, our arms loaded with plates, as we raced to clear the table on Christmas Eve. "Fifteen minutes!" I yelled to the kids, who were jostling to claim the mirror in the bathroom.

Dillon flew into the kitchen. "Can you help me with my tie?" I gestured for my husband to handle it.

"I still need you to do my hair!" Faith wailed.

Dumping the casserole dishes on the counter, I turned to my mother. "Would you put the ham in a Ziploc bag while I curl her hair?"

Exactly fifteen minutes later, we somehow managed to buckle into the minivan with the children in their Christmas outfits and the leftovers in the refrigerator.

"Why isn't Daddy driving with us?"

"He has to go to work for a little bit." I backed out of the drive. My husband and I had a special surprise for the kids, one we had no intention of blowing before the big reveal.

Our children loved dogs. We joked that Faith was obsessed with them. Her favorite stuffed animal was a puppy, and she shared a special bond with my parents' Cocker Spaniel. When Faith was a tiny two-year-old, we decided to add a dog to the family, but the rambunctious Golden Retriever proved too feisty and three months later we sold him to a farmer with two preteen boys. It had crushed our little girl, and we promised ourselves we'd consider another dog someday. Now our children were finally old enough to handle the responsibility of one, and we were determined to make the event special.

I pulled into the church parking lot and escorted the kids to a classroom for their rehearsal. Both sets of grandparents joined me in the pew, and my husband arrived right before the service began. Our hearts were moved by the children's retelling of the story of a baby born in Bethlehem. All too quickly, the children sang the final hymn, and my husband gave my hand a quick squeeze to let me know Operation Christmas Puppy was underway.

Our friends bred miniature dachshunds, and they had six puppies ready to leave their mama. At exactly nine weeks old, the friendliest female in the litter was about to be introduced to her new home. My husband had picked up our new addition right before church, but he needed to take her outside to do her business and get her in a special gift box before I took the kids home. I had no idea how to stall the children that long!

We kissed the grandmas and grandpas goodbye, and I slowly drove away.

"Can we please open one present tonight?" Dillon begged from the back seat.

"We'll have to ask Dad, but I think that would be okay." My spirits soared, thinking of their reactions when they opened the gift waiting for them.

"I can't wait to change out of this dress," Faith said. "And I'm hungry. I was too nervous to eat much dinner."

Both kids were more than ready to go home, get comfortable, and anticipate the next phase of Christmas — the presents. But would my husband have enough time to get the dog situated? I was running out of options when inspiration struck.

"Look at those pretty lights." I pointed to a yard with twinkling white reindeer. On a whim, I turned into the subdivision next to it. "Let's drive around and admire the displays."

"Aw, Mom, do we have to? I just want to go home."

I ignored them and crawled past the houses with multi-colored lights. We drove through another subdivision, and I popped in a lively Christmas CD. Too soon, the tour ended.

"Mom, we've seen enough lights."

I still had time to kill. The stoplights didn't help. Where was a red light when I needed one? I remained stoic, keeping the minivan at a good five miles per hour under the speed limit.

Out of options, I finally entered our subdivision, and Dillon pressed his face to the window when we passed our home. "You passed our house!"

"I just want to see the lights behind us." I made sure we drove down every street, praying I could safely return home soon.

Thank goodness my husband's car was in the driveway. As soon as I parked the van, the kids raced to our porch and scrambled inside, ignoring the Christmas tree on their way upstairs to change. I quietly asked my husband if everything was ready. He grinned.

"Hey, wait," my husband called up the staircase. "Don't you want to open one gift?"

Thump, thump, thump. Still in their dress clothes, they charged down the steps into the living room. "Really? We can open one?"

That's when they saw it. The huge wrapped box with the big red bow on top, sitting in the center of the room. Would the puppy bark and give it away?

The package remained quiet, and the kids hesitated as they neared it. "What is it?"

"I bet it's a PlayStation," Dillon said.

"It's too big to be a PlayStation," Faith said in her superior tone.

"It could be one."

"Well," I said. "Open it and find out."

Faith tore at the paper, but Dillon lifted the box. To their surprise, the top lifted right off. They peered inside and gasped.

Seconds ticked by in silence. The shock on Dillon's face kept him from speaking. Then Faith looked at us, her eyes brimming with tears, and she whispered, "A puppy. Can we pick it up?"

My husband assured her, yes, she could pick it up. Tenderly she lifted the precious black and tan dog. With a small sob, she cradled the tiny body to her chest. I got teary-eyed watching them. Then she passed the calm bundle to Dillon, equally awed.

For ten minutes our house existed in hushed pleasure. The cinnamon scented candles, lights on the tree, and soft Christmas music playing in the background created a kind of wreath around us. The children set the puppy on the floor and pointed to her fluffy bed, which she launched into as if she knew it was hers.

We named our Miniature Dachshund Sophie, and she's been a treasured member of our family since that special Christmas Eve. We might have taken the long way home, but the kids agreed it was worth it for Operation Christmas Puppy.

~Jill Kemerer

"I'd like a boy of my own!"

Our Lucky Christmas

Dogs are not our whole life, but they make our lives whole.

~Roger Caras

It was Christmas Eve in the Kootenays, British Columbia, in a place called Nipika. The sky was white, and it was snowing, the fluffy flakes descending lazily like battalions of miniature parachutists. Inside, I was curled up on the couch by the fire, reading about that poor orphan, Oliver Twist, who starts life slaving in a workhouse and gets tossed from good fate to bad, the bad being particularly nasty and the good being marvellous. Before I could see what fate befalls Oliver, I was distracted by the sound of barking and sat up to look out the window.

There outside was an urchin of a dog, with crooked ears and a bushy tail like an electrified squirrel, charging about in the snow—a furrified firecracker.

He was a jolly dog, and since he seemed so hard up for company, I went outside to throw him sticks. He loved to be petted and talked to and was distraught at the many little ice balls clinging to his paws. As I helped him to remove them, I found friendship in his intelligent bark-brown eyes. My husband joined us, and an afternoon of doggie romping went by, until suddenly our new friend galloped off, probably to curl up beside his owner's wood stove.

We ate a quiet Christmas Eve dinner and afterwards headed to the Nipika lodge to share a glass of cheer with the owner, Lyle, and the other guests. The moment we stepped outside, our furry friend materialized and galumphed with us all the way to the lodge. Inside, as the fire blazed, we asked everyone, "Who owns that long-haired reddish-brown dog with the fluffy tail?" Silence. "We thought it was your dog," said the couple from New York. Nobody knew to whom he belonged, but he seemed to have a firm sense of belonging here. When we returned to our cabin, the dog had disappeared in the snowy night.

Next morning, Christmas Day, I glanced out the kitchen window to see the dog huddled under the only dry spot—a dirt patch underneath a tiny pine. He looked marooned on his winter desert island. When I opened the door and called to him he careered down the hill, ears flapping, paws flailing up and down, a steamroller of fur and enthusiasm. But when he reached the door, he came in politely, as if someone had taught him good manners, then plunked down on the mat like a sack of potatoes.

Since he belonged to nobody at the camp, we figured he hadn't eaten since at least the day before. So he got a Christmas supper fit for an orphan: ham, Brussels sprouts, mashed potatoes, and gravy, which he promptly inhaled to my intonations of "You lucky dog!" That was when we started calling him Lucky. He was lucky to get lost in a place whose owners were dog lovers, and lucky to find the two big softies in the furthest cabin.

Yes, we were smitten by that pair of doleful eyes. We even thought—scandalously—about adopting him into our one-cat family. Lucky must have understood he had found his angel benefactors.

That night, Lucky slept near our bedroom door. Whenever we stirred, he stirred, his nails clicking on the wood floor. He heaved sleepy, contented sighs that kept me ever so slightly awake, like a mother with her new babe.

On Boxing Day morning, Lucky ate sour cream and chive noodles with... Brussels sprouts and ham. All day, he was our constant companion, accompanying us on a hike, waiting outside the sauna, or lying inside with his head on my feet as I followed the exploits of that other orphan, Oliver, whose brush with good fortune, alas, proved to be all too brief.

On the 27th, a pick-up truck pulled into camp. It was the security man from the mine twenty-five kilometers down the road. He was looking for a dog named Nuke, he said—our dog. Nuke was supposed to be at the mine, tied up, alone, doing his guard dog duties, but a few days ago he had escaped. Our Lucky was a fugitive. That explained the ice balls on his feet. I turned to look for Lucky but our orphan runaway was hiding. Clearly, this lonely mining job was not an apprenticeship that suited him at all. My heart broke for my poor brown-eyed friend.

With a special whistle, the security man located Lucky, lured him into his pick-up and drove away. Suddenly our beloved dog's name seemed utterly inappropriate.

I said to my partner, "If this was Dickens, Lucky would run away again from his evil captors, appear barking at our door, and I would embrace him saying, 'Oh, Lucky! You came back!'" But we knew that wouldn't happen. Some gifts are not for keeping. Lucky was gone.

Gloom settled over the household. When I went to bed I even cried. What kind of spell had Lucky—a dog—cast over us in so short a time? I lay in bed and spoke to him in my head. I told him if he wanted to come back, we were here waiting. Even if he didn't come, we would always love him.

All night I slept fitfully, missing his doggie sighs and clicking toenails. Then, at 2 a.m., I heard a thump, as if someone had stepped—or jumped—onto the porch. "Could it be?" I asked myself. "Don't be ridiculous! The mine is twenty-five kilometers away!" Still, I couldn't resist going downstairs to check.

At the side door I squinted out—that's where Lucky usually waited. Nothing but gaping blackness. With a dwindling sense of hope, I went to the front door, cupped my hands over the cold glass and peered into the night. A pair of soulful eyes stared back at me. Lucky! He had come back! The dog with the squirrelicious tail had run twenty-five kilometers in the middle of the night to be with us! I let him in and he burst into the cabin, exploding with doggie joy.

Now, this story has two endings. When we left Nipika two days later, Lucky, with his one ear up and his one ear down, was still there. Lyle, the resort owner, had also grown very fond of him but agreed that the mine—his rightful owners—had the last say. We said we would adopt Lucky, although our city house hardly seemed the place for him. Besides, what would the cat think? We left not knowing his fate.

A week passed, and our fondness for Lucky never faded. Then we received an e-mail from Lyle. He told us that through a marvellous stroke of luck, our Christmas orphan had been freed from the mine. Lucky now lives with his new family in doggie freedom in the wide-open spaces of Nipika Mountain Resort. It was truly a Christmas gift for all of us.

~Barbara L. Black

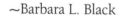

Our Miracle Puppies

Miracles, in the sense of phenomena we cannot explain, surround us on every hand: life itself is the miracle of miracles.
~George Bernard Shaw

We raised Miniature Fox Terriers and loved every one of them. We gave away our puppies to good friends and never put a monetary value on them. "It would be like selling your own flesh and blood," Eddie said. We jokingly called them our kids, and when one of them left us to go to another home, it felt much the same. A member of our family was missing.

When Little Bit became pregnant with her second litter, we were excited. Her first delivery had been uneventful, with four healthy pups, So when her delivery date neared, we took Little Bit from her outdoor kennel and put her in the 10' x 12' building we called the nursery. There we had prepared a nice straw bed for her complete with plenty of food, fresh water, and a doggie door for when she needed fresh air and sunshine. That way, we could keep an eye on the mother-to-be, who was due three days after Christmas.

Little Bit loved her new home and had spent the last few days hollowing out a nest in preparation for the puppies' birth, just like she did with her first litter. The mild December nights, much warmer than normal for Kentucky, had created a perfect environment.

Christmas Eve morning was damp and cool. Temperatures had

fallen more than expected overnight, hovering just above freezing. Eddie had gone out to feed the chickens and dogs like he did every morning, but he noticed right away that Little Bit didn't come out to greet him as usual. Something was wrong.

He lifted the door to her private quarters and found Little Bit had given birth to five puppies during the night. Two strong males, thriving and strong, nursed at her side. One little fellow was stillborn and under-developed. It never had a chance, as sometimes occurs in nature. But, two perfectly formed females lay over in the corner, wet, cold, and, worse than that, not breathing. During the night, they had gotten separated from the warmth and comfort of Mom.

I watched out the window as Eddie walked toward the house carrying a small bucket in his hand. I could see it on his face when I opened the door. "Look, Linda," he said sadly. "She had five puppies and three are dead. These two should have made it."

I looked down at the tiny black-and-white bodies with guilt and regret. If only we had brought the mama inside the house before the puppies came. "Are you sure they're dead?" I asked.

"I'm sure. Why didn't I put her in a crate last night and bring her in?" Eddie asked, shaking his head.

I knew how he felt. With a little intervention on our part, the puppies' deaths might have been prevented.

He picked one up and handed it to me, his eyes full of sorrow. He took the other pup and we held them close. They felt like small chunks of ice. I held mine to my ear. There was nothing—no heartbeat, no breathing, no movement. The lump in my throat grew larger. We should have brought her in, I thought. It would have been so easy.

As I walked the floor with the soft puppy, I thought back on the scene in *101 Dalmatians*, when Roger revived one of Pongo and Perdita's newborn pups. Only in the movies. Something that amazing could never happen in real life. But, when I mentioned it to Eddie, his eyes lit up.

"It's worth a try," he said. His positive attitude never faltered.

Working together like scientists on a mission, I warmed a bath towel in the clothes dryer and Eddie grabbed the blow dryer. We gently bathed the puppies' backs and tummies in warmth, praying it would work. Minutes seemed like hours before I heard a faint squeal. "I heard something!" I yelled. Although the sound was weak, it was a definite sign of life.

For thirty minutes, we continued our vigil, rubbing and massaging their tiny chests until I felt unmistakable energy pulsing in my hands. My little girl was coming to life. Suddenly, her mouth opened and she breathed her first breath.

"She's alive!" I shouted as tears streamed down my cheeks.

With renewed hope, Eddie worked even harder to save the remaining pup. "You can do it, little girl," he said as he thumped her lungs and rubbed her body vigorously. It seemed like forever, but within a few minutes of her sister's first breath, she gasped for air too and wriggled in his hands.

He nuzzled the pup next to his face. "Nothing smells sweeter than puppy breath," he said. I had heard him make that comment many times before, but now it had a much deeper meaning. He handed me the puppy, grabbed a basket, and hurried out to get the others. We had done all we could. Now, it was time for the power of mother's milk to work its magic.

Back together in front of a heater, Little Bit licked the two girls, nudging them to her breast for nourishment alongside their brothers. We stood in awe watching the cozy contented family, each searching for the best position. Before long, they were lined up nursing like nothing had ever happened.

But, something had happened to us, something we had trouble putting into words. And, when I tried to tell my family later that day, the words lodged in my throat. Finally, I knew there was only one way to explain it. "Come and see Popsicle and Icicle for yourself," I said. Their names fit them to a tee.

When the day came to go to their new homes, the owners not only got a puppy of a lifetime, they got the incredible survival story along with it. We hear from them often. The puppies are all grown up, happy and healthy, cherished by their new families. We stay in touch, making sure they are okay and well cared for.

Today, our Christmas holidays continue to be filled with lots of love. Our family and friends bring wonderful heartfelt presents and we love them all. Still, when I think back to that one incredible Christmas Eve morning, I can't quite believe it. My husband and I had seen something we would never forget—life where there had been none. No amount of money or all the gold in the world could buy such a gift. And, to make it even better—it came just in time for Christmas!

~Linda C. Defew

The Boogie Man

Sometimes imagination pounces;
mostly it sleeps soundly in the corner, purring.
~Terri Guillemets

I think I was close to five years old the Christmas that the Boogie Man came. I had always imagined him to be the ugliest thing that ever lived, with big teeth and horns, a long forked tail, and a pitchfork for poking little girls and boys. He turned out to be a whole lot cuter.

Our Christmas tree that year was just beautiful. I would lie on my back under the tree and gaze up into the branches, and it felt like I was in another world with all the lights and sparkly objects. There was snow on the branches, and it smelled like a forest of pine trees. The angel on the top would move and look from one side of the tree to the other, keeping watch over this wonderland of my imagination.

On that Christmas Eve, my mama could not drag me away to bed; even bribery would not get me there. I begged and begged to stay up. I just wanted to look at the tree and wait for Santa to come. Mama finally got me to lie on the couch and just rest, as she put it, knowing I would fall asleep. She untied the belts of my dress and covered me with a blanket and I watched and waited for Santa to come. Finally, I drifted off to sleep. My tired mama just let me sleep there and went to bed herself.

During the night, I was awakened by noises in the house. It

sounded like someone running from room to room, stopping every so often to see if anything moved. I just knew it was the Boogie Man looking for me. I'd been told he looked for little girls who won't be good for their mamas and go to bed. I covered my head with my blanket and tried not to move, barely breathing. I tried to call for help but not a sound would come from my mouth. The sounds kept getting closer, until he found me.

One of the belts to my dress had fallen over the side of the couch and he had seen it. Grabbing the belt, he began to pull on me, trying to drag me off the couch and carry me away to some hideous place where I would never see my mama and dad again. My fear was running rampant. He would pull and I would move as far away as I could, but it didn't stop him. He would let go long enough to growl at me and then grab my belt again and pull. I must have been stronger than I thought, because no matter how hard he pulled or how much he growled, he didn't pull me off the couch.

It was hot under my blanket, sweat was running off my body and my hair was ringing wet. I have never been so scared in my whole short life. This tug of war seemed to go on for most of the night.

Once more, I lifted the blanket, sucked in a breath of fresh air, and tried to scream. To my surprise, the word "Mama!" sounded loud and clear. I called again and again; once I got started, there was no stopping me. Finally, the door to my parents' room opened, and my mama came running out to see what was wrong. The Boogie Man scampered away.

I had never been so glad to see my mama. Sobbing, I told her the whole story while she hugged me, wiping sweat and tears from my face. I knew the Boogie Man would not come now that my mama was there. I finally felt safe.

My mama went in search of the so-called Boogie Man. When she came back, there he was—a rambunctious puppy! Mama said she and Dad decided I needed a puppy for Christmas, and they got me a very lively one to keep up with me. They had put him in the laundry room, never dreaming he would escape. He wasn't trying to be mean—he just wanted to play with me.

Thanks to a mischievous puppy, I was given my Christmas present early that year. My little Boogie Man and I had many more games of tug of war over the years—it was his favorite game. Sometimes he won and sometimes I won, but it didn't matter to us. We just loved being together. I will never forget the Christmas that the Boogie Man came to visit.

~Louise McConnell

49

A Furry Little Secret

There are few things in life more heartwarming
than to be welcomed by a cat.
~Tay Hohoff

I grabbed a potholder and pulled the tray of blackened star-shaped cookies from the oven. Well, that about matched my holiday mood. Dark and up in smoke! Money was tight, schedules were hectic, the house was a mess. And the shopping list! I wanted to do something special, but I had no idea what to get my mom for Christmas.

Recently Mom had remarried and moved to Canada. With work, family schedules and limited vacation time, I didn't get to visit her very often. So I did my best to keep in touch with her on the computer via chat.

"The holidays are too stressful," I typed that night.

"Oh, dear. Don't worry about all that," Mom typed back. "Think about the carols, and the pretty snow... just think about the positives."

Well if that wasn't a mom thing to say! Over the next few days, I ran around shopping, helping with the kids' school programs, volunteering at church and making sure everything got done. I didn't take time to stop and listen to the cheerful music piped into the stores or to appreciate the beautiful snowflakes that decked the evergreen outside my kitchen window.

Instead, I worried about my gift list. I'd already shopped for my husband and the kids, but I still needed to get something for Mom.

Mom lived in a townhouse with her new husband, Hans. The transition to a new home and a new marriage hadn't been easy for her. She had Darlene—a friend from church—and a few others, but she still missed her old friends and family. She especially missed having pets.

To be fair, Hans was a cat lover, and had a cat of his own—an old black-and-white longhaired feline named Susie. But Susie didn't like Mom. Not one bit. Apparently the cat didn't want to share her affection with anyone but Hans.

"Why don't you get a cat of your own?" I'd asked.

"Nah, that's okay," Mom had responded. "I have enough here to take care of." But I knew the real problem was that Mom wouldn't do something special for herself.

Hans didn't get out much and hadn't thought of getting another cat for Mom. But a cat of her own would make Mom so happy. I wondered—could I get Mom a cat for Christmas? It's not like I could order one from a catalog. The idea lurked in the back of my mind.

"What are your Christmas plans?" I typed one day.

"I'm going to a party with Darlene," Mom responded. She went on to tell me about the church Christmas party and something called Secret Sisters. They drew names, and would exchange secret gifts at the party.

I stopped typing. Secrets? Gifts? A smile spread across my lips. Could this be my way to get Mom a special surprise?

I hurriedly signed off the chat so that I could set to work on my new idea. I found Darlene's address and tapped out an e-mail. "Dear Darlene," I wrote, "I have kind of an unusual request..."

From that day on, Darlene and I began plotting in secret. I found myself smiling and humming Christmas carols. I paused while washing the dishes and noticed how delicately the new-fallen snow laced the windowpanes. I made it to both the kids' holiday concerts, and even managed to bring a plate of un-burnt cookies for the bake sale! And when I chatted with Mom, I fairly burst from keeping the secret.

"Things must be going better," Mom typed. "You don't sound as stressed."

"Yeah, I guess you're right!" I typed back. "Maybe I just took some good advice."

The day of the Secret Sister party arrived. That night I logged onto my computer, wondering how the party went and if the details of the surprise had all worked out. I didn't have to wonder for too long. The chat messenger pinged.

"Hi!!!" Mom wrote. The number of exclamation marks she used suggested that she was very happy. "I just got back from the party. Guess who is here helping me type?"

"I couldn't guess," I teased.

"It's a beautiful little gray kitten! She's sooooo cute! I named her Misty, short for Mistletoe."

"Glad you like your surprise!" I wrote.

"She stole my heart," Mom wrote back.

I beamed, imagining Mom at her computer far away, with her little gray kitten purring beside her. She told me about the party and how Darlene placed before her a box with holes in the sides. When she'd reached into the box and felt the soft ball of fur, she'd been so happy she couldn't stop the tears. She couldn't write for too long; she had to do some important work getting her little friend settled down and accustomed to her new home. "Now, how'd you arrange something like this?" she asked.

"It must have been some Christmas magic," I replied.

After we signed off, I addressed a few last-minute cards. Only a week until Christmas. Everything wasn't ready; everything wasn't perfect. But that was okay. When the holiday stress built up, I knew the cure. I had taken Mom's advice a step further. Don't just think about the positives, do something positive. Like a little secret act to make someone else happy. Even if it involves a lot of miles, a box with holes in it, a secret sister, and one perfect gray kitten.

~Peggy Frezon

50

Dr. Christmas

Miracles don't just happen, people make them happen.
~Misato Katsuragi

"Angie, you have to understand," my mother pleaded, tears in her eyes. She reached for my hand, which I promptly pulled away.

Oh, I understood all right. My very own mother was a murderer. I stared at her in disbelief as she tried to justify her reasons for killing my best friend. It was too much for my nine-year-old brain to comprehend.

"Angie, please don't look at me like that," she said softly, her voice breaking up, "Teeger was very sick. He had a bad bladder infection. The operation was too expensive and the veterinarian couldn't guarantee that it would work anyway. I had no choice but to have him put to sleep. It's better this way. He's not in pain anymore."

Teeger was a big, fat, roly-poly, orange cat who I loved like no other. And now he was gone. I wanted to close my eyes and make it all go away. This would be the worst Christmas ever.

"You didn't even let me say goodbye," I finally choked out.

Teeger had come into my life at a time when I really needed a friend. It was shortly after my dad had moved out for good. I was the only kid in my class whose parents weren't together, so there was no one I could talk to who would really understand what I was going through. I had a hard time making friends as it was, since I was painfully shy. Moving once a year didn't help. Being overweight also didn't help. My mother saw how much I was struggling, but she didn't know how to make it better. She did, however, know how to cheer me up. Enter Teeger.

Teeger and I had bonded instantly. He was a lot like me, actually. Shy... chubby... loved Cheezies. He had a playful side—but only when no one was looking. If you caught him chasing his tail, for example, he would stop and pretend that he was just cleaning himself or doing something equally sensible. What I loved most about Teeger, though, was how special he made me feel. He preferred me over everyone else he knew and he wasn't afraid to show it. He made me feel like the most important person in the world.

As the years went on, my bond with Teeger grew even stronger. When I was home, he followed me wherever I went. He sat beside me on the piano bench as I practiced for my upcoming lesson, occasionally putting a paw on the piano keys to remind me that he was there. He slept at my feet every night. He licked away my tears when I told him about the kids at school who made fun of me or about how much I missed my dad. He was my best friend.

One fateful morning, I woke to find that Teeger was not beside me and I immediately knew that something was wrong. I jumped out of bed and ran from room to room, frantically calling his name. I checked every nook and cranny in our little farmhouse, but Teeger was nowhere to be found. For two more days I searched like this, refusing to accept the possibility that he might actually be gone. On the third day of searching I was in the basement, looking for the hundredth time, when I heard a faint "meow" coming from up above. I looked up and suddenly saw those familiar green eyes and orange fur. Teeger was in the furnace duct!

I called for my mom, who ran down the stairs as fast as she could, and I pointed out the unlikely hiding spot where Teeger had been this whole time. We instantly got to work. It took a while, but I finally got him down. And then panic set in. He didn't look like the Teeger I knew. His fur was matted, his stomach bloated, and his eyes seemed quietly desperate.

"Angie," Mom said quietly, "I think Teeger is very sick. Sometimes cats go off into hiding when they know they are going to die."

I could not accept this. I had already decided long ago that Teeger was a miracle cat and he would live forever.

"He's not going to die," I said firmly. I held him close, comforting him as he had done for me so many times. "You're going to be okay, buddy," I told him over and over. "You'll get better, I just know it. You can't leave me yet."

Mom looked at me sadly and promised to take him to the vet right away.

Looking back, I understand why my mother didn't talk to me before making the decision to have Teeger put to sleep. How could she possibly have said no to a teary-eyed, inconsolable girl begging her to save her best friend? I likely would have told her to keep my allowance and to take back my Christmas presents so we could afford the operation. She might have taken a third job just to pay for it, even though she was exhausted working the two jobs she already had just to make ends meet. No, she really didn't have much of a choice at all. I understand that now.

In the weeks that followed, my mother did her best to try to cheer me up. She sang. She baked. She decorated the house for Christmas, going "all out" like she always did. But this time there was no cheering me up. I didn't want to get into the Christmas spirit. And besides, I wouldn't get what I wanted for Christmas anyway… my best friend back. No one could give me that. Or so I thought.

And then I got a phone call that I would never forget.

"Angie, the phone's for you," my mom said, handing it over to me with a puzzled expression on her face. "It's the veterinarian. He asked specifically for you."

"The veterinarian?" I echoed, equally puzzled. I had never even met him before. Why would he ask for me? Hesitantly, I picked up the phone.

"Hello?"

"Hello, Angie," a deep voice greeted me. "I… well… I wanted you to be the first to hear what I have to say. Your mom told me that

Teeger was very special to you. So... in the spirit of Christmas... I gave Teeger the operation for free."

Could it really be true? Was Teeger alive this whole time? It was a miracle! A Christmas miracle!

"I'm sorry that I didn't call sooner," the veterinarian continued, "but I wanted to make sure that Teeger was completely better and stabilized before I called you to let you know. He's ready for you to pick him up now. I think he misses you."

It seemed an eternity before I was able to blurt out the words, "Thank you! Thank you so much!" Tears of joy streamed down my face and I had my shoes on before I could even explain to my mother what was going on.

When we got to the animal clinic, the veterinarian was waiting for us. I immediately ran over and hugged him, thanking him over and over again. He looked over at my mother and blushed, unsure of how to handle my display of emotion. He brought out Teeger, who immediately began purring so loudly you'd swear that a car with a bad muffler had just driven through the office. My heart felt like it was about to burst with happiness.

Thanks to that wonderful man, I got to spend twelve more years with Teeger by my side. And I got to learn at an early age that the true spirit of Christmas has nothing to do with spending money or getting gifts; it's about giving to others from the kindness of your heart with no expectation of getting anything in return. And I learned that sometimes... just sometimes... angels come disguised as veterinarians who make Christmas miracles happen and little girls' wishes come true.

~Angela Rolleman

Chapter

6

It's Christmas!

The Naughty List

He who has not Christmas in his heart will never find it under a tree.

~Roy L. Smith

The Ghost of Turkeys Past

Just because something is traditional is no reason to do it, of course.
~Lemony Snicket, The Blank Book

For years, our family Christmas feast has consisted of a standing rib roast with all the trimmings, paired with an abundance of side dishes and desserts. But it wasn't always that way. Before the Christmas of 1970, we served a big roast turkey on both Thanksgiving and Christmas. Only the desserts changed—from pumpkin pie in November to mincemeat pie and Grandma's special butter rum cake in December.

The tradition changed that fateful Christmas in 1970 when the turkey was set out to brine. Grandma had always done this. Mom did this. So, I followed the tradition and did it. The sink was filled with cold, salted water and the bird was placed in it to soak.

The bird for that Christmas was a beauty—huge, almost thirty pounds. My father had paid a fortune to a local turkey farm to get us the biggest, best bird possible. It would be a true feast for all. The cookies, pies, cakes, and puddings had all been made. The candied yams were ready for the oven and the cranberry sauce was chilling in the refrigerator. All that was left was to brine the turkey a few hours, then pat it dry and refrigerate it while I made the stuffing to get it ready for an early morning oven. Due to its huge size, it needed to be rotated in the brine because it was too large to actually soak the whole bird at one time. The brine only came halfway up the body of the bird as it soaked, breast down in the sink.

I was just about to go in and turn the bird in the brine when a scream from the kitchen changed my plans entirely. My three girls came running out shrieking that the bird's ghost was there and the monster was going to get them! Their father and I ran into the kitchen to see that the "dead bird" soaking in the sink was hopping all over the place and splashing water everywhere.

My husband approached the bouncing bird with caution and made a grab for it. It slipped from his hands, as heavy as it was, and bounced onto the floor where it continued to do a jig across the tile.

The girls continued to scream while our two Collies started barking and jumping at the naked, dancing bird. I managed to push the dogs and now hysterical children back into the living room and held them at the doorway while their father continued to try to control the giant bird. Finally, it hit a corner between the sink and refrigerator and got wedged in. It continued to bounce up and down, breast side down, until finally something started poking through the back of the bird.

A smear of black appeared through a small hole near the spine of the fowl. Then a set of whiskers and a paw appeared. Our little cat Johnny had actually climbed into the open cavity of the bird and was happily chewing his way out. His little black and white head popped out through the hole in the back of the giant bird and he looked straight at us as he continued to gnaw off another chunk of raw turkey.

Of course, we could have removed the cat, washed the bird out (which was now stuffed with cat hair) and salvaged the dinner plans with none of the guests the wiser, but somehow, none of us wanted to eat turkey after that. I called my dad and told him what had happened. He made an emergency run to the local butcher and came over with two large standing rib roasts, enough to feed the crowd.

Thus began the new family tradition that my children now follow in their own homes with their own families. Johnny is long gone, but to this day, everyone who is still around to laugh about it remembers the day the turkey jumped out of the sink. And to this day, we still have turkey on Thanksgiving, but we always have roast beef on Christmas.

~Joyce Laird

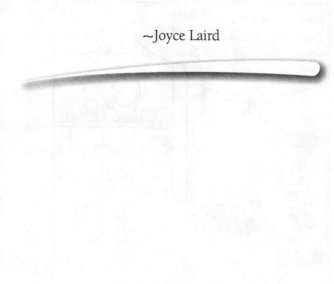

Reprinted by permission of
Off the Mark ©1993

On the Roof with Santa

Perhaps the best Yuletide decoration is being wreathed in smiles.

~Author Unknown

My eighty-four-year-old mother has always loved Christmas. It's her favorite time of the year. My parents' home at Christmastime looks like a Norman Rockwell painting—very Christmassy. People rave about it.

I never realized how much time and work my father put into it until I had to start doing it myself four years ago. That was when Alzheimer's began taking its toll on his body and mind, and I moved back in with my parents to help out.

A few years after I moved in, my father's physical and mental health deteriorated so much that he needed to be placed in an assisted living facility. That was in August. I decided Mom's first Christmas alone needed to be especially nice.

I hate doing all of it—it could turn a normal guy into a real Grinch. But what I hate doing most of all was stringing those outside lights along the gutters of the roof. Since childhood, I've been terrified of heights. I hate heights—and I hate that darn plastic Santa Claus, too. That little yuletide creep has become my nemesis. It's still laughing at me. See, the last three Christmases, when trying to position Santa between two rose bushes in front of the house, I have stepped back and gotten stuck by a branch from one of those rose bushes—and it hurt, too.

Well, I vowed that that wouldn't happen to me this year. I decided to place that smiling, hand-waving, Chucky-inspired Christmas bugger somewhere else.

Sure, it took me an entire week, but on the cold winter day of November 22nd, I had all of that "Christmas cheer" up on both the inside and the outside of the house. I had it all done—except for figuring out where to place that darn plastic Christmas devil, the Santa Claus.

It was two o'clock and Mom had just left to visit Dad. I was cold and tired—I had been working on decorations since eight o'clock that morning—and I still couldn't figure out where to place the Santa Claus. Then, I looked up at the roof, at the chimney, and it all made sense to me. Yes, that's where he belongs—against the chimney.

Armed with three extension cords, white masking tape, and Santa, I climbed the ladder and got on the roof. I didn't feel scared at all. I foolishly thought I had finally conquered my fear of heights.

After securing that smiling, waving, fat, red-and-white, plastic piece of stupidity to the chimney with masking tape, I connected the three extension cords together and went to the edge of the roof to toss the third extension cord over the gutter. And that's when my vertigo kicked in.

Suddenly, everything looked narrow; my knees began to buckle. I felt light-headed and like I might faint. At least I had the presence of mind to fall backward instead of forward.

I lay prostrate on the cold, tiled roof for ten or fifteen minutes before I felt the blood return to my brain and I could sit up. I didn't know what to do. I couldn't go near that ladder. I didn't have my cell phone.

It was getting colder, and the clouds were darkening more—it looked like it might rain or snow. I zipped up my winter coat.

One hour turned into two hours, and still I sat on the roof.

A car passed by and I shot up and waved my hands at him anxiously. He merely waved back at me, as if he were wishing me Merry Christmas.

I sat back down, despondent. More time passed.

Then, when I had almost resolved that I would be spending the rest of my life on the roof, I looked across the street and saw the front door open. It was the neighbors, Mr. and Mrs. Johnston. Mrs. Johnston, a white-haired, slight woman in a white blouse and black dress slacks, stepped out onto their cement porch, holding a fluffy, white bathroom rug. She shook the rug hard.

I shot back up and shouted, waving my arms and hands above my head: "Mrs. Johnston! Mrs. Johnston!"

"Hello, Alan," she shouted back to me in that high-pitched, cracking voice of hers. "Well, you've come up in the world."

"Mrs. Johnston," I shouted, "can you come here for a second?"

"Wait a minute," she said. Then, after turning around and opening the glass storm door, she tossed that bathroom rug into the living room.

When she came abreast of the ladder, I gingerly crawled to the edge of the roof so that I could glance down at her.

"Mrs. Johnston," I said to her, "if I give you the phone number of my brother, would you call him for me?"

"Why do you want me to call your brother, Alan?" she asked, perplexed.

"Because I can't get down from the roof," I replied, feeling terribly embarrassed. "I placed this Santa Claus on the chimney there and now I can't get down."

"Why can't you get down?" she cried, even more perplexed than before. "Are you sick or something?"

"No," I replied. "I think I'm just scared."

"Scared?" she replied. "Oh, what nonsense.... Here, I'll come up."

"What?" I cried. "Mrs. Johnston, don't do that. Just call my brother—or the fire department. Mrs. Johnston, don't do..." But before I could protest, she was already scrambling up the ladder.

When her chest was even with the top of the ladder, she said: "Now, Alan, get down on all fours."

"What?" I said, having no idea what she was talking about.

"Get down on all fours—get down on your hands and knees," she said. "Go on, do it," she commanded.

I didn't want to, but I did as she instructed.

"That's it," she said. "Now, turn around and have your legs facing me. Go on now, do it."

I did as she said.

"That's right," she said. "Now, start crawling backwards towards me."

I did.

"That's it," she said. "Keep coming. You're such a good boy."

When I came to the edge of the top of the ladder, she said: "Now, I'm going to take your leg and place it on the top rung of the ladder. When I do this, you shift your weight on that leg and then give me your other leg and I'll place it on the rung below that one. Okay?"

"Okay," I replied and did as she said.

"There!" she cried joyously. "We're doing it," she continued, and as we descended the ladder, I could feel her liver-spotted, thin fingers on my hips.

When we were finally on the ground, Mrs. Johnston hit me playfully on the shoulder and said: "See, we didn't need to call your brother. We got down. Say," she added, "how are you going to get that Santa Claus down from the roof?"

"Oh," I replied with a nervous laugh. "I'm not going to worry about that until after Christmas."

It's now April ninth and Santa is still on the roof. I can almost here him taunting me, saying, "I'm still up here. Summer's coming. Why don't you throw me a pair of sunglasses?" I don't know. If it's still up there by summer, maybe I'll see if Mrs. Johnston will help me, again.

~Alan Zacher

53

Monster Truck Warrior

We acquire friends and we make enemies,
but our sisters come with the territory.
~Evelyn Loeb

I was seven years old, and I was about to give my sister a rather painful and unintended haircut in front of the Christmas tree, though I didn't know it. What I did know was that I wanted a little battery-powered monster truck, just like I'd seen at my cousin's house. The box in my hands was wrapped in candy cane wrapping paper, and it was about the right size. And it passed the shake test—were those little rubber tires I could hear bouncing against the plastic within?

I opened the wrapping paper gently, removing each piece of tape one by one, so as to not disturb the treasure within. Behold! It was a blue plastic monster truck, battery operated. But no batteries! Those were wrapped up separately, and once I found them, I entered make-believe bliss. As Elvis Christmas songs blared from the stereo, I made a stack of my parents' tapes and exulted as my truck crushed them to smithereens (or at least rolled over them awkwardly with a lot of help from me).

After the tape demolition, my truck moved on to the coffee table, and made a wasteland of the hapless sugar cookies and the cardboard

Advent calendar. Then I spied the ultimate monster truck challenge: my sister Heidi's head. What could be more glorious than seeing my truck ride roughshod over my know-it-all older sister?

Heidi was oblivious, sitting cross-legged in her pajamas and blocking out the Elvis Christmas music via her brand new portable tape player and brand new Bon Jovi cassette. Heidi, the responsible one, who was never caught unaware, who wouldn't even let me walk with her to the store, would feel monster truck domination.

I clicked the switch on the bottom of the monster truck to "on," lifted the truck, and slowly let it descend toward her wealth of blond, curly hair. The moment it touched down I knew I was in trouble. Her voluminous hair instantly wound around all four tires and the motor ground to a halt.

"Ah!" she screamed, and scrunched her shoulders, as I tried to pull the truck away, pulling her head with me.

My father was on us in a second. "Ronald! What did you do?" Heidi screamed as he tried to disentangle her tightly wound hair, and my mother, the most rational human being on the planet, stepped in, stopped my father and laid a hand on Heidi's shoulder.

"We're going to have to cut it out. It's the only way."

To her credit, Heidi did not cry as the long steel scissors did their work. To her discredit, she did pummel me in the back yard when I went out to play later. As for my monster truck, I painstakingly cut and pulled the long blond hair from the little metal axels, only to find that its brave little engine had given out.

Monster truck Christmas was over, but my champion had met its fate honorably, in combat with one of the greatest arch nemeses known to boyhood: the older sister.

~Ron Kaiser, Jr.

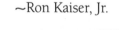

54

The Bare Necessities

Let us be of good cheer, remembering that the misfortunes hardest to bear are those which will never happen.

~James Russell Lowell

"You've heard the old saying, 'It's like pulling hen's teeth?'" I asked my dear friend Anna Marie.

"Uh-huh."

"Well, finding help to set up the Christmas tree makes pulling hen's teeth seem like child's play."

"Quit whining," she said. "Just throw a party and invite all your tall, non-acrophobic friends to come over and celebrate 'the trimming of the tree.' Either that, or make up your mind, once and for all, that a six-foot tree is every bit as nice as one that reaches clear to your twelve-foot ceiling."

"No way." I shook my head. "That yearly twelve-foot tree is a symbol of my independence. When I got divorced, I swore I wouldn't scale down just because I didn't have a live-in tree-trimmer. It's a matter of principle."

"Principles or not," said Anna Marie, "I'll help you with the ornaments, but that's it."

"Terrific!" I beamed. "I've got the crew in place to bring the tree into the house and set it up, another contingent to man the ladders and get the lights on it, and you'll nicely round out the baubles and balls brigade."

The only thing left was tinsel. What is it about tinsel anyway? Even the mention of the word sends grown men and women screaming for asylum.

"Wait!" I implored the hordes of so-called friends abandoning my living room. "Think of it as a 'growing experience.' After tonight you can tell everyone you have looked tinseling square in the eye and come away unscathed!"

"I promised my sitter I'd be home by nine."

"I came over here right after dinner, and I'm sure the dishes are through soaking by now."

"My laundry is piled three feet higher than the washer."

"I've been neglecting my cat. I promised tonight I'd spend some quality time with him."

"Face it, Jan," said Anna Marie, the last rat to leave the ship. "It's not that we don't love you, we just don't do tinsel."

So now I had a decision to make. Could I live with a non-tinseled tree, or would I have to put it all on by myself? I decided to sleep on it.

Everything looked rosier first thing in the morning—a clear, crisp, December day. I pulled on my robe and opened the drapes to survey the monolith dominating my living quarters. What a glorious tree! But yes, I determined, it needed tinsel.

I fixed a cup of cocoa, turned on the stereo, and opened the first of two-dozen packages of icicles. A twelve-foot tree takes twenty-four packages; it's in the rulebook.

Several hours later, and about two-thirds finished, I realized that static cling was causing my clothing to remove as much tinsel as I put on with each trip around the tree. I looked like a giant foil orb.

No problem. I had only a few more turns around the fir to complete the job. I set my glasses on the coffee table and shucked off my robe and nightgown. I live in the woods; I was not expecting company.

Singing along with Mitch Miller and his band, I worked my way once again around the back of the tree. The back of the tree, of course, is against the front windows.

Suddenly, my peripheral vision caught a movement in the

driveway. Something far bigger than my cat was out there, and here I was, caught buck-naked tinseling to the tune of "Silent Night."

I dropped to the floor. I hadn't seen a car pull in, but perhaps someone had walked into the yard from the road. My robe, draped across a dining room chair, was miles away. I couldn't even get to my glasses without risking further exposure.

Gathering courage, I raised up to peer, like Kilroy, over the edge of the windowsill. At the same time, whatever it was out there also raised up to get a better look.

And there we were, nose to nose, with only the plate glass window separating us; bare on the inside, and bear on the outside.

I don't know which of us was more startled. But I do know which one of us quickly got to her feet, retrieved her glasses and robe and watched a very large, very confused, black bear lumber off into the woods.

I'll never know what possessed that bear to rouse itself from hibernation to pay me an early morning visit. The only thing I know for sure is that this is one woman who is never, ever going to be caught tinseling in the nude again by either man or beast!

~Jan Bono

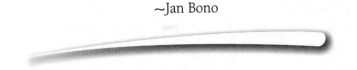

55

The Christmas Hostage

The secret to humor is surprise.
~Aristotle

Typically a man of quiet spirit, my husband morphs into Mr. Christmas after we take down our Thanksgiving decorations. It's like he's saved up all his playful fervor behind a mask of reserve all year. And then, bam! Passing neighborhood children stop to gawk at his obsession—oversized hollow figures that light up, including a complete nativity scene. The baby Jesus is his most challenging piece, requiring not only a stake of wood like the larger pieces, but also wire to strap him in.

I've seen dormant competitive streaks awaken during this time of year, and it peaks with my husband Joe. "Kathleen's got her manger scene out already," he said coming home from a drive by his sister's lawn.

I played along, taking my husband's side of course. "Yours is always bigger and brighter."

"She didn't strap down the baby Jesus. It might blow away."

"You've told her before and she didn't listen. When she has to pay $50 for a new one like you did, she'll learn." I am jealous of his sister. They have a shared childhood history in a tight Philadelphia row home neighborhood, cementing their relationship. It sometimes makes me feel like an outsider.

December is always a blur of happy busyness. But come early January, the excitement of retro childhood fantasy dissipates as the decorations come down.

We were leaving Kathleen's home on January 6th one year, after a 50th birthday celebration, and reminiscing. Joe checked his sister's nativity scene as we passed it on our way down her porch steps. "She's lucky no one stole her baby Jesus. She didn't zip-tie him tight enough to the manger."

I hated to see my husband's playful side go back into storage for another eleven months. His antics with his sister back inside the house were infectious, inspiring me to become an accomplice.

"Take it," I goaded as we strolled along Kathleen's driveway to the sidewalk.

Joe laughed. "No." He stole a glance to see if his sister had gone inside.

"Why not?" I pushed. "I dare you."

He stopped and said, "She'll need it for next year."

"Joe, you'll give it back." I knew he was thinking she'd be as upset as he was when our original one was stolen. "And you can leave a note or call her in a disguised voice saying you're holding him for ransom." I could tell he was interested. "Come on. She'll know it's you right away. And she'll love the fun you'll have with her."

St. Joseph said no more and adopted his sister's plastic doll for a year. We hid it in our home and took it out for photo opportunities. The first photo I snapped was of Joe behind the wheel of his pick-up with the doll atop the truck above his head. He's smiling as if about to drive away unaware of it. He left the picture inside Kathleen's mailbox.

Joe works in a rail yard, so he brought the poor baby to work and put him on the tracks. Click. That photo arrived at his sister's with a playfully written suggestion.

We also used the doll to lighten up a serious family situation. Our daughter was admitted to the hospital and needed emergency surgery. We brought the doll to her hospital room. I saw a twinkle in her eye as she mustered a smile while posing with the abducted plastic. Her smile gave way to chuckles when her dad took another picture of the thing on the windowsill as a helicopter landed on its pad just outside. The note attached to this picture was most fun because our recovering daughter and her visitors helped write it.

There's a picture of the baby Jesus presented to the camera by Kathleen's own teenagers, taken at Easter time when they stopped by to visit our teens.

Kathleen responded to the fun by taping a poster of her missing decoration to a milk carton and passing it around to family who knew all about the prank.

The year of the missing nativity piece extended family playfulness in such a uniting way that surrendering the hostage was almost sad. But as preparations for the next Christmas began, Joe returned the decoration with gratitude for the love — and mischievous streak — of his family.

~Dawn Byrne

56

Woman Versus Tree

There is little success where there is little laughter.
~Andrew Carnegie

One Christmas, I found myself solely responsible for our family Christmas tree. Of course, our daughter, Elizabeth, was more than anxious and excited to help me with this task. Her fourth birthday was nearing—a mere five days before Christmas itself. All of our decorations were already lovingly placed throughout our home, yet there was an empty corner of the family room awaiting the tree.

For a number of reasons, my husband Ted and I would not be sharing this particular tradition. As December rolled on and Elizabeth's excitement grew, I knew that I needed to take action. I thought to myself, "This can't be that difficult. I certainly can handle this." I had helped, or rather watched, Ted erect many a tree. I had helped, or rather watched, my own father erect many before that.

So I made the decision that on that upcoming Friday evening, our Christmas tree was going to fill the family room corner as it rightfully should.

I placed the plastic bins of tree decorations in the family room in anticipation. I set up the tree stand with open arms as if anxiously awaiting a visiting friend.

When Friday arrived, I bundled Elizabeth up and she and I hopped into my four-door sedan destined for the nearby church's

Christmas tree lot. Elizabeth bounded out of the car as soon as her car-seat belts were unbuckled. I raced behind as she scrutinized the nearest trees. Not surprisingly, the first tree that Elizabeth saw, and insisted on having, was probably a good three feet higher than our ceiling and wide enough to encompass half of our family room. I convinced her that there were so many other trees to consider and we really should look around for the "perfect" tree.

With that, she and I wandered up and down rows of various pines—some with most of the needles already on the ground surrounding the base and others with tiny drooping branches that appeared to have lost their needles months ago. We continued our search until we did, indeed, find our perfect tree. Elizabeth jumped in delight when I told her, "Yup my dear! This one is coming home with us."

The kind volunteer attendants at the church lot carried the tree and placed it in my trunk. Actually, it wasn't really in my trunk, but rather my trunk was supporting the middle while both ends stuck out the sides. We only had perhaps a quarter of a mile to get home so, again, the kind volunteer attendants provided rope to hold both my trunk lid and the tree in place. I hadn't even considered that previous years we used Ted's pick-up to get the tree home. Regardless, with both the tree and Elizabeth strapped into my car I drove ever so slowly back home.

Once arriving home, and assisting Elizabeth out of the car while she squealed with excitement, I ran into the house and grabbed a pair of scissors. As I snipped the rope that the volunteer attendants had so kindly fastened, my trunk lid popped up like a bouncing ball and the tree plopped out onto the driveway. I wasn't discouraged. After all, the tree was going to be coming out of the trunk anyway... this just made it less work for me, right? And my daughter certainly found it amusing from her vantage point in the garage as I could hear her peals of laughter.

With that, Elizabeth and I began our journey lugging our Christmas tree around the house to the sliding glass door that led directly to its new home in our family room. I did the lugging while

Elizabeth skipped joyously through the dusting of snow on the ground, following the trail left by the dragging tree. I hadn't exactly anticipated the weight of the tree and had to take more than a few breaks along the way on our trip around the back yard to rest my back and arms. Elizabeth's pure enthusiasm continued to boost my energy and after a moment here and there, we continued on our way.

Once arriving at the door, I felt quite relieved. Certainly the worst was over and now I would simply pick up the tree and place it in the stand. I had Elizabeth sit on the couch while I made my first attempt at this task. Taking a deep breath, I wound my arms around the prickly branches and hoisted the tree a few inches into the air, placing it in the stand. I then bent to tighten the screws at the stand base and our perfect tree attacked! Down it went tumbling onto my back as I flung my arms to catch it and keep it from falling completely to the floor. Elizabeth laughed.

"Mommy should have held the tree while I tightened the stand," I commented to Elizabeth. She didn't really understand what I was talking about but nodded in agreement. Again, I hoisted the tree mere inches into the stand base. This time I balanced the tree with my left hand and awkwardly bent to tighten the stand base screws with my right. My left hand was just a little too high up on the trunk of the tree and as I bent, our perfect tree again went tumbling down on my back. This time I was to my knees on the floor before I could catch the falling tree. Again, Elizabeth laughed.

"Okay—I'll get it this time!" I said as much to myself as to my daughter. I truly believed that I had this entire thing figured out and completely forgot that when Ted and I set up the tree, one of us would balance the thing while the other tightened the stand. I was determined that this could be done. For the third time, I hoisted the tree, bent to tighten screws, and our perfect tree again plummeted down. This time I was face down on the floor with the tree completely flattened on top of me. And, again, Elizabeth laughed.

I gave up. I called my dad to the rescue and within fifteen minutes he and my mom arrived grinning at the door. Dad showed up with a small hand saw, cut the tree trunk so that it was even, placed the tree in the stand, and tightened the screws to hold it erect in what seemed to be a blink of an eye. My mom delighted in Elizabeth's hysterical recanting of how the tree kept falling on Mommy. Elizabeth was nearly rolling on the floor trying to tell the entire story.

And I smirked, sitting exhaustedly on the couch pulling pine needles out of my hair. Naturally, since the tree was beautifully set up in the corner, we had to put some colorful ornaments, lights, and a garland on it, and Grandmom and Pop-Pop joined us. We listened to Christmas music and just had to smile. Every once in a while, amidst the decorating of the tree, you could hear Elizabeth chuckle: "The tree kept falling on Mommy."

When Ted arrived home, Elizabeth rushed into her Daddy's arms. She was most anxious to show him our tree and repeatedly chanted in her sweet singsong voice, "The tree kept falling on Mommy, the tree kept falling on Mommy!"

Now, many years later, with Elizabeth nineteen years old, we have transitioned to an artificial, yet very natural looking, tree that I can actually put up alone without finding myself pinned underneath its branches. Yet each Christmas season as we decorate, Elizabeth asks, "Remember when the tree kept falling on Mommy?" It is almost as if I can still hear her little girl squeals as we hang each and every ornament.

~Lil Blosfield

Two wise men & one wise guy

Shopping at The Loft

The best gifts come from the heart, not the store.
~Sarah Dessen, Lock and Key

"I t's the thought that counts," my daughter Meredith chided me as I studied potential gifts stacked in our loft. "I think Miss Joyce will love it."

True. But should I re-gift a present I had received? "I can't," I said. Or could I?

I loved holiday decorations, cantatas, parties, shopping, and especially the gift giving. I put a lot of thought into selecting gifts the recipients would enjoy. Had they, in turn, wondered, "What in the world am I going to do with this?"

Even the latest edition of *Emily Post's Etiquette* approved re-gifting in the right situations. But would my traditional Southern mother who sent me to charm school think it tasteless, tacky, and downright insulting?

This year, family health issues and lots of extra hours working meant little time to shop holiday sales or to browse online.

"I'm desperate," I said to Meredith. "I don't want friends and family to say 'Really, you shouldn't have,' and mean it."

She suggested I peruse the items we uncovered when downsizing. All were now stored in the loft of our home until we decided to keep them, sell them, or give them to charity. Clever gadgets mingled with unwanted sweaters, stacks of books, and one interesting vase in a delicate shade of blue from an out-of-town friend. Beautiful, though not my decorating color scheme.

This vase seemed perfect for my best friend Joyce.

"Think of it as recycling," Meredith said.

"Well, it is 'new' as in 'never used.'" I wavered. "It's not like Susan will see it in Joyce's house since they don't know each other." I studied the vase. "But I don't know if I'll feel right."

Meredith shrugged.

"I bet your friends re-gift you." She grinned at me.

What? I pondered the thought as the final shopping days wound down. No telltale signs had made me feel re-gifted. But I became obsessed with the idea.

My husband had given me the same book, *Failing Forward*, three years in a row. Could I get away with giving one back to him?

Had the bath salts with the questionable expiration date been fizzing and festering for years before they landed under my tree? The gold lamé fanny pack, glow-in-the-dark PJs, and the fruitcake door-stopper had to be re-gifts. What other white elephants had I received? Just how many Scrooges had tricked me?

Perhaps I would "shop" in my own stuff. But, each item had to pass the re-gifting test: nothing handmade for me, no monograms, and no autographed books. Everything must be unopened, in good condition, and given with the best intentions.

Re-gifting would be my little secret.

I plunged into shopping in my upstairs store. "The Loft" offered a whole new experience. No lines. No credit card remorse. No qualms.

I inspected the unique blue vase. It screamed, "Pick me for Joyce!" I envisioned her oohing and aahing over the gift I selected especially for her. Albeit, one from The Loft, but only Meredith and I would know.

"I can do this," I said, gathering the gift-wrapping paraphernalia. "I think she'll love it."

A few days later, Joyce met me for lunch to exchange gifts. White lights twinkled, soft music wafted through the restaurant, and aromatic candles flickered and scented the busy dining room. Crystal glasses clinked. We laughed, gabbed, indulged a little bit, and opened our gifts.

"You first," I said with a twinge of apprehension.

Joyce tore into the package, ripping the exquisite paper. She removed the gold bow and matching grosgrain ribbon and wadded the paper into a ball.

"I can't wait to see," she said.

She opened the box, pushing tissue paper aside, and lifted the vase.

I held my breath.

"Oh, it's lovely," she said and turned the vase around in her hands, admiring the intricate design. "I love it!" She beamed at me. "Where did you find it? I'd love to get another one to have matching vases on each end of the mantle."

"I bought the last one at The Loft," I mumbled and avoided eye contact.

"Ann Taylor's Loft?"

"No," I said as she continued to drill me.

I broke down and blabbed everything. My little secret tore across the table like a runaway holiday train before landing in Santa's bad-girls-who-get-coal pile.

"A friend gave it to me last year," I stammered. "It wasn't the right color for me, but I thought it would work for you."

Joyce leaned back and laughed a belly laugh, then dabbed at her eyes.

"Your gift is a re-gift, too," she confessed. "My sister gave it to me last year. I love it, but more for you than for me." She jumped up and gave me a warm hug. "That's why we're best friends. We're not two old biddies who'd never consider re-gifting because of some antiquated ideas." Joyce reexamined her gift. "I would have hated to miss this vase," she said. "It's perfect."

When I got home, I checked my list again. Three hard-to-buy-for relatives remained. And by now, I'd stretched my last dollar and my last nerve. Finding the perfect gift had shifted to "get 'er done" via a trip to The Loft.

I settled on John Maxwell's book. *Failing Forward* was perfect for them, and I just happened to have three. With any luck, I'd receive another copy from my husband real soon.

~Debra Ayers Brown

Southern Hospitality

Christmas is doing a little something extra for someone.
~Charles Schulz

Hurrying to meet my sister Heidi at her gate, I had to grin. The airport may have been smaller than many Manhattan subway stations, but nearly everyone was smiling. Gone was the New York City "time is money" frenetic walking pace. Here folks meandered as if they had all the time in the world. The attentive car rental employee gave us a complimentary upgrade to a convertible. When he said, "Enjoy your trip!" he looked me directly in the eye. His sincere tone lingered long after we'd left the rental counter. Had we stumbled onto a movie set?

Off we went in the direction of the condo we'd rented for the long weekend in Charleston, South Carolina. I like driving. I really like driving fast. And that car begged to be driven quickly. The pothole-free freeway tempted me, but I held back from racing until I became more accustomed to the different freeways and local driving habits.

After wandering off to get the keys from the building manager, we received another surprise. On the kitchen counter the owners had left a nice bottle of wine and a box of chocolates with a "Happy Birthday!" note. How thoughtful. I had only mentioned in passing that

Heidi and I were there to celebrate her birthday. Being a Sagittarius, she gets ripped off, her birthday lost in the hoopla of Christmas celebration. We'd decided to change that this year and enjoy her big day in late November instead. So far, so good.

On the coffee table in the living room, underneath a cute "Please smoke outside" sign, was a black binder stuffed with helpful information, complete with menus. Wanting nothing more than to curl up on the comfortable couch and watch movies, we agreed to go out the next night and ordered a pizza. Heidi didn't need their tutorial on how to work their plasma television and we chose a film.

The beaming pizza delivery guy was college student age. Our un-Southern accents said that we were visiting, so he welcomed us and said to have fun.

"Goll-eee!" he exclaimed when I gave him the customary twenty percent New York City tip. "That is mighteeee generous. Thank yew."

We were so thrilled to have a hot veggie pizza with extra sauce that I'd have gladly given him more. I didn't tell him that the pizza cost as much as a draft beer in my local bar.

The next morning we went to a local coffee shop, taking time to savor our delicious homemade chocolate chip pancakes, while noticing that all the patrons were genuinely pleasant. Touring the plantation homes was informative. I learned more Southern history, something the Northern school systems tend to teach differently. At least both sides agree it's a dark chapter of American history. Our walking tour gave us an even greater appreciation of Charleston. People on the streets sold handmade baskets, treats and souvenirs. How would we ever squeeze in a round of golf on the Jack Nicklaus-designed course on Kiawah Island?

Time passed too quickly. Regrettably we handed back the keys to the convertible and checked in for our flights home. Such a great birthday celebration. I wanted to return. As the old adage warns, "Be careful what you ask for."

A week later I received an early Christmas gift in the mail. After opening the envelope, I cursed my invitation asking me to kindly come back... and appear in court. One of those hidden cameras had caught me in the rental car going way too fast.

"What?" I took another look at the dollar amount of the speeding ticket. What a costly mistake, even by the standards of North America's most expensive city. I sat down and wrote a polite letter to the judge. Starting with how much I had thoroughly enjoyed my visit to his charming town, I shared highlights of our trip. Because of our incredible time, I was more than willing to come back down and visit Charleston again.

Unfortunately the court appearance scheduled in two weeks didn't give me enough time to get days off from work and book a reasonably-priced plane ticket, reminding him the holidays made fares exorbitant. If he'd please move the court date further into the future, I'd happily return. I admitted that I was speeding, but only "slightly above" the limit, not a "reckless" number of miles over. Alternatively, if he'd reduce the fine, I'd pay it and we could call it even. I ended with, "Please let me know what action you'd like to take. Enjoy your fabulous city for me. I love Charleston."

A week later, my hands quivered when I saw his reply had arrived. I couldn't believe what I was reading and had to read it again. My face broke into a huge smile. Written by hand were the words, "Your ticket has been forgiven. Merry Christmas!"

Now, regardless of the time of year, whenever anyone mentions Southern hospitality, I think of that very kind judge and smile all over again.

~JC Sullivan

The Canning Shed

In some families, "please" is described as the magic word.
In our house, however, it was "sorry."
~Margaret Laurence

Christmastime is over, we're basking in the glow
Of Yuletide fun and memories, some made so long ago
The presents have been opened, the turkey has been carved
We've joined the kiddies on the hills, in winter boots and scarves

And though the years are flying by, we never will forget
The year that Grandpa lost my grandma in the canning shed
The snow was softly falling, the stars were shining bright
My grandpa finished up the chores, and came in for the night

The turkey it was roasting, Grandma's cooking smelled sublime
The tree was loaded down with gifts; soon it would be time
The family was coming, with new babies, cats and dogs
The neighbors were invited to join the Christmas throng

Grandma then decided to the canning shed she'd go
Grabbed her boots and flashlight, and trundled through the snow
The wind was howling 'round her as she opened up the door
To find a turkey platter that she'd been looking for

It wasn't in the kitchen, this was her last resort
And she couldn't call on Grandpa, he was busy doing chores
Just as she found the cupboard, where the dish would likely be
Her flashlight died and darkness was all that she could see

Just then Grandpa left the barn, and saw the open door
He slammed it shut and locked it, knocking Grandma to the floor
He could not hear her hollering above the blizzard's roar
(Sometimes I wonder if he did and decided to ignore)

Grandpa cleaned the milk pail, then went upstairs to change
He thought about it later, and something did seem strange
Potatoes simmered on the stove, the turkey almost done
Headlights showing in the lane, the party had begun

When Grandpa came back down the stairs, the family was there
But no one could find Grandma; she had disappeared
The family was worried and searched the house anew
Grandpa looked distressed and wondered what to do

Suddenly, he stopped and slapped his forehead, said, "Aha!"
"I think I know where Grandma is, I bet she's good and mad!"
Sure enough, she'd been locked in the frozen canning shed
She'd found the platter in the dark and hit him on the head

That Christmas we spent warming Grandma by the fireside
And Grandpa had a goose egg on his head and two black eyes
We had our meal and opened gifts and got the kids to bed
But today we laugh about our Grandma in the canning shed

~Gloria Jean Hansen

It's Christmas!

A Little Help from My Friends

*The best gifts in life will never be found under a Christmas tree,
those gifts are friends, family, children and the one you love.*

~Author Unknown

It Takes a Village

You can always tell a real friend: when you've made a fool of yourself
he doesn't feel you've done a permanent job.
~Laurence J. Peter

I got up at the crack of dawn that morning. I expected about thirty people for Christmas dinner, and the meal would consist of a twenty-pound turkey with all the trimmings.

Though the house was clean, dessert was made, and everything was cut, diced and sliced to make the cooking chores go as smoothly as possible, I still had a lot of work to do. My husband, son and I had opened our gifts from each other the night before knowing that this day would be a hectic one.

I wrestled the huge bird out of the refrigerator, dragging it to the sink. As I rinsed it, I noticed that the legs resisted my tugs. It was still a little too frozen to stuff, but I guesstimated that an hour defrosting in my cool office would thaw it completely and keep it safe from the curious cats gathered around my ankles sniffing at the air.

I placed it on my desk and shut the door. Then I busied myself with other assorted tasks, setting my timer so I wouldn't forget the main dish. I threw the tablecloth and placemats I planned to use into the wash, and gave the carpet another once over when I noticed some glitter from the previous evening's gift exchange clinging to the fibers.

The timer went off as I finished layering the scalloped potatoes in the baking dish. I wiped my hands, turned on the oven to preheat, pulled the stuffing out of the fridge and went to retrieve the turkey. As I placed my hand on the doorknob, I heard a loud belch come from behind the door and my heart sank.

I knew what I'd find even before I saw it. Intent on banishing the cats from the room earlier, I didn't notice the dog lying in the warm rays of his favorite morning sunbeam... in the office! I had closed him in with the turkey. I never heard the sounds of his feeding frenzy over the noise of my appliances, or I might have saved the main course. Unfortunately, now, it was too late.

What was left of it lay on the floor resembling the carnage of a wildebeest slaughter by lions in the Serengeti. My dog, Jack, sat licking his lips next to it. He had the grace to look slightly ashamed, but I knew that, deep in his heart, he thought the transgression was well worth any consequence.

I only needed to point to the area of his doggy bed. He slunk by me, head bowed, while his grotesquely engorged belly swayed from side to side. I knew he'd be okay after eating that much. A similar past experience with an entire ham left me feeling pretty confident that he'd expel what he couldn't digest. I could only hope that happened long before my guests arrived.

I approached the remains with tears in my eyes and with some concern. A quick inspection told me two things — the first, that there would be no danger of Jack suffering any mishap from bone shards or splinters, and the second that I couldn't salvage even a wing. Every bone was intact, yet the turkey was picked clean. The rib cage could have been used in a veterinary anatomy class, there was so little meat left on it.

What was I going to do? It was Christmas. There wasn't a store open anywhere, and even if there was, any replacement I'd manage to get would be frozen solid. I had less than seven hours to come up with an alternate plan, and I knew nothing in my own freezer would suffice.

At that moment the doorbell rang. I answered it to find my

neighbor and friend, Amy, standing there with a platter of brightly decorated cookies.

"Merry Christmas!" she sang, and I promptly dissolved into a lump of quivering hysteria.

"Oh my goodness!" she cried, pushing past me. She dumped her tray on my kitchen table and pulled me close. "Talk to me," she demanded. My husband and son, having heard my meltdown, rushed into the room from downstairs.

I couldn't speak. I could only make incoherent, choking sounds as I led them to the office to point to the carcass. The cats were circling it, trying to find even a tiny overlooked morsel. My husband shooed them away and immediately discarded what was left. From the other room we heard a gagging splashing noise and I knew Jack had relinquished his feast.

"I have thirty people to feed!" I sobbed. "I can't possibly cancel now," I wailed as my husband scurried off to clean the mess.

Amy patted my back gently, deep in thought. When she spoke, it was with calm firmness.

"You leave everything to me," she murmured. "Keep getting the other stuff ready. I'll call you in about an hour," she assured me.

She whirled around and charged towards the door, averting her eyes from the deposit my husband was cleaning. "Trust me and don't worry," she called over her shoulder. "Oh, and spray some air freshener!" she advised before she disappeared.

She called right on time. By then, I had calmed down enough to put the finishing touches on some side dishes and made sure the meat pies were thawing in a safer place.

"Okay, problem solved," she announced. "We'll be there about four. Don't stress anymore," she said, and hung up without further explanation.

As promised, she showed up with two other neighbors, Sarah and Judy, grinning from ear to ear. She carried a huge foil-covered roasting pan. The other two juggled large chafing dishes. They all walked in as I stood there gaping.

"Ta-da!" Amy exclaimed dramatically, pulling the wrapper off the pan to reveal orderly piles of turkey parts.

"What on earth?" I gasped.

Everyone chipped in," she explained. "All our friends up and down the block donated a leg here, a wing there, until we managed to pretty much come up with a whole turkey and then some," she said, pointing to the extra three drumsticks and two breasts.

"I made gravy," Sarah proclaimed, pulling out a gigantic jar from one of the food warmers.

"And I brought stuffing, in case you didn't make any." Judy offered.

I was speechless. The food smelled delicious and was still steaming, so the girls set up the chafing pans and filled them.

"Keep everything warm," Amy directed. "It's all cooked and the dishes will keep the turkey moist until you're ready to eat. Just tell everyone you sliced it early. We'll leave now before your company gets here. Merry Christmas."

"Merry Christmas—and thank you so much," I whispered, hugging them all. "You have to tell me who contributed so I can thank everyone else too," I insisted through happy tears, waving goodbye.

As they drove off, my first guests pulled into the driveway. My husband put his arm around me and winked at my son. Thanks to the kindness of friends and neighbors, and polite guests who never questioned the various flavors and extra turkey appendages, our Christmas went off as planned.

~Marya Morin

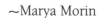

61

The Light of the Carolers

Healing requires from us to stop struggling,
but to enjoy life more and endure it less.
~Darina Stoyanova

As I drove into the garage on a snowy winter's day, Bing Crosby was crooning "I'll Be Home for Christmas" on the radio. The lyrics stung, as it would be our first Christmas season without our eldest son, Davis, who had been killed in a traffic accident six months earlier.

Decorating the tree was one of our favorite family traditions. I thought about the carols that would be playing as we untangled the tree lights and laid out our collection of ornaments. Each ornament had a history and a story. How would we get through Christmas without Davis?

Our friends, Jim and Fiona, knew how difficult this "first" would be for us. They, too, were facing their own Goliath. Jim had been diagnosed with a cancerous brain tumor the year before and was in full battle mode. He and Fiona understood how precious life was. Yet they were determined to brighten our home by bringing over a home-cooked meal and spending an evening with us.

As I looked out the window into the neighborhood, I noticed our neighbors' homes outlined in colored lights and festive displays.

Our house was usually one of the earliest to be decorated. Not this year; we were the hurting house. I went back into my kitchen to put the finishing touches on the appetizers I was preparing.

The doorbell rang a little earlier than I expected. My husband and I met at the entrance, ready to greet the Prestons. To our amazement, our snow-covered yard was filled with flickering candles and familiar faces singing, "We Wish You a Merry Christmas." There were carolers as far as the eye could see. The sound was angelic. One carol followed another in beautiful harmony, with faces aglow in the candlelight. As tears flooded my eyes, I felt such gratitude for this meaningful gesture of love. All was calm, all was bright.

Several of our neighbours opened their doors to the songs of the carolers and joined in. After another carol had been sung on this cold winter's night, someone piped up with, "Well, can we come in now?" The initial dinner plan had been a ruse to gather together our friends and colleagues in a Christmas experience we would never forget, one that we needed so desperately. Within minutes, a potluck of Christmas dishes appeared from the back seats of cars or from their hidden places under bushes.

We stoked the fireplace, brought out the eggnog, and filled our home to capacity with the large group that had gathered. Christmas would never be the same as it had been during our eighteen years with Davis, but I realized something that night. Joy can trump sorrow. Love came down and gathered on our doorstep. Jim and Fiona had given us the wondrous gift of community to fill the gap. It set the tone for the Christmas season that followed. Even though Davis wouldn't be home with us, God compensated for our loss with a love so evident in this gesture of friendship and support. Each caroler had taken a piece of our heartache from us. As I looked around at the smiling faces in our crowded house, I knew I wanted to decorate the tree tomorrow, assured that Davis would be present with me in a different but meaningful way. He'd be home for Christmas—if only in my heart.

~Sally Walls

62

The Penguin Christmas

A single rose can be my garden... a single friend, my world.
~Leo Buscaglia

What could have easily been the saddest Christmas of my life turned into my most cherished holiday memory. Christmas of 2005 was the Christmas that I had been dreading all my life; it was my first Christmas in a nursing home.

I was born with cerebral palsy, a condition that left me totally dependent on my parents, who did their best to take care of me. But as they became older, they decided that it was time for me to find a new home. I was only forty-eight years old.

Although my family had chosen a very nice nursing home for me, a Catholic home where I could attend daily Mass, it was still a nursing home. The nurses' aides were nice enough, but they were on a tight schedule, so they had very little time to talk. Besides, a lot of the CNAs were teenagers who worked after school. These girls were sweet, but hearing them giggle about boys night after night got to be old.

I also found it difficult to relate to the other residents. Most of them were too sick to carry on a conversation. There was one sweet lady whose company I enjoyed very much, but Eleanor died just a few weeks after my arrival. All of this, combined with the fact that my family wasn't visiting me as often as they had promised to, left me feeling very lonely.

Then one night, an aide who I had never seen before came into my room. This middle-aged woman, who introduced herself as June, had bright blue eyes and a smile that lit up the room. Somewhere deep in my heart, I felt connected to her.

Over the next few weeks, the bond between June and me grew even stronger. Since June was closer to my age than any of the other CNAs were (in fact, she was nine years older than me), I found her very easy to talk to. June must have felt the same way about me, because every night, as she put me to bed, we would have a nice chat. June would tell me stories about her grandsons, whom she adored. Hearing about the antics of these three young boys would always make me smile. June just seemed to have a gift for cheering me up. No matter how sad my day had been, I would usually be laughing hysterically by the time June tucked me into bed.

Once in a while, June would pop into my room early in the evening, just to see how my day had been. "Why are you always watching penguins on that little TV of yours?" June asked me one night.

I couldn't help but smile to myself. Since my sweet friend was extremely computer illiterate, I wasn't about to try explaining YouTube to June. "Penguins have always intrigued me," I said. "They walk upright. They remind me of toddlers, and they seem so cuddly."

"Have you ever seen a penguin in person?" June asked as she got out my nightgown.

"No, but I'd love to."

"Haven't you ever been to the New England Aquarium?" June asked. "I thought that every kid in Maine had gone there."

Without knowing it, June had brought up a painful subject. "My parents thought that traveling with me was too much work," I said quietly. "They always waited until I was away at camp before they took my brother on family vacations."

I could tell that June was fighting back tears as she put her arms around my shoulders, and kissed me softly on my head. "It won't be for a long time," she said. "But maybe after I retire, you and I can go see some penguins. Would you like that?"

I could only nod. The idea of getting to see penguins was exciting. But if June and I ever traveled to Boston, I would have her all to myself for a whole day, maybe even two. I would be in heaven.

Over the next few months, I began to adjust to living in a nursing home. As the holidays approached, I enjoyed all of the Christmas activities that were offered. (Since my grandparents had died, my family had very few holiday traditions.) I loved the carolers, the parties, and the crafts that we worked so hard on. We even put on a Christmas pageant. I was really enjoying the holidays until reality set in.

Christmas Eve in a nursing home is one of the loneliest nights of the year. All of the little carolers who brought us so much joy during the past few weeks were at home celebrating with their own families. Everything on TV is a rerun, because hardly anyone watches TV on this holy night. But there was one thing that made this Christmas Eve bearable for me: June was working.

June was running late that evening, and I was wondering why. It was almost an hour past my bedtime before she came into my room. But when I saw the huge gift bag that she was carrying, I knew that June had put all her other residents to bed first so that she could spend some extra time with me. Maybe this wasn't going to be such a bleak holiday, after all.

"It will be quite a while before we can go to Boston," June said as she placed the bag on my lap. "But maybe having these will make the waiting easier."

Until that moment, I hadn't noticed that there was a picture of a penguin on the gift bag. As June helped me empty the bag, I saw that there was a definite theme to the bag's contents. The bag held a penguin doorstopper, penguin socks, penguin pajamas, penguin-shaped chocolates, and penguin knickknacks. Even the card that June had signed with love was a penguin Christmas card.

My eyes filled with tears as I pictured June going to different stores, and picking out all these things for me. These little guys that now filled my room showed me that June had put a lot of time, thought, and love into shopping for me. I had never received such a precious gift.

That Christmas was six years ago, and June still has to work two more years before she can retire. But every year, when those precious penguins reappear in my room, I'm reminded of the vacation—and the time together—that June and I will someday share.

~Jamie Henderson

The Perfect Gift

Those who bring sunshine into the lives of others,
cannot keep it from themselves.
~James M. Barrie

Christmas was fast approaching. The houses in our neighborhood looked like ladies going out on the town, with necklaces of garlands and colored lights. In the spirit of the season, my father bought the most beautiful tree he could find and spent hours lovingly decorating every bough with lights and ornaments. Some of the ornaments were crafted by artists, some were collected on trips, and others were priceless creations that my parents had saved over the years: things like a tiny handprint in clay or the photograph of a toothless kindergartner surrounded by glitter.

On Christmas Eve morning, my father brought my mother home from the hospital for the holidays. Her long battle with cancer was coming to an end and we knew, with heartbreaking certainty, that her forty-ninth Christmas was going to be her last.

It was a melancholy reunion. In many ways, my mother, who had once been so full of life, had already left us. She was weak from the disease, the pain medication left her foggy and lethargic and, as hospice had predicted, she had withdrawn into herself in preparation for death. She sat in her wheelchair in front of the Christmas tree for hours, lost in thoughts she couldn't express.

At the same time, my brother, sister, father and I also carried wounds from her battle. We had spent long hours in hospital rooms, had lived through terrifying emergencies that sent ambulances racing to our home and had ridden the roller coaster of hope followed by disappointment and despair. We moved about the house with heavy hearts and a deep exhaustion that the gaiety of the season made almost too painful to bear. There was no Christmas feast planned, no shiny packages under the tree. For what could possibly be put into a box for someone with so little time to live?

As the day slipped into evening, the doorbell rang. Word had gone out in the neighborhood that Mom was home for the holidays. For the next few hours, friends and neighbors trickled in. Chairs were arranged in the family room, the fire was stoked, and carols were softly playing on the stereo. The conversation soon turned toward those special moments when my mother had touched their lives in some way. Some of the stories were new to me; stories that hadn't been told because she never advertised her acts of kindness.

"Remember the time I was shorthanded at my alterations shop and mentioned it when I ran into you at the mailbox? You were on vacation from your job, but when I got to work the next morning there you sat in front of a sewing machine, helping out."

"How about the time I took the roast out of the oven and dropped it at my dinner party? I was devastated!" said another. "You knew how hard I'd worked on it so you made me serve it right off the floor!"

"When my daughter got pregnant you insisted on keeping her baby in the morning so she could finish high school and you wouldn't take a dime for doing it. Without your help she would have had to drop out of school. It would have changed her whole life."

"Remember the time you dropped me off at the bus station? You were waving goodbye so enthusiastically, the bus driver thought you were flagging him down and backed up!"

It started slowly, but as the words began to paint a picture of deep, abiding friendship and love, something magical happened. Each story drew my mother a little further out of the fog and back into the light. A vacant nod turned into a smile. Her brown eyes began to twinkle with warmth and awareness. She even chuckled at the stories about her foibles, as she had always loved to laugh at herself. As she drew nearer to us, my heavy heart lifted.

Our college-aged friends who were home for winter break began to arrive. They also had stories to share.

"We loved being in your house. There was always something fun going on; football in the back yard, *Euchre* inside at the game table. Plus you always fed us!"

"You were the best baker in the neighborhood," my best friend added, "I couldn't get enough of your cinnamon rolls!"

"You don't know this," said one of my brother's friends, "but I always wished I had been born into your family. You guys were always laughing. It was a great place to be!"

"I wish I had known," my mother quipped softly. "I could have worked out a trade with your parents." The room erupted into laughter and taunts toward my siblings and me. They thought it was hilarious that she could have so cavalierly tossed one of us aside.

It was in that small joke that I realized my mother had returned to us. Against all odds she was truly present, surrounded by the family and friends who treasured her. She always said she was just a simple woman living a simple life. Those who view their lives as "simple" seldom see the impact they have on those around them. Our neighbors took the time to let her know that she had made a difference to each of them, and in doing so, softened the razor-sharp edges of my own grief.

There hasn't been a December since that year when I haven't thought of the night our friends postponed their own traditions to demonstrate the true meaning of Christmas. Six days before my mother would pass away, they gave my family the perfect gift. It couldn't be boxed, bowed, or stuffed into a stocking, and cancer couldn't take it away. It was the gift of love that had been nurtured for decades. It was the one gift, I know beyond a shadow of a doubt, that she carried with her into Heaven.

~Vicki Kitchner

64

From Worst to Best

Friendship is a sheltering tree.
~Samuel Taylor Coleridge

Everyone knew that this Christmas would go in the family books as the worst Noel in Johnson family history. I was nine years old, and my family had made the move from Los Angeles, California to a completely invisible, forgettable town in northwestern Ohio. Both of my parents, my little sister, and I were living with my aunt as my dad struggled to find work as a minister. All the while, I was fighting a rare blood disease that kept me confined to the hospital most of the time. On the days when I was able to attend school, I kept to the library and isolated myself by the swingset, trying to keep my distance from the strangers I called my classmates. As the Christmas season approached, I was again confined to the medical ward and my parents still hadn't found any work. Yes, this would be the worst Christmas ever.

It was December 16th and my classroom was in a tizzy, preparing and decorating for the class Christmas party, to be held the next week before we were released for winter break. I had the lonely job of cutting out paper snowflakes while I watched the other children hang garlands and discuss how they were finally going to sneak up on Santa this year. My teacher, Miss Endicott, called for me across the room, but I shook my head and averted my gaze to the white printer paper shreds in my hand, pretending not to hear. Of everyone in my school, Miss Endicott was the individual who was always encouraging me to interact with my classmates, and I could almost see her shoulders sag a little at my avoidance of company.

It would be the last time I would see my class until February.

Early the next morning, my parents drove me to the operating room where I was scheduled to have another tumor removed. I could see Christmas decorations out of the corners of my tear-filled eyes, hear "Jingle Bells" playing over my begging to go home, and the faint smell of mint mixed with the sickly sweet stench of anesthesia. As a masked face loomed over my field of vision and said, "You are being such a good girl, you will be home in time for Christmas," I prayed that God would take away Christmas and carry me from this terrible place.

The surgery was a success, but I experienced complications and was confined to bed for several days. As my body recuperated, my boredom was satiated by homework my dad picked up for me from school.

On the last day of classes before school ended for holiday break, my dad brought home a stack of textbooks, folders, and atop the teetering pile of paper, a VHS tape. My mother lay beside me as my dad pressed play, and I became confused as the first image to appear on my television screen was my classroom. All of the decorations were up, and my classmates were all lined up against one wall. My teacher's warm face appeared in the corner of the screen and explained that since I couldn't come to the class Christmas party, then the party would have to come to me. The camera panned back to my peers who were holding up a bright yellow sign with "Get Better Soon" scrawled in crayon. One by one, Miss Endicott placed each classmate in front of the camera to say uplifting words, wishing me a Merry Christmas, asking if I would play with them when I came back, saying they would leave my gifts and candy on my desk until I got back to school. My mom's hand gripped tighter around mine as she whispered through tears, "This is incredible, this is so incredible."

I was shocked that I was cared for by people I barely knew. I watched the video again, just to be sure it was real, and my first day back at school I hugged Miss Endicott and thanked her over and over again. I don't remember what gifts I received, whether it snowed that year, or even the rest of my recuperation. What I do remember is that the Christmas when I was nine years old remains the greatest Christmas I have ever had.

~Nan Rockey

65

The Christmas Spirit Strikes Again

Blessed is the season which engages the whole world in a conspiracy of love!
~Hamilton Wright Mabie

I always dreamed of pulling off the surprise prank of a lifetime. You know, the kind you see on TV, or laugh about late at night with friends? Well, thanks to a little determination, some luck, and a generous helping of Christmas Spirit, my dream became a reality.

My family is Canadian, although my sister moved down to Australia a few years ago to study speech pathology. She was graduating just before Christmas, but due to my own scholarly schedule back home, I would not be unable to make it down in time for her graduation. She was understandably disappointed, and I felt guilty that I wasn't able to be there for her on this most special of occasions.

While I was talking to my supervisor the week before my sister's graduation, the conversation drifted toward Christmas plans. When I mentioned that I would be missing my sister's graduation by less than forty-eight hours, she commented, "Well, if you want to go, I have no problem with it, so go ahead!" I couldn't believe my luck! I nearly jumped for joy. "Just make sure you get permission from admin," she added. My heart sank. The administration at my school was notorious for denying any sort of time-off requests, and last-minute pleas would undoubtedly draw nothing but ire. I almost didn't bother asking, because I knew it would be a waste of time and I didn't feel like a thorough chastisement. Plus, I knew the answer already: no. But something in me decided to try, just in case. Maybe it was the hope that the Christmas Spirit would somehow permeate the administrative office at this time of year.

When I returned home to find the Associate Dean's reply in my inbox, I steeled myself for disappointment. I gritted my teeth, opened the e-mail, and started to read. And re-read. And re-read, just to make sure I'd understood. Approval? I could actually go? I rubbed my eyes—there must be a mistake. But no. I was flabbergasted. There was no logical explanation. I couldn't believe my luck! The only explanation I could possibly come up with was that the Christmas Spirit had been lurking in the heart of my Associate Dean when she'd read my request.

Immediately, I called the airline. Miraculously, even during the busy Christmas season, I was able to change my ticket to arrive the day before my sister's graduation.

With news this fantastic, I was bursting to tell my sister. But, fingers on the dial, I paused. Wouldn't it be so much more fantastic if I could surprise her? I pictured myself just showing up, knocking at her door. What a state of shock she would be in! I laughed gleefully to myself as I pictured her face when she opened the door and saw me. She loves pranks and practical jokes of all sorts. Pulling off a prank like this would certainly be the ultimate gift, and if I were successful, she'd probably be more excited about my unconventional arrival than even my attendance at her graduation.

Slowly the idea evolved in my mind. For a surprise of this grand a scale, I needed a much more dramatic arrival than just a ring of the doorbell. For me, Christmas surprises are epitomized by presents. Or at least boxes. What if I could arrive in a box? I started to plot. Then, brilliance struck. Getting delivered in a box to my sister's house by couriers! I knew if I pulled this off, my presence at her graduation and my grand arrival would be the best Christmas present I could ever give my sister. No one appreciates a prank like a prankster!

Although I was leaving in less than seventy-two hours, I frantically jumped on my computer in Halifax, Nova Scotia, Canada, and started Googling courier companies. One of the first I came across, and the only one willing to go along with my Christmas surprise, was CouriersPlease. At first the branch manager said no, pointing out that Christmas was their busiest season and he couldn't spare a courier for this rather unorthodox request. But he suddenly and inexplicably warmed up to the idea and actually volunteered to dress up and deliver me himself. The Christmas Spirit strikes again!

Upon arrival in Australia, the manager met me in full uniform, but that wasn't all. He'd brought one of his couriers, plus a CouriersPlease van along for the ride as well! They even had a reinforced box prepared for me that they'd already tested at the office. I'd thought it would be easiest to walk up to the doorway, and then jump in the box while they rang the doorbell. But no, they insisted; my sister might see me through the window and they certainly didn't want to jeopardize my Christmas surprise. Instead, they parked a few hundred meters up the street, where they loaded me in the box and carried me all the way up to my sister's, where they rang the doorbell and announced they had a delivery for her.

I couldn't see the look on my sister's face as she opened the door to couriers with a surprise delivery, but I could tell from her voice that she was more than a little perplexed. This soon morphed into utter disbelief and shock when the box was opened and she saw her older sister sitting inside smiling up at her. She was at a complete loss for words, and I will never forget the look on her face as she opened those flaps on the box.

It was such a gift to be able to attend my sister's graduation, and to show her my love by giving her the most unique, unconventional Christmas present in the history of our family. It was a memory both she and I will cherish forever. It also served as a lesson for me: never, ever underestimate the power of the Christmas Spirit. It can move hearts, minds, and yes, even people in boxes.

~Heather Thompson

A Flood
of Blessings

*A lovely thing about Christmas is that it's compulsory, like a thunderstorm,
and we all go through it together.*
~Garrison Keillor

I t was the Monday before Christmas, and the first really cold
day of winter. My seven- and nine-year-old sons and I pulled
up to our brightly decorated home, excited to go in and wrap
more gifts. We tromped over the snow, past the herd of lit-up
reindeer and elves and through the front door. I smelled it before I
saw it—there was moisture in the air.

Before I could puzzle it out, the boys had already run downstairs
into our basement family room and were yelling the bad news up
to me. The basement had flooded. We made our way down to find
four inches of water on the floor, and more pouring in from a pipe
that had frozen and burst. Fortunately the boys were so caught up
in rescuing our hysterically mewing kittens they failed to hear the
colorful words from their mother's mouth. All I'll say here is that I
was not feeling very merry.

In our basement were my desk, computer, TV, pool table and a
brightly lit Christmas tree (it was on a timer), surrounded by beautifully wrapped gifts. Thank God the tree was on a stand, so the gifts
were okay. But other than the pool table, everything else resembled

cookies that had been dipped in milk for too long. And the water was still pouring in. I dashed through the icy flood and yanked the power cords from the wall. I hadn't considered the likelihood of becoming a cautionary tale about what *not* to do when you're standing in ankle-deep water.

Surviving that, I needed to figure out how to get the pipe shut off. I called the local water agency, and the message I was forced to leave was not about their awesome crisis support. Next I started rifling through the Yellow Pages for a plumber. As I found out firsthand, the first freezing day of the season brings lots of floods throughout our city. Needless to say, they were only minimally interested in my problem.

When I finally got someone to talk to me, he promised to be there in an hour or so. Worrying about what "or so" might mean, the boys and I rushed our valuables upstairs and started bailing as fast as we could. By the time the plumber arrived two hours later, the water level had risen by several inches and we felt a lot like Jack and Rose on the Titanic. The cats, being cats, had quickly figured out this was a human issue and headed upstairs with no more than sardonic cat-smirks for goodbyes.

The plumber, God bless him, shut the water off, mended the pipe as best he could, and called in his restoration partners to take over the next phase of the "Keeping Jackie from jumping off a ledge" project. Those wonderful men spent the next four hours (until well past midnight) hauling dripping carpet out onto the snow outside. Of course they discovered mold, which meant even more destruction was in order. By this time, the boys had shrewdly joined the cats and retreated to their upstairs bedrooms, which were relatively spa-like in comparison to the rest of the house.

The next morning, striving for normalcy, I dropped the boys off at school. Then I went to work completely exhausted, both physically and emotionally. I tried to go about my regular business, but my mind was very much on my basement and that poor, beautiful Christmas tree surrounded by the not-so-beautiful wreckage. As the workmen were not as emotionally invested in my tree as I was, I knew its time was limited. I decided we would take down the tree that night and move the presents upstairs.

Very pleased with my logic and emotional control, I shared the flood story, along with my aquatic heroics, with two male co-workers in a meeting that day. I explained to them that it made no sense to have a tree when there were so many other, more important, things that needed to be dealt with—not the least of which was fungus-free air.

My co-workers listened patiently and nodded carefully, like negotiators trying to coax a jumper off her ledge. After more of my "reasoning," one co-worker finally asked how I thought our family, who decorated like maniacs for every season, could possibly go without a tree on Christmas. I explained that the tree was in the basement because our living room was too small, and there was no way it would fit upstairs, and we'd just tape up a picture of a tree, and that the kids got it, and I got it, and everyone else would too—ha, ha, ha, ha... ha. Talking about it was obviously a bad idea, and I finally lost control. The tears I'd been carefully holding back fought their way out and streamed down my face. Not at all happy about crying at work, I sped to the bathroom, blotted my eyes and returned to the meeting. Nothing more was said of Christmas trees or flooded basements.

I picked up my boys early that day, so we could head back to our cold, sodden family room and start dealing with the mess. When we arrived home, what should be waiting for us on the front porch but a small Christmas tree, wrapped in a bow, with a card attached. It was a note from Santa, explaining how it was not acceptable for the Sheltons to be without a Christmas tree. He had specially selected this one to fit in our living room.

The boys were thrilled that Santa had dropped in early, while I was overwhelmed at the thoughtfulness of my co-workers, bringing the tears streaming back. But this time, in a good way. I felt very much like George Bailey, and yes, it was wonderful. We brought it inside and set it up in the same spot I'd planned for the tree picture. Santa had guessed well—it fit perfectly.

That night we reenacted the ritual we'd performed just weeks before, with one small difference. We heated up hot chocolate, cranked the Christmas tunes, and spent hours moving ornaments and gifts from one tree to the other. As we enjoyed our evening, I thought about how much different that night would have been if we'd been packing up the ornaments into boxes, and how blessed we were to have such amazing people in our lives. There was no way that night could get any better... until my nine-year-old turned to me and said, "Mommy. How lucky are we that we get to decorate *two* Christmas trees this year?" And just like that, our worst Christmas turned into one of the best.

~Jackie Shelton

Santa in the 'Hood

Christmas, my child, is love in action.
Every time we love, every time we give, it's Christmas.
~Dale Evans

I was pregnant and my husband had just started a new job driving a transport truck. We weren't sure our finances were going to get us through the holidays. Things were tight and we already needed to make a nice Christmas for our first child and my husband's daughter. I felt as though I was failing as a parent in some way. We didn't have enough money for food and our marriage was going through a bumpy patch at the time. Being pregnant and alone a lot only served to deepen my depression, and I even mentioned to a friend how low I was feeling.

One day, I was babysitting for another friend. I was doing everything possible to earn a little extra money. I was in the bathroom when I heard a knock on the door; the kids must need me, I thought. I called to them to let them know I would be right out. I was shocked to hear a male voice answer me saying, "Hurry up! Get dressed. We are going for a car ride."

When I came out of the bathroom, I was surprised to see my friend Wayne standing in my living room smiling broadly at me. "I can't just go for a ride, I am babysitting and we don't have any car seats or anything," I replied. The truth was I wasn't feeling up to company and didn't feel like going anywhere.

Wayne was a persuasive man and always seemed to have answers to such problems. "Oh, that's no problem... I can just use my grand-daughter's seat." He smiled at me, almost bouncing out of the house. "I'll be right back. Be ready, okay?"

Realizing that my friend was not going to take no for an answer, I quickly brushed my hair, grabbed my coat, and got the kids dressed for the weather, just in the nick of time. In mere minutes, Wayne was knocking on the door. As I walked to the car I realized that it was my neighbour Stu's car, and he was there, smiling in the front seat.

"Where are we going?" I asked my friends.

Wayne quickly replied, "Oh, Stu needs to go into town to pick up a few things, and we just thought it might be good for you to get out of the house."

When we got into town, Wayne pulled into the grocery store parking lot, parked, and proceeded to get the kids out of the car.

I told them I would just wait in the car, but they wouldn't hear of it. I got out of the car, took the kids by the hand, and followed them into the store.

As we walked through the doors of the store, Stu and Wayne each grabbed a shopping cart and turned to me. I stood there waiting for them to start their shopping. "I'm ready," I said, trying not to hold up their shopping. They looked at each other mischievously, then back at me. "What?" I asked.

Stu smiled. "Okay, since you're ready, let's do your shopping." I was dumbfounded. I just stood there staring, as tears began to run from my eyes.

"Wh-wh-what?" I stammered.

"Let's do your grocery shopping, and no looking at price tags. Just buy what you want. I'm paying," Stu replied with a boyish grin.

"You can't do this," I said quietly.

"I can and I am," he replied, still smiling.

In a quiet whisper, smiling through tears, I told Stu, "I'll get you back for this." Slowly, I started to follow them.

As the two men ushered me through the store buying all manner of food, drink, candy, chocolate, and anything they deemed we needed, I couldn't wrap my head around it. Why were they doing this?

At the checkout counter, it suddenly dawned on me what was actually happening. I started to cry again, and the cashier asked timidly, "Are you alright?"

Yes," I replied. "These two have just done my Christmas shopping for me."

"I'm paying," Stu stated proudly. The cashier smiled and said, "Well, it's nice to meet you, Santa!"

Once we were packed in the car (believe me, there wasn't much room) and on our way back home, I asked Stu why he did what he did. He told me that since he didn't have children of his own, and his wife had passed, this was his way of celebrating Christmas.

It took me three days to find room to put all the food away.

In January of the following year, Stu was diagnosed with esophageal cancer. I had to let him know how much everyone in the community loved and appreciated him. Stu was a bit of a philanthropist in our small town. What could I do? How could we show him? We had to do something before it was too late.

Eventually, I came up with the idea that we could make him a quilt and have each of our families' names embroidered on a square so that he could be "blanketed in the warmth, love, and kindness" of us all. We called Wayne, who then got in touch with many of the people around town who knew, loved, and respected Stu. He planned a bit of a party and had the quilt embroidered. I told Wayne that I didn't want anyone to know it was my idea. We just all needed to let Stu know we loved him.

A year later, it was a snowy December evening near Christmas. My mom and I got the kids ready and walked to the community center to join in the festivities. When we arrived, we noticed Stu sitting at the front of the hall.

Then, Wayne took the microphone. "Tonight would not be happening without the thought and care of one person...."

Oh no, I thought. Here it comes. I stood there staring at Wayne, shaking my head slowly at first and then more violently. "Connie, can you please come up here?" I'm going to die I thought, everyone is looking at me.

"Go on, Con," my mom whispered.

When I got to where Stu was sitting, tears were streaming down his face. I leaned down and hugged him. "I told you I would get you back," I whispered to him.

"That you have, darling, that you have. Merry Christmas!"

A month later Stu passed away from the cancer. Twelve Christmases have passed since he died and every year I think about him and say a silent prayer of thanks to him for being Santa to me all those years ago.

~Connie I. Davidson

It's Christmas!

Holiday Hijinks

At Christmas, play and make good cheer,
for Christmas comes but once a year.

~Thomas Tusse

The Stinky Gift that Kept on Giving

The poets have been mysteriously silent on the subject of cheese.
~G.K. Chesterton

When our family reminisces about our favorite Christmas food, it's not pies, cookies, or even the oyster casserole my mother used to make before oysters got too expensive. The food we remember with glee is a food we never ate: a jar of Limburger cheese.

Like families who pass around hardened fruitcake, our family's jar of pungent cheese traveled back and forth between Pittsburgh and Ashland, Ohio for nearly eighteen years before it was finally laid to rest.

The stinky cheese story began more than thirty years ago at our rehearsal dinner in August 1979. Uncle George Fike wrapped up a jar of Limburger cheese and gave it to us as a gag gift. I grew up with his four daughters and since I was an only child we were almost like the classic book, *Little Women*—plus one.

Meals on the Fike farm were fun times, when my mother's brother would sneak pickles onto our hamburgers, or threaten to feed us horseradish and Limburger cheese. None of us ever ate Limburger, so we had no way of knowing what it was like—but it sounded horrible.

After our wedding, when Rick and I moved our wedding gifts into our first apartment, we discovered that my mother had sent the cheese. We put it in the refrigerator.

"What shall we do with the cheese?" I said to Rick one day. He laughed and said, "Let's give it back to your uncle for Christmas."

Thus began a tradition that provided endless entertainment at every gathering of our extended family for the next eighteen years. Of course, the gift was always disguised as something nice. My husband particularly got into the creative presentation. When our children came along, they did too. Early in the fall, we would ask each other how we should wrap the cheese.

One year, the jar was inserted in various tubes of cardboard until it looked like a Super Soaker squirt gun when wrapped up. Another year, it was a gift for George's woodshop—a handsaw and a C-clamp, with the jar of cheese wedged in the clamp. There was even the time when two fancy fishing lures hung out of the top of his gift, looking like it was going to be a new fishing rod. The reel turned out to be a jar of much ripened cheese.

This cheese always added some anticipation to our holiday fun. At some point it would pop up, such as the year my husband unfolded the decorated sweatshirt George's wife had made for him and the cheese clunked to the floor from the sleeve.

One year, all the presents were unwrapped, and everyone sat there glumly thinking Uncle George—or Rick and I—had forgotten. Then across the room a voice boomed, "Hey, Rick, how about passing around some of that candy?" My husband plunged his arm up to the elbow and he came up with the dreaded jar. The Limburger became one of the most carefully wrapped gifts, since no one was quite sure how rancid the aged cheese had become. All it would take was one hard hit on the floor.

As my uncle's health began to fail, my husband broached the subject. I couldn't imagine the grief I would feel without my mother's only brother. "When it does happen, I just hope we have the cheese," he said sorrowfully, then laughed.

One Christmas, our presentation—complete with a personalized song—particularly delighted my uncle. We wrapped the jar in a brightly colored holiday box with a gold partridge in a pear tree embossed in gold. One of a set of twelve boxes, each box held the appropriate number of other items, from five brass rings to eleven sugar-free lozenges. My four cousins told me that the Christmas box—with the contents stored safely in the refrigerator—remained on the dining room buffet table almost all year.

Uncle George told everyone who entered the farmhouse how he was really going to "get us good" come Christmas. But life doesn't always go the way we plan. Uncle George died of a heart attack in November that year, at almost the exact time that our daughter Elizabeth was born.

We couldn't be at his funeral due to our new baby, but thanks to the Christmas cheese, a part of us was, indeed, present. My cousin Judy lovingly placed the cheese back in its box—as a final resting place for our Christmas tradition—and sent it into eternity with Uncle George.

Of course, the rest of us wonder if we've truly seen the last of the Limburger. We imagine arriving at heaven's gate and being handed a gaily-wrapped Christmas box... filled with a pungent surprise.

~Jane Miller

The Sweet Smell of Christmas

It is Christmas in the heart that puts Christmas in the air.
~W.T. Ellis

This is going to be a perfect Christmas," I said to myself. Family and friends had been invited to share the first Christmas in our new home. It was a hectic but controlled chaos as I decorated, cooked, and left Post-it notes to myself all over the house. You see, I can be sort of semi-organized at times, and this task deserved my best effort. Nothing could go wrong.

My fantasy of the perfect Christmas included a huge fresh Christmas tree, decorated in splendor to make our new home look warm, cozy, and inviting. We found the perfect tree that would almost reach the high ceiling of the living room, and were excited to discover a new product that was "guaranteed to keep the tree fresh and green throughout the entire holiday season." All we had to do was add it to the water in the tree stand. What could be easier?

The tree was just as awesome as I had dreamed it would be as we added the final touch—our Christmas angel. Sparkle Plenty, the pitiful plastic dime store angel, resembled an ancient Barbie on drugs, but she had graced the uppermost branches of the family tree since my husband was a small child, and was given to us by his mother for our first tree as newlyweds. It has been perched on top of every tree since that first year forty-six years ago. Anyone who saw this sad angel specimen and wasn't aware of her history would probably wonder why we hadn't replaced her, but we've had her longer than our children, so she deserved her rightful place on top of our tree.

Blue lights were hung from the eaves outside, wreaths decorated the doors, and candles glowed in each window. It was beginning to look very festive, warm and inviting. Greenery was everywhere and candles were placed strategically throughout the house and on the mantle in preparation for our family Christmas Eve dinner. Almost ready to show off our new home, we added one more finishing touch as we filled the fireplace with wood and hung the stockings from the mantle. It was a beautiful sight, reminding me of Norman Rockwell paintings I had seen as a child. I could hardly wait for the family to see it all!

As the famous biblical saying goes, "Pride goeth before the fall."

Two days before the "great event," we began to notice an odd, rather unpleasant odor in the house that we were unable to track down. Searching everywhere, and unable to discover the source, we resorted to room deodorizers which only added a sickeningly sweet smell to the already disgusting scent.

By the time Christmas Eve came, the smell was pungent and growing worse with each passing hour. It actually smelled like vomit, and was the very worst in the living room where the family gathered around the Christmas tree. I had prayed the aroma of homemade bread and turkey would overwhelm the still unidentified stench that was taking over our new home, but that didn't happen. "Something must have died in the wall or attic," I moaned.

The Christmas Eve extravaganza ended early and we were sure everyone was glad to leave our beautiful, festively decorated home to breathe the fresh December air.

Christmas morning we opened our immediate family gifts and the aroma was even worse! As a nurse, I have smelled some pretty disgusting things, but this smell topped gangrene, old blood, and burned flesh. How could we continue to live here if this continued?

As the last package was removed from under the tree, I noticed the trunk of the tree had greenish-black, mossy-looking algae all over it, reminding me of *The Blob*, a movie I had seen as a child. I imagined the poor tree pulsating with the disgusting stuff, as it tried to rid itself of the powerful evil force! Eureka! It was the Christmas tree that was creating the hideous stench, and it had to be the caused by the "amazing new additive guaranteed to keep your tree fresh."

We couldn't get that tree out of our new home quickly enough! We even considered not taking the decorations off and simply dragging the entire tree to the street just the way it was, minus Sparkle Plenty of course. But my frugalness got the best of me and I did remove the trimmings, taking several fresh-air breaks along the way. By Christmas afternoon the tree was ready for pick-up by the garbage man, who probably turned every shade of green when loading it in his truck.

Artificial trees have decorated our home every year since that disaster, still topped by old Sparkle Plenty of course. Sometimes people will say, "Oh, but you miss out on that wonderful smell of a fresh tree." I just smile and say, "Exactly. We had a live tree once, and that is one smell I can do without, thank you!"

It has taken me twenty-five years to see the humor in this situation, but one thing is certain. Our family will always remember that Merry (cough, gag) Christmas in our new home with the beautiful live tree from hell!

~Liz Every Cook

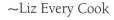

Home Invasion

Many of our fears are tissue-paper-thin,
and a single courageous step would carry us clear through them.
~Brendan Francis

It was Christmas Eve. Or Christmas Day, technically. The glaring backlight of my phone reminded me how late it was as it guided me into my house. I quietly closed the back door behind me and snuck up the stairs, wincing at every groan of the floorboards. My parents knew I was going to be out with friends late, but I still didn't want to wake them. I made it to my room and crawled into bed, exhausted. I fell asleep quickly.

The next thing I heard were hoarse, terrified whispers from my sister across the hall.

"Oh my god, oh my god, oh my god..." I heard my sister Erika say slowly and quietly.

What was happening? I guessed it was around 4:30 a.m. I was still waking up, but I could hear the terror in her voice. She repeated her words over and over again, speeding up and getting louder. I had no idea what was going on.

"Oh my god, oh my god, oh my GOD..."

I was still groggy and confused. Was she dreaming? Sleepwalking?

"Who are you?" I heard her say.

I woke up instantly. I knew then what had happened: our house had been infiltrated. The possibility of expensive items waiting under the tree must have been appealing to burglars, and no one would expect a robbery on Christmas Day. The perfect crime.

I don't know how much time had passed since I woke up. Erika was still sobbing, calling out to the figure standing feet from her. I felt a rush of aggressive bravery. My sister was in danger. Maybe my parents were too—I had no idea if the intruders had made it into their bedroom or not. But me—I was alive, and I was the only one who could help her. The only one who could save my family.

How could I defend her? What weapons did I have? I had no idea, and no plan at all. In my bed, I needed to go for two items quickly: my glasses and my light. I'd be blind without either. I only needed one swift move to get to both. Once the light was on, I would have only seconds before her attacker realized I was awake and coming. Seconds to find a weapon and charge into Erika's room. Seconds to survive. I flipped over in my bed and reached to my nightstand.

But I didn't make it to the light, or to my glasses. To the weapon, or to Erika. Instead, I froze in horror, because in front of me stood a blurry and dark figure, feet from my bed.

They were in my room too.

The panic kept me frozen for seconds that seemed like hours. I could still hear Erika, but my room seemed so still, so quiet. It was just me and the man in my room. I didn't move, and neither did he. It was horrifying.

"WHO ARE YOU?" Erika screeched.

Suddenly, the blood rushed through my entire body, unlocking my joints and pushing me forward. I struggled with the light, turning it on while I searched for my glasses. I tried to hide a terrified sob while I fumbled around on my nightstand. What was I going to do? What was he waiting for?

My palm smashed into my glasses. Shaking, sweating, and crying, in what I assumed would be my last moments, I jabbed my glasses onto my face and looked up at my attacker.

Before me stood a cardboard cutout of teen heartthrob Edward

Cullen. The singer Justin Bieber was in Erika's room. They were Christmas presents from our parents.

~Monika LaPlante

Seek and Ye Shall Find

Home is where you are loved the most and act the worst.
~Marjorie Pay Hinckley

My family did it, still does it, and will probably always do it. It's a little pre-Christmas tradition that has gone on for years. It's the thrill of the hunt, the victory of the find... peeking before Christmas! There, I said it. My family has complete and utter ignorance for the "Do Not Open Until Christmas" tags on gifts.

One Christmas, my dad bought my mom a wooden rocking chair. She had hounded him all year for one. A solid oak chair with a cushion seat for the corner of the living room. He found exactly the one she described, wrapped it ever so carefully and tucked the wrapped box under the tree in the back. One day, as he was putting other gifts under the tree, he noticed a small tear in the front of the box. The hole appeared to be about the size of a finger poke. The next day he noticed the hole was a little longer, and the day after that it was even longer! My dad knew not to ask if my mom was snooping, though. She'd never admit it. But when it comes to my mother, really, why bother wrapping? She must have figured out what it was at some point, because the hole mysteriously didn't get any bigger.

I can't help it either; I suppose the temptation is too great. But I can just smile and say, "Well, Mom does it!" if I ever get caught.

One day, I was at my uncle's house when he had just returned from holiday shopping. He walked briskly past me, on a mission to hide gifts in his bedroom before anyone saw. He came out quickly, shutting the door behind him, and headed to the kitchen.

What was in there? I had to know. I approached the bedroom door, opened it slowly, and peeked in. On the bed were brand new winter coats for everyone! Oh, what to do, what to do? I had to tell someone. Someone who would understand the pleasure of my discovery and savor this experience... my mother!

I snuck into the living room and told her what I saw. She scolded me at first for peeking in his bedroom. "You're not supposed to be looking in there!" she said, and couldn't help adding, "But tell me what you saw."

My brothers crossed the line one year. Mark was twelve and Jim was eleven. They wanted a new Nintendo for Christmas in the worst way. One day, while my parents were out, their curiosity got the best of them. They began searching the house, top to bottom, like a couple of wild animals on the hunt. Mark scoured the attic, and Jim rummaged through closets. Finally, they found it! A brand new Nintendo system sitting on the top shelf in my mother's bedroom closet. They didn't stop there. They yanked the Nintendo off the shelf and stared wildly at the box, in awe that they were really getting a Nintendo for Christmas! During their triumph, Jim looked over and noticed a camera on my dad's nightstand. He turned on the camera, pointed it at Mark, and said, "Hey Mark, hold up the box, say cheese!" Mark grinned widely, evidence in hand, as Jim snapped the scandalous picture. Then Jim returned the camera to the nightstand. They placed the Nintendo back in the closet and ran outside to play.

It was a week before Christmas, and my brothers and I came home from school to find my parents sitting at the kitchen table with an envelope of newly developed photos. Mark and Jim went pale. Both started to giggle nervously and couldn't stop. They suddenly remembered their adventure from the prior week. They realized they had been caught. My dad had a serious look on his face as he pulled the pictures out of the envelope. The picture on the top of the stack was the incriminating photo showing Mark holding the Nintendo system, sporting a smile full of braces. So nailed!

My dad let out a loud sigh and started to say, "So I picked up some pictures today..." but he started laughing so hard, he couldn't finish the sentence. Finally, catching his breath and clearing his throat, he said, "What were you two thinking? Were you hoping I wasn't going to develop these until after Christmas?" and laughed some more.

My brothers had no answer, except for shrugging their shoulders and mumbling. Mark and Jim were fortunate enough to still receive the Nintendo for Christmas; my family understands the curse of temptation. They were grounded, however, for going through Mom's closet.

When my dad finished laying out their punishment, he turned to all of us and said, nonchalantly, "Oh by the way, thanks for the drill, it's just what I wanted. I promise to act surprised when I open it on Christmas." Then he casually walked out of the room, laughing the whole way.

~Michele Christian-Oldham

Pajama Party

*You know children are growing up when they start asking questions
that have answers.*

~John J. Plomp

Every Christmas Eve, Mom let us open one present. I
always hoped that the one I got to open would be a
book, or maybe a toy, to keep me occupied the next
morning until everyone else was awake.

But no, every single Christmas Eve it was the very same thing:
pajamas!

When Mother handed each of us the selected gift to unwrap, she
knew exactly which present held each kid's nightwear. But how did
she know? It just couldn't be a coincidence!

At first I thought maybe she was stacking the gifts in a certain
area under the tree to make sure all four of us got new PJs when it
was time to get ready for bed. So one year I mixed up the placement
of all the presents. No change. The girls still got nightgowns, the boys
still got action figure designs, and it was all still flannel.

The next year I ruled out the color of the wrapping paper, since
everything was wrapped in different designs. So I examined the tags
of every package. Written on each tag was one of our names and a
funny-looking squiggly design. Some squiggles looked like an exclamation mark with a twist. Some looked all loopy and flowery.

Two days before Christmas, I saw that there was one package

for each of us with the same specific matching design on it. And that year, those were the very packages we got to open! It must have been some kind of secret code!

Try as I might, year after year, I couldn't make any kind of sense of the squiggles. By my junior year in high school, my problem-solving skills had sharpened somewhat. Christmas Eve I asked Mom if I could be the one to select our "night before Christmas" gifts to open.

"Okay," she said slowly, "but I have to approve your choices first."

I quickly picked out all four presents. She smiled. "You know which ones, but you're not sure why, are you?"

I agreed that that was the case.

My senior year in high school I took several secretarial preparation classes. I didn't want to be a secretary, but I wanted to be sure my typing and other skills would serve me well in college.

Mid-December rolled around, and suddenly the Christmas code made sense. I picked up package after package from under the tree and knew exactly what was inside.

Smugly, I went into the kitchen and confronted my mother. "The jig's up, Mom," I told her. "You're going to have to stop writing what's inside the presents on everyone's gift tags."

She looked up from her cookie icing, tilted her head and said, "And why's that?"

"Because..." I smiled and stole a frosted cookie from the racks, "...I'm taking shorthand this year, and I'm at the top of my class."

Her eyebrows nearly hit her hairline and she jumped to her feet. "Janet Marie!"

There were no more squiggly marks on package tags after that day, but I still got a new nightgown to wear on my last Christmas Eve at home. Marked in bold blue felt pen all across the red and green wrapping paper, it clearly said, "PJs for Jan."

~Jan Bono

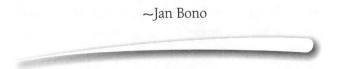

A Christmas Story Revisited

Siblings: children of the same parents, each of whom is perfectly normal until they get together.

~Sam Levenson

"So, Mom, I've got this great idea," my son Jon announced on the telephone. I heard the deep giggle that usually punctuates one of his "great ideas."

"Amy and I found a website that sells adult-sized one-piece pajamas. For Christmas we're going to buy four of them in pink—for Andy, Dana, Kate and Mike." I held my breath. When he mentioned his siblings, I sensed a practical joke coming on.

"And—we found hoods that tie under the chin. We're going to get four of them and sew long pink ears on them." Now he was chortling. "We'll sew bunny faces on the foot coverings. We'll wrap them up and those will be their gifts on Christmas Eve. And they're going to have to put them on! It'll be like..." An explosion of laughter interrupted him.

I finished his statement, "Ralphie in *A Christmas Story*." Shaking my head, I smirked at the vision of my son and daughter and their poor spouses dressed in these ridiculous costumes, not to mention Jon's hysteria and his forethought. I mean, it was September—way too early to think about Christmas.

While I raised my family to honor traditions of our faith and ancestors at Christmas, we also adopted a tradition of pop culture: watching the now-classic movie, *A Christmas Story*, about a family preparing to celebrate the holidays in 1940s Indiana. The older son, Ralphie, wanted nothing more than a Red Ryder BB Gun, but his mother disapproved, uttering, "You'll shoot your eye out."

Every year we watched the movie at least once during the month of December, memorizing the dialogue. Certain scenes have become favorites: when Dad wins a major award, famously known as the leg lamp; when Santa's elves terrorize Ralphie and his kid brother at the department store; or when the neighbor's dogs devour the Christmas turkey, forcing the family to eat at a Chinese restaurant. Jon, of course, loved it when an embarrassed Ralphie modeled the handmade pink bunny outfit sent by a doddering aunt.

"It's going to be great!" Jon assured me about his prank. "Remember, you're sworn to secrecy."

"Absolutely." Still shaking my head, I sealed my lips.

In November my daughter Kate phoned. "Mom, I was shopping on the Internet, and you won't believe this. I found a pair of pink pajamas for adults. They're one piece, and they have feet and a hood attached, like a baby's onesie. I am going to get that for Jon for Christmas. I'm going to fix it up with bunny ears and a bunny tail."

"You mean like in *A Christmas Story*? Where did you get that idea?"

"I was online, trying to find a gift for Jon, when I saw it. I think it'll be hilarious." She giggled. I imagined the way she crinkled her nose on such occasions. "I told Andy about it, and he thinks it's good. What do you think, Mom? Should I do it?"

"Oh, sure. He'll get a big kick out of it."

"You won't tell Jon, will you?"

"What, me? Spoil a surprise? Never."

This was going to be great.

I revealed the madcap Christmas plots to my husband Joe because the secret was too good to hoard. I relished the thought of watching this zany fun. For years as parents, Joe and I put forth the effort and made the fun and the magic for the kids. Now they were giving back.

On Christmas Eve, the house smelled of sauerbraten and spiced red cabbage and twinkled with tree lights when the young folk arrived. Around the table, we said grace and made a toast for a merry Christmas, then chatted and joked through dinner. Jon and Kate played it cool. Near the meal's end, Kate left the dining room, only to make a hurried return and whisper into Andy's ear. His head recoiled slightly, his brow furrowing. I shot a quick glance at my husband, who raised an eyebrow back at me. Good, we're gathering steam now, I thought. Andy and Kate hovered over the gifts placed under the Christmas tree, directing their attention to four identically sized boxes, wrapped in candy-cane-striped paper.

The party moved to the family room to exchange our gifts. Kate rose from her seat, grabbed a box, and handed it to Jon. He tore the wrappings and lifted the top of the box, the crisp tissue crinkling. Shock registered on his face with the first peek inside.

"Wait!" said Amy. Seated next to Jon, she folded the corner of the tissue paper back, ran to the tree to pick up four boxes from under the tree, and presented one each to Andy, Dana, Kate, and Mike. "Okay, now open them!"

The recipients, looking as bug-eyed as Jon, tore the gift wrap. Their mouths gaping, they lifted pink fleece pajamas by the shoulders for all to see. My husband and I clapped furiously, howling, enjoying the release of three months of built-up anticipation.

Andy stood up. "All right, let's go. Let's put them on." They excused themselves to work their legs and arms into the pink fleece in private. One by one, five adult-sized pink bunnies emerged from bathrooms and bedrooms. They looked like confused Easter bunnies at the wrong holiday.

Appraising each other's ears and cottontails, they exploded laughing, including Jon, who laughed loudest at his own reflection.

The five pink bunnies lined up and posed in front of the Christmas tree, while we snapped several pictures. Whether they are the craziest Christmas photos ever taken is debatable, but for me, they are a precious reminder of a Christmas when my children strengthened our family bond with the sweet gift of shared laughter.

~Dorothy K. LaMantia

A Christmas Surprise for Everyone

A new baby is like the beginning of all things —
wonder, hope, a dream of possibilities.
~Eda J. Le Shan

When the company transferred my husband back to our home state, we were delighted to once again be close to our family, especially the grandchildren. We moved into our new house the first of December and decided to have the whole family come to our home for Christmas that year.

Two weeks before Christmas, our oldest daughter Kathy called to tell me she was pregnant with their third child. Since I was the first to be told, we plotted to announce the new arrival to the whole family on Christmas Eve. I would purchase a little gift, wrap it, and hide it in the lower branches of the Christmas tree for the new addition to the family. Since Kathy already had two children and our youngest daughter Cindy had been married almost a year, everyone would assume Cindy and her husband Alan were expecting.

On Christmas Eve, everyone arrived and gifts were piled around the tree with excitement and anticipation. After dinner, we gathered in the living room. My husband handed out gifts. We watched as our two grandchildren quickly opened all their packages and became engrossed in playing with their new toys.

After the adults finished opening their gifts and everyone said thank you, I sat down on the floor next to the Christmas tree, trying to look casual as I straightened the tree's skirt. Accidentally finding the little package in the branches of the tree, I announced, "Oh, look, here's a gift we missed." I pulled it out from its hiding place and read the tag: "To the new addition to the family."

We were all shocked at what happened next. Cindy began berating Alan! "Why did you tell them? I told you not to tell anyone! I wanted to wait till after Christmas!"

Poor Alan, as surprised as the rest of us, pleaded innocent, "I didn't tell anybody anything!"

"Yes, you did!"

"No, I didn't!"

Confused, other family members chimed in: "Tell us what?" "Wait a minute!" "What's this all about?" "What's going on?"

Kathy began telling Cindy, "Alan didn't tell us anything. It's me that's expecting."

"You? No, I am," Cindy said.

"I am, too."

"You are, too?"

"When?"

"End of August," Cindy proclaimed.

"First of August," Kathy said.

Kathy and I had planned to surprise everyone else. Instead, we were all surprised and delighted to hear there would be two new babies in the family. As for me, I breathed a sigh of relief that they weren't due at the same time... it was a five-hour drive between them!

~Janie Hall

A Dangerous Mission

Two things are infinite: the universe and human stupidity;
and I'm not sure about the universe.
~Albert Einstein

"Any ideas?" my husband Jeff asked as we walked around a mall several weeks before Christmas.

"No. Everything looks so boring," I complained. "We already bought the small stuff. We need something big." The truth was our sons were both grown men with wives and homes of their own. I'd always found men difficult to buy for and this year was no exception.

"I've got an idea," I offered. "I'll shop for the girls if you take care of the boys." Sounded easy enough to me. Mentally, I went through the list of things I could get for our daughters-in-law. No problem.

"Nothing doing. We're in this together," Jeff reminded me. We trudged on. And on. And went home with nothing once again.

"Are we really stuck with gift cards for our own kids?" I asked feeling defeated as we dressed for our next shopping trip.

"No. We'll find something. Let's go." We bundled ourselves up and headed out for yet another shopping experience. I was so distracted by our lack of a big present for each of our sons that I didn't even want to hear Christmas music.

We entered the sporting goods department and I saw a smile on Jeff's face. "I've got it," he exclaimed. I followed him as he headed over to the freestanding, outdoor basketball hoops. Yes! This would work. We still had a basketball hoop on our garage and they still played when they visited. Neither of them had yet put one up at their own homes. We were sure we'd found the right gift.

"Do you think they'll fit in the car?" I asked, looking at the large boxes and thinking of our Hyundai.

"Sure. The trunk's big and the back seat goes down. No problem."

We hauled the large, heavy boxes onto a wagon, took several minutes to catch our breath and feel our limbs again, and headed for the checkout.

Did the boxes fit? No way. One lay nice and flat. The other would lie on top but only the wrong way with the end sticking out.

"We could tie it down," I suggested.

"Nothing to tie it with."

I glanced at the store we'd just left. Naturally, they'd have something to tie down a trunk but Jeff's mind was working on some other solution.

"I've got it. I'll put the second box on top of the first and I'll lie on top of the two of them. They won't move with the extra weight on top. I can hold on to the passenger seat until we get home."

'We've got a big hill to go up," I reminded him. "Why don't we just leave one here and come back and get it?"

"This will work," he said with determination.

So, with me driving and Jeff lying across the boxes and holding onto the back of the seat, we began our trip home. At five miles an hour, it was a long trip.

"I'm slipping," he yelled. I pulled over immediately. Relieved drivers raced past us.

"You're going to get hurt," I stated again.

"No, I'm not. We're almost there. We can't give up now. All right. I can feel my arms again." He got back into the same position. "Throw that blanket over my hands. They're freezing." At last, we were ready to move on.

"The top box is sliding." Once again, I pulled over. We rearranged the boxes. Then, looming ahead was one of the largest hills in the area. And we lived at the top of it. The only other option was to go through a lot of traffic and spend at least twice as long on the road. We had to get up the hill. There was no choice.

I turned the corner slowly, hearing the boxes shift. "Should I stop?" I yelled back."

"No. Keep going. If we stop again I don't think I'll be able to get back on here. I'm freezing and my shoulders are about to dislocate."

Then, we started laughing. It was stupid but it was funny. Picture a retired schoolteacher lying on two huge boxes in the back of a small car, the edges of the boxes and his feet sticking out, the door to the hatch back flopping up and down and him holding on to the front seat for dear life while I drove slowly enough for turtles to pass.

At last, we did make it home. It was the most dangerous trip to get presents we'd ever experienced. I'd like to say it was the last one but we now have two grandsons and I'm afraid of what may come next. Ah, Christmas memories.

~Jane Lonnqvist

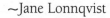

76

The Spider Tree

Laughter gives us distance. It allows us to step back from an event,
deal with it and then move on.
~Bob Newhart

The first Christmas tree is the most important tree any couple will ever have. It will be discussed at length, photographed for history, and represents an important milestone for a couple.

And ours was covered in spiders.

As a brilliant twenty-year-old head over heels in love with my college sweetheart, I picked out the perfect Christmas tree. Well, at least I thought I did. It was a gorgeous tree, the best tree in the store's parking lot the day after Thanksgiving. There, amongst scraggly pines and brown-tipped spruces, I found a prime specimen of Christmas in all its pine glory for the glorious price of $20. I paid and hauled it out to my car, gently loading it into my trunk and through the back seat of my Jetta on a tarp my dad had provided for emergencies.

This was definitely a holiday emergency.

After all, this was the first Christmas I would spend with my college sweetheart. While we'd be spending the actual holidays and most of the break with our respective families, we were going to spend a week after finals together. With visions of sugarplums and cheap felt stockings dangling from apartment walls, I was determined to make it perfect.

My sweetheart, and now husband, Ben, wasn't as confident.

"Where did you get this tree?" he asked, helping me haul it from the parking lot to his lower-level apartment. We carried it through the front door, settling it on the cheap carpet.

"The store." I beamed. Pulling off the orange wrap with a flourish, I whirled around. "Look, isn't it pretty?" Fluffing the branches, I stepped back. "It's so full and nice! And it was only $20!"

"I'm not surprised," Ben muttered. He eyed the tree. "Where did it come from?"

"Santa," I teased. "I'm going to go get the decorations out of the car. Can you set it up for me?"

"Sure." As I hurried out the front door, I hid a grin. He was scratching his head as he inspected the tree and the $5 metal stand I had bought to display it.

I returned fifteen minutes later to disaster. Ben was rolling about on the floor, clutching his eye. "The tree stabbed me!" he bellowed. Jabbing a finger at the offending foliage, he shouted, "It's a vicious tree!"

I dropped the bags of ornaments on the couch and hurried over. "How did it stab you?" I bent down, trying to peel his fingers from his face. He simply clamped harder.

"I was trying to help you wind the lights around," he pointed to the strands dangling from the branches. "And I bent down to wrap a branch and..." he snarled, glaring at the tree, "it stabbed me! A needle poked me in the eye!"

"Let me see." Sighing, he moved his hand. I peered at his eye. "I don't see anything."

"What?" Ben rocketed to his feet, rushing to the bathroom. "What are you talking about?" he bellowed. "It's red and watering. And there's a hole!"

"A hole?" I swallowed a giggle. "How is there a hole?"

"There's a hole! In my eye! That tree stabbed a hole in my eyeball!" Water streamed from the sink and he splashed his face. "There's a hole in my eye!"

"So I take it you don't want to help me decorate the tree?" I winced as his offended roar shook the apartment walls.

"It'll just stab another hole in my eyeball!" Clutching a washcloth to his face, his good eye glared at me. "That tree is out to get me! I know you think I'm paranoid, but there's something very strange about that tree!"

If only I had known how right he was.

After I decorated the tree alone, I kissed Ben and left him and his sore eye to rest. I returned the next morning, bursting with holiday cheer and plans for a sunny, crisp Saturday.

"Hi, honey! Listen, I was thinking..." I froze, staring at the tree.

"What?" Ben twisted, his one eye still red. He squinted at the tree, which was hard to do with one good eye. "What is that?"

"It's..." I crept closer, goose bumps popping up on my arms. Peering closely at the branches, I gulped. "It's... spider webs."

"Spider webs?" Ben's eyes widened. "Those are spider webs? I thought it was tinsel or glitter or something!" He shuddered.

I shook my head, forcing back the bile rising in my throat. "Nope. Those are spider webs."

And indeed they were. Our festive, perfect first Christmas tree as a couple was covered from the tip of its plastic star to the bottom branches with white, perfectly spun spider webs.

"But where there are spider webs there are..." Ben gagged, "...spiders! Tons of spiders!" He rushed over to the patio door, throwing it open. Before I could even grab a single ornament, our first Christmas tree was flying onto the lawn, landing in the tiny grass square outside his apartment. Red bulbs shattered across the sidewalk as white lights blinked in the bright sunlight.

As Ben hurried to find the bleach and mop, I stared at the tree through the patio door.

"I'm sorry, darling." I lowered my head, tears springing to my eyes. "I just wanted us to have a perfect Christmas, and the perfect Christmas tree. I wanted us to have a great Christmas."

Hurrying to the door, Ben stopped to give me a kiss.

"Tree or no tree, any Christmas with you is perfect." He leaned his forehead against mine. "Because all I want for Christmas is you."

And just as my heart swelled, he turned and glared at the offending tree. "But not trees with spiders. Or trees that stab eyeballs." He raised the broom and opened the bleach, slamming the patio door behind him.

The tree was in the dumpster two hours later, ornaments and all.

Needless to say, that was our last Christmas tree until our first Christmas as a married couple, after graduation.

We purchased an artificial tree, which we still use every year.

Ben is happy to report it is spider free and does not poke unsuspecting eyeballs.

~Miranda Koerner

"IS THAT ANY WAY TO TAKE DOWN THE TREE ?! "

Reprinted by permission of
Bruce Robinson ©2010

77

The Twelve Martians of Christmas

I always find beauty in things that are odd and imperfect—
they are much more interesting.
~Marc Jacobs

Nearly every year Mom gives my sister and me something extra special for Christmas—our "big gift," she calls it. When I turned sixteen, she bought me a cedar chest. Another year she bought me a brass daybed. Sometimes we get jewelry. Whatever the gift turns out to be, Mom puts a lot of effort into planning the perfect "big gifts" for her girls.

A few years ago, just before Christmas, I knew Mom was up to her usual Christmas antics. Each time I stopped by her house for a visit, she scurried into her sewing room and closed the door behind her. The muffled sounds confirmed my suspicions... my "big gift" was behind that door. Because she needed my help to find a pattern, she gave in and revealed the big secret—she was making me a gingerbread man quilt for Christmas.

My gingerbread man craze began the year I got my first teaching job. I could afford a little luxury, so my husband and I went on a weekend getaway. While shopping, I stumbled upon a store called

Elder-Beerman, and that's where I first set eyes on an all-gingerbread-man Christmas tree.

The tree dazzled me. Stuffed gingerbread boys and girls dangled from every branch. Some of the gingerbread boys wore chef hats. Some held rolling pins or cookie sheets. Some wore Santa hats. Some had buttons or vests. Gingerbread girls sported holiday dresses with holly and bows and candy canes. These scrumptious delights entertained me for hours.

Growing up, our Christmas tree was a mishmash of ornaments. Felt Santa ornaments, Styrofoam snowmen, gold angels, Christmas mice, elves, sleds. Nothing matched. Anything Christmas meshed together. If I decided to buy this tree, it would be the first themed Christmas tree in the family. I had to have this tree! But we didn't need a tree. But I did have the extra money. What would my husband say? I could certainly find more useful things to buy. But it would last for years and years — an investment in our future. Finally feeling justified, I bought an all-gingerbread-themed Christmas tree.

Although my obsession with gingerbread men grew, I did not have a gingerbread quilt, and I couldn't wait to receive the one my mom was making. It would be the perfect addition to my Christmas collection.

Christmas had finally arrived and although I knew what my "big gift" was, I felt like a little kid. Carefully, I unfolded the quilt and held it up for everyone to see. I was expecting to see a twelve-block gingerbread quilt. Instead, I saw twelve blocks of oddly shaped extraterrestrials!

The first thing that jumped out at me was how each gingerbread man looked different; each had its own deformity. Most of their heads were too big or shaped like extraterrestrials. There were some missing necks, and some with outrageously long necks. A couple of them appeared to have a fat roll just above the legs. Then there were those whose right legs and left legs weren't the same size or shape.

Mom even went through the trouble of sewing on buttons for their eyes. The only problem was that most of the buttons were cockeyed or they were placed too far apart. The poor things!

Even with all of these disfigurements, none was worse than the lips. Mom used red rickrack for the lips, so they looked like bloody vampire fangs. These extraterrestrials scared me a little, and some looked scared themselves.

Despite the misshapen gingerbread men, I know my mom worked diligently on my quilt. The last thing I wanted to do was hurt her, so I complimented the beautiful fabric and thanked her for all of her hard work.

Mom realizes my "big gift" won't win any prizes, but we get a good laugh out of it every time it's mentioned. Hence the name we gave it... "The Twelve Martians of Christmas."

~Jeannie Dotson

It's Christmas!

Bittersweet Christmas

What is Christmas? It is tenderness for the past,
courage for the present, hope for the future. It is a fervent wish
that every cup may overflow with blessings rich and eternal,
and that every path may lead to peace.

~Agnes M. Pahro

Comfort and Joy

Let your tears come. Let them water your soul.
~Eileen Mayhew

It was a sad Christmas. My twin sister Sue had died suddenly the spring before. I missed her every day. But nothing broke my heart more than missing her at Christmas.

Decorating the tree had been tough. While Marc and the kids unloaded boxes of ornaments, I made cocoa and placed the mugs on the coffee table along with a plate of sugar cookies.

I tried to be cheerful for the sake of my family. It was Christmas after all. Christmas was supposed to be a time of joy and good cheer.

My husband touched my arm and gave me a hug. "How are you doing, hon?"

"I'm fine," I answered bravely. But was I?

Marc unraveled the Christmas lights. I put our favorite Christmas carol CD in the player. Karen Carpenter's "Have Yourself a Merry Little Christmas" began to play. I quietly braced myself for the lyrics I knew were coming: "Through the years we all will be together, if the fates allow." My insides started to churn, but I kept a smile on my face and continued to hang ornaments with the children.

The children chatted away. "Oh I bought this one at the craft show!" Caroline squealed with delight, holding up a wooden snowflake painted snowy white. Lauren hung a favorite soccer ornament with her name on it.

"Mom, do you remember this one?" Dan asked, finding the red cable car ornament we had picked up in San Francisco a few years back. They worked thoughtfully on the branches of the tree as they reminisced.

I reflected quietly. Joyful memories of Christmases long ago with Sue flooded my mind. But I didn't mention the memories out loud for fear of breaking down and crying. This was Christmas. I was going to be happy and enjoy this! No tears!

However, the more I tried to hold in my feelings, the harder it became. The ornaments felt like weights as I hung each one. The children had no idea how quickly I wanted to get this over with. It had become a chore instead of a pleasure.

Finally we were finished. Our younger children, Caroline and Dan, scooted out the front door to play in the bright winter midday sun. Our oldest, Lauren, headed up to her room to get ready to go out with some friends from college.

I began to pick up traces of tinsel, scattered hooks and empty candy cane wrappers. Marc was across the room. He was organizing the boxes that previously held tiny colorful Christmas lights, years of treasured ornaments and the somewhat gaudy but beloved red, green, and silver blinking star that graced the top of our tree each year.

"Oh no!" Marc suddenly shouted as he looked toward our beautifully decorated Christmas tree. I turned just in time to see our six-foot Scotch pine come crashing down.

Miniature nutcrackers, reindeer, snowmen and Santa ornaments were launched through the air as some of the blue and silver Christmas balls shattered on the floor. Pine branches snapped and water splattered everywhere. After a moment of stunned silence, I just shook my head and laughed. "Well, there you go!" I said to my husband. "And that is how I really feel about Christmas this year!"

Strangely, as I looked at the mess on the floor, I felt relieved! When the tree came crashing down it somehow validated my feelings.

Lauren had heard the crash and had come down the stairs, "What happened?" she exclaimed. As if on cue, Dan and Caroline came through the front door. Caroline cried when she saw all the broken ornaments and Christmas balls. Dan just stared.

"Okay, on the count of three." Marc said. We carefully lifted the tree back into the stand. This time, we made sure the tree was completely secured in place.

I gathered up all the unbroken Christmas balls and ornaments off the floor and placed them on the table between leftover cookies and empty mugs of cocoa. I swept up broken glass and pine needles, as Marc mopped up the wet floor and refilled the stand with fresh water. He then restrung some of the twinkling lights that had come undone.

I hesitated for only a moment before putting the Christmas music back on. When "Have Yourself a Merry Little Christmas" came on for the second time, I decided to let the tears flow. Marc gave me another hug.

I felt comfort in releasing my tears. I let the Christmas music wash over me. This time decorating the tree seemed more like healing than a chore. Sharing my feelings had actually lifted my spirits. As Marc and I decorated, I began to chat about some of my favorite Christmas memories of Sue.

"When we were little girls," I began, "Sue and I would sneak out of our beds early in the morning. We'd giggle and shush each other as we tiptoed down the hallway and slowly opened the door so it wouldn't creak. Our hearts leaped with joy as we gazed at our Christmas tree and caught a peak of what Santa had left. After a few moments we closed the door carefully and just as quietly walked back to our room whispering until we got the official okay from Mom or Dad to get up."

Marc smiled and nodded knowingly, since he had heard this story and others many times before. Now that Sue was gone, he too cherished my memories of her.

The last decoration I picked up was a needlepoint ornament of a rocking horse pressed in a small brass frame. I sighed. Sue had made it for me. I placed it with love on the tree.

We finished the tree for a second time. Marc plugged in the

lights and we admired our work. "Two trees in one day. Not bad," Marc said.

As I looked at our lovely tree I spotted Sue's rocking horse ornament. It made me smile. Then it occurred to me. So often at Christmastime tears and joy are intermingled. It doesn't have to be one or the other; it can be both. Bringing joyful memories and tears to the surface instead of suppressing them brought Sue a little closer to me. I felt comforted. I felt joy. I felt the love of Christmas.

~Donna Teti

Still Sheldon

You don't have to suffer to be a poet.
Adolescence is enough suffering for anyone.
~John Ciardi

"Oh no, God. This is a big mistake, isn't it?" I prayed silently while waiting for our teenage son to take his turn. We were going around the dinner table on Christmas Eve, telling our family members what we admired most about them or thanking them for something. It was our family tradition. Now we all sat waiting for sixteen-year-old Sheldon and it looked as though he was not going to participate.

When had our relationship become so strained? We were so close when he was younger. Where had my fun-loving, chattering little fellow gone?

This year the silence had descended upon us like a wet blanket. Sheldon became quiet and withdrawn. I often wondered what was going on behind those big blue eyes. His sixteenth birthday came and went and he refused to acknowledge it. He didn't care to get his driver's license either. I couldn't believe it.

"Lord, what is going on in his head? Please help me to understand," had become my constant prayer.

I began to dread Christmas with this heaviness hanging over our home. I was sure this sullen teenager would choose not to participate in our family Christmas traditions. I could just picture him staying in his room and shutting us out as he played his CDs or strummed his guitar for hours behind a closed door. What could I do to reach him?

How could I break through to him? What was he thinking?

I went through the usual motions of getting ready for Christmas, but my heart was heavy whenever I thought of how much things had changed over the past year. Would we be able to have our special time of sharing around the table, as we always had?

Now we were gathered around the table on Christmas Eve. The candlelight reflected on each face as we ate our traditional French onion soup and bread. It was a tradition we had started at the request of the children when they were small. They wanted to eat something different—not a big meal where I had to spend all day in the kitchen. They wanted time to read stories and play games together.

Tonight, when it came time to share, we had purposely started with my husband who was sitting on Sheldon's left. That way Sheldon would be last, so even if he chose not to participate it wouldn't spoil the atmosphere for all of us. We had each taken our turn, telling each member of the family what they meant to us. Now it was Sheldon's turn. I silently prayed for strength to respond in a positive way, no matter what he said.

He cleared his throat and just sat there. I found myself nervously picking at the tablecloth and trying not to make eye contact with the others.

The he began.

"Dad, I love how you skate with me and play hockey... you are fun to have for a father..." He continued, but I was lost in thought.

Had I totally misunderstood Sheldon?

Just then I heard "Mom..." As I looked up I saw Sheldon was now looking directly at me. He paused again and appeared to be unsure what to say. With our relationship feeling so rocky, I was afraid of what he might say. Then I heard him speak.

"I love you Mom, I always have."

I was shocked and elated. He hesitated again, and I looked up to meet his eyes, hoping to give him the confidence to continue.

Unbelievably, in the soft candlelight, I saw tears glistening in his eyes.

"Thank you for being so supportive of me and whatever nutty thing I have decided to do"—by this time the tears were rolling unheeded down his face—"...and at my games, I can count on you to be there in the stands. I feel your love and encouragement and you support me, whatever I do. Thank you..." He choked, unable to go on.

Oh Lord, forgive me—I was so wrong! With tears streaming down my own cheeks, I got up to hug him, and found myself in a group hug. What a beautiful answer to my desperate pleas—and just in time for Christmas.

~Annie Riess

Together at Christmas

In true love the smallest distance is too great,
and the greatest distance can be bridged.
~Hans Nouwens

The tree was trimmed and illuminated with multi-colored lights—some sparkled, some stayed steady, and some were burned out. Ornaments, both fancy and kid-friendly, clung to the branches above a pile of presents. My famous fudge had been made—both the traditional flavors, along with a couple of new concoctions. Yet, despite the decorations, treats, and presents; despite having grandparents join us at our home for the festivities; and despite all the music that filled the air, it wasn't quite right—something was missing. More accurately, someone was missing.

My husband Greg had been deployed in Iraq for over five months, with four more months to serve before he could come home. Our children, Josh and Sydney, were four-and-a-half years old and three years old, respectively. This was the first year that they were both really into Christmas and Santa, and Greg was going to miss it! Even though I e-mailed daily and planned to take many pictures in order to keep Greg updated on the happenings at home, it just wouldn't be the same as having him with us.

In addition to keeping Greg updated, I had to work to keep the concept of Daddy as a fixture in our kids' minds. Josh and Sydney, I had hoped, were the perfect age to endure a deployment. They were old enough to remember Daddy, but too young to understand the concept of time. Because the time difference required Greg to call us late at night, Josh and Sydney rarely got to talk to him. Thus, we talked about and looked at pictures of him all the time. I wanted his presence to be a constant. Also, since I hadn't been through a deployment before, I really didn't know what to expect. I had no idea if all my efforts would deliver the result I had hoped for: that Josh and Sydney would feel just as connected to Greg when he returned as they did when he left.

Even though Greg couldn't physically be with us during Christmas, I knew I had to do something so it felt like he was. I took two of the pictures Greg had sent me from Iraq and framed one for each of the kids to open on Christmas morning. Sydney got a picture of Greg dressed in camouflage, standing in front of a beautiful and lush oasis, while Josh got a similarly clad Greg standing in front of a military plane. They were great shots of Greg that showed the kids where Daddy was for his "Hero Job."

As we began opening presents Christmas morning, we got about halfway through when I realized I had forgotten to have the kids open the pictures first. While I loved my gesture and was hopeful the kids would too, I was also realistic. Josh and Sydney were really into presents that year, and I knew that pictures of Daddy might be overshadowed by toys. I grabbed the pictures and gave them to the kids to open. I braced myself for a lukewarm reaction.

Josh opened his picture first, with all eyes on him. As the paper gave way and his daddy's image appeared, his eyes widened and he whispered, "Daddy!" He quickly freed the picture from the wrapping to get a full look and pulled it in tight, closing his eyes while he hugged the frame. Then, as if to be sure he saw what he thought he saw, he released the picture from his hug, looked at his daddy again, and hugged it close once more. Sydney, upon opening her picture, followed suit.

And me? Well, it was the only time that Christmas I cried. Only I didn't cry tears of sadness from having to spend our Christmas as a separated family. No. I cried tears of joy... and relief, because the kids were obviously just as connected to their daddy on Christmas as they were when he left. That was the greatest gift I could have received for Christmas, and the greatest gift I could give to Greg.

~Andrea B.

Angel Unawares

To live in the hearts we leave behind is not to die.
~Thomas Campbell

As always, Christmas cards lined our living room the season I was sixteen. And as always, I marveled at the masses of them. This year they were swirling in, even more abundantly, like gentle snowflake messages meant to remind us we were loved. But nothing about this year was like always. For it had only been eight months since my nineteen-year-old brother, Greg, had been murdered.

Mom stood back from decorating the tree, and said, as she had through every one of my growing up years, "Isn't it just like a fairyland, Pam?" Tears glistened in her eyes, like the room reflected in the shining red balls hanging from the tree.

"Yes, Mom," I agreed. If anything could ease my pain, it just might be the wonder of turning off all the lights except the tree and letting the glow flow over us, as Andy Williams crooned of silver white Christmases, one Holy Night and sweet Noel—a balm to our souls.

But could anything wipe out the memory of our last six years? They'd seemed like one long rumbling earthquake in our family life as Greg looked for friends in all the wrong places....

Just then, the doorbell startled us both and we laughed uneasily. Lately, the thought of unexpected visitors set my heart pounding.

Dusty, our usually calm Sheltie-Beagle mix, started barking. I grabbed her before Mom could open the door. No use scaring whoever that was on our doorstep.

From over Mom's shoulder, I could see a young girl about four years older than I was—slim, blonde, with a nice smile. She held a potted poinsettia. I'd never seen her before.

"My name's Gloria," she introduced herself. "I was a friend of Greg's..." Her voice cracked slightly and she paused. "I've been wanting to stop by for a long time now... to tell you... how sorry I am. May I come in?"

Mom opened the door wider. "Yes, certainly," she said. Then to me, "Pam, take the flowers from Gloria." I put Dusty down as she woofed a little softer in her "I don't know you so I'm watching you" tone. But Gloria just commented on her beauty, stooping down with confidence to pet her long soft fur. Dusty's tail swished, a sure sign of acceptance. I caught Mom's eye, certain we were both thinking the same thing. We'd learned to be wary of Greg's... friends.

I reached for the flowers and met Gloria's smile, as Mom led her to the couch. I sat across from them to listen. Dusty moved to sit protectively at Mom's feet.

"I don't remember Greg ever speaking of someone named Gloria," Mom began.

Gloria relaxed back against the cushions comfortably. "We knew each other in grade school," she explained. "I hadn't seen him in years, but I just wanted to tell you about what a wonderful boy he was back then."

As we talked, Gloria's open laughter and sweet reminiscing about my brother warmed us, melting a little of the ice around our hearts. "Greg was one of my first 'dates,'" she confided. "We were just kids, but he impressed me because he was such a gentleman. He opened doors—always so thoughtful—even brought me a rose."

Again, I could almost read Mom's thoughts. I knew the sorrow devastating her all these months since Greg's death. The idea that she'd done something wrong in how she raised him, somehow failed him. The constant self-questioning. How had he changed from a happy kid to a reckless teen? And even more importantly, could she trust he was now at peace with God? As for me, I loved God, but he seemed somehow so far away and I wasn't sure how that could change.

As Gloria recalled the Greg she knew, it was like she somehow brought him back into the room with us. Not tormented, as in recent years. But as the young boy we'd almost forgotten existed. She spoke of all the values my parents had taught each of us kids—faith, compassion, gentleness—and how she had seen them all in Greg. Her words became sorely needed proof that he had been a boy of character and values.

Time flew, and before we knew it, the dark of evening was on us. I got up to turn on the soft lights of the tree. Gloria stood to leave, moving to hug Mom as Dusty eyed her carefully. She had to go, but it was one of those moments you felt you didn't want to lose. A sense that it shouldn't just end there. Gloria met our eyes and smiled. "I'd like to come back," she said, "to stay in touch."

"I'd like that, too," Mom said, warmly.

We picked up the empty decoration boxes after Gloria left, clearing things out from under the tree to leave room for presents. A soft feeling hung in the air for the first time that season—Christmas-y, like the scent of incense in church when every candle was aglow and all was quiet and peaceful. A benediction.

"I think we'll start baking the oatmeal cookies after dinner tonight," Mom said.

"And Russian teacakes?" I asked, mouth watering. Those had always been my favorite.

"First things first," Mom laughed. "Dad and your sister will be home soon. Let's get dinner started."

Beginning that night, and carrying throughout the season, it was as if a candle had been lit. A little light to melt our sorrow. Carols flowed from the stereo, and from us, as we sang of angels bending near the earth with their song of peace. Soon, we started hearing the familiar hum of Mom's sewing machine again, as she worked long into the night on our presents—lovely new nightgowns for Christmas Day.

Gloria became a part of our lives for several years, stopping by regularly, seeking out Mom as a second mother. Others after Gloria came to us with their own peace-giving puzzle pieces of Greg's life.

Healing comes in stages, of course. But that one Christmas, we received a blessing of God's assuring love from an angel so wondrously named Gloria.

~Pam Depoyan

Green Pickle Christmas

A child needs a grandparent, anybody's grandparent,
to grow a little more securely into an unfamiliar world.
~Charles and Ann Morse

It was three weeks before Christmas and I was mixing a batch of snicker doodle cookies, when the "Movin' Train" ringtone on my cell phone let me know that Alexandria, my nineteen-year-old granddaughter, had sent a text message. She and her younger sisters, Mary and Victoria, were driving in from out of state and had been expected an hour earlier. Praying that nothing was wrong, I read the message.

"Gma b there at 7. bad traffic. bff with us. hide pickle. lol. ily."

Chuckling, my eyes focused on the refrigerator door to examine the cheat sheet of text codes. For me, texting was like a foreign language, so Alex had made the decipher list when the family sent me an iPhone as an early Christmas present. It did everything but read to me. All the strange icons and abbreviations on the screen made me nervous, but I knew I'd lose out if I didn't accept the challenge of a new way to communicate with them in their fast, high-tech world.

A pleasant feeling gripped me when I found "ily" on the list and whispered, "I love you. Awww! It's been too long since I've heard that."

Reading the message again, I snickered at their new name for me—Gma. What started out when they were babies as Ga-Ga had evolved over the years to Gammy, Grams, Gramcracker, and Grandma.

The clock above the refrigerator read six o'clock. I plowed through the storage boxes to find the item that had been a part of our Christmas tradition for many years. From a black velvet bag, I slid the dark green glass ornament shaped like a small whole pickle. In the living room, the festively decorated long-needle pine filled the house with fragrance. Peeking between the boughs, I found the perfect hiding place and clapped my hands together at the thought of playing our game again. "There, it blends in so well on this tree compared to my old artificial one. I can't believe it's been two years since we did this."

My daughter was a single mother who had to work long hours to support her kids, so the girls grew up with very little. The original German legend on the card that came with the pickle said that the child who finds it on Christmas morning gets an extra present. These girls had needed something more positive, so I changed the rules. In a basket, I put little brown paper grab bags of inexpensive fun things that I knew they would like—things that I'd shop for throughout the year. Included in each bag were handmade coupons that allowed each one to spend time with me—trips to a museum, the beach, concerts, or picnics. Also, each bag contained a one-, five-, or ten-dollar bill.

Our game was played almost a month before Christmas. The one who found the pickle selected a bag, then hid it again until all the bags were gone. The next day we all headed to the mall to choose a child from the Salvation Army Angel Tree. According to the rules, each girl had the option to use all or part of the money to buy what the child listed.

"Now, what will I do for grab bags?" My fingers snapped as an idea formed.

Forty-five minutes later I heard, "Grandma, we're here." Mary, the middle child who always wanted to be first, hurried to hug me. "Oh, it smells so good!" She grinned and reached for a cookie.

"Not yet." I gently slapped her hand.

Alex and Vicky came for their hugs and then motioned to the teenager who was hanging back. With a welcoming smile, I hugged her. "Hi, you must be BFF."

Her eyes narrowed with confusion as she shook her head. The girls looked at each other and shrugged. Alex's eyes widened and she bent over with laughter before she caught her breath and said, "No, Grandma, 'bff' means 'best friends forever.' This is my friend, Tori."

Joining their laughter, I said, "Put your things in the guest bedroom. Someone can sleep on the sofa."

"Sleep? Isn't this a party?" Vicky said. "Did you hide the pickle?"

I set out hot, spiced cider, little finger sandwiches, snacks, and a pile of cookies on the table. Mary looked around. "Where are the bags?"

"We're playing it differently this year," I said. "The one who finds the pickle gets a cookie."

Groans drowned out the Christmas music playing in the background. Alex asked, "We're not going to do the Angel Tree?"

Tori's face lit up. "Angel Tree?"

"Oh, no," Mary said. "Why not?"

I put my hand up to signal "stop" and adopted a mysterious tone. "I'll give you a hint. Be very careful when you eat your prize." My hands rubbed together as I cackled like an old witch.

All four girls rushed to the tree, giggling and pushing. In less than three minutes, Vicky squealed, "I've got it!" She did a winner's dance and grabbed a cookie to hold in the air like it was a gold medal. Biting off half, she chewed, yelped, and spit into her hand.

Mary stepped over to look. "Yuck. What's that?" Her nose wrinkled.

"I told you to be careful when you eat." I pulled a dime from the mess in her palm. "In each cookie is a penny or dime. I was afraid a nickel would be too heavy. For each coin I'll give you one or ten dollars to go toward our angel."

Tori gasped and covered her mouth. Her eyes brimmed with tears as she asked, "You play this for Angel Tree money?"

"Are you okay?" I put my hand on her shoulder.

"It's just..." her head tilted back to look at the ceiling. "My dad does the Angel Tree. He said it's because someone did it for my brothers and me five years ago when he couldn't work while he was taking care of Mom before she died. He says he'll never forget the happy look on Mom's face when we woke up with presents even though we didn't have a tree."

"Why didn't you tell me about this?" Alex sounded hurt.

Tori shrugged. "We were just starting to hang out then."

Alex hugged Tori, and we all joined her. If it hadn't been for "Jingle Bells" playing in the background, tears would have flowed. Mary eagerly bounced to the beat and said, "Hey! We need to celebrate. There's a real angel from the tree right here."

"Yeah," Alex said. "Let's get this game going, so we can find another angel tomorrow."

"But watch out for Gramcrackers's money cookies." Vicki giggled.

They stared at my Cheshire cat smile before I said. "Remember, a little ingenuity never hurt anyone. At least you'll have something to lol about with your bff for years."

~M.M. Jarrell

Daddy's Still Here

People can be more forgiving than you can imagine.
But you have to forgive yourself. Let go of what's bitter and move on.
~Bill Cosby

The twee! The twee!" Three-year-old Ana Lu sprinted toward our three-foot-tall Christmas tree.

"Isn't it adorable?" I knelt down next to my daughter and wrapped my right arm around her waist. I wasn't exactly sure who I was trying to convince, because I couldn't believe we were decorating the tree without Daddy. Something was missing. Then the hopeful, motivated mom in me encouraged the exhausted, saddened ex-wife in me: You can do this.

The fact that our petite tree could easily be mistaken for a tree topper in comparison to our old Christmas trees did not bother Ana Lu. And relative to our 300-square foot apartment, our mini-tree rivaled the one in Rockefeller Center.

"I want hang dis one!" Ana Lu exclaimed, pulling out a wooden snowman with a stethoscope that a friend had given me the year I graduated from nursing school, some twenty years before.

Ana Lu giggled, "Ha ha ha—look at dis one, Mommy! It so silly, Santa no swim!" Ana Lu dangled a two-inch-tall Santa Claus figurine a few inches from her amused little face. Santa's big belly hung over his red floral swim trunks, and he wore a snorkel mask and large black flippers. My ex-husband Charles and I had bought it while on our honeymoon in Hawaii six years earlier.

I headed to the kitchen for more eggnog. As I filled my glass, I watched a jovial Ana Lu bounce around the room searching through the bins for the next ornament to hang. I leaned into the wooden kitchen island, thinking about how I wished I could protect her from the pain of the separation and missing her daddy during Christmas. I felt horrible that I couldn't offer her a big tree with the scent of real pine, like the one she had at her daddy's house. Not only was our tree miniscule, it was fake.

I reminded myself that our tree was super-special because it was the one Charles and I had ever since Ana Lu's first Christmas. She was just four months old so we decorated it in a pink sugar-and-spice theme with pink booties, a pink teether, a white rattle, and a host of "sweet" ornaments like cute sparkly gumdrops and a reindeer with teeny-tiny candy cane antlers.

I refilled my glass, wishing the stores sold eggnog year-round, and then headed back to join Ana Lu. I plopped down in front of our coffee table, sat with my legs crossed, and started to sift through the ornament bin labeled "FRAGILE." I selected two and added them to the top of our tree. I picked up the next ornament and peeled back the layers of the red tissue paper as if peeling an onion. I knew what was inside. Maybe if I held it far enough away while I took off the layers it wouldn't make me teary.

It was a small, personalized, ceramic ornament with a candid glossy photo of my ex-husband bonded to both sides. It was taken on his 30th birthday while he was blowing out the candles on his cake, a great shot because it captured his charming smile without being a cheesy "I'm posing" type picture. I felt a pang of sadness. Not because I doubted our separation. I was confident both he and I were happy with our decision. But my heart ached for Ana Lu. Was she missing out on something now that her parents lived in separate homes? I didn't want Ana Lu to see it. I hated the thought of her missing her daddy. I folded the red tissue paper back around the ornament and tucked it away.

"The twee's ready! Can I plug the lights in, Mommy?" she asked.

"Yep, it's ready. But this is very special, okay?" I answered in my annoying, authoritative Mommy tone to let her know we don't play with outlets, but this time she was ready to handle the responsibility of lighting up the tree.

"Yes. Special. Special," she replied, clearly humoring me. Ana Lu plugged the lights into the wall outlet. The tree lit up, it really did look adorable.

"Wow! It's got lots of colors just like twee Daddy house. We show him dis one. Soooo pretty..." Ana Lu marveled at the colorful tree.

Then it hit me. Daddy wasn't missing. Her daddy was with her this very moment. Maybe he didn't live here, but he wasn't missing. He is in her. He is in me. And most important, he is a part of us.

The ornament! My mind raced through pros and cons. If I had a picture of him up in the house, what would people think? They'd think I'm nuts... they'd think I want to get back together with him... they'd think it was ridiculous to have a picture of my ex. My rationale brain took over. Who cares? My girlfriends are great. They would understand when I explained. And anyone who didn't, well, their opinion didn't matter. I know what's best for my family. And in this moment every cell in my body was telling me to acknowledge that Daddy is always with us. Always.

Focused, I walked to the bins stacked at the door, pulled out the one labeled "FRAGILE" and grabbed the Daddy Ornament. Determined, I walked back to the tree and unlike all of the other fragile ornaments that dangled from the top branches, I hung this one on the bottom. The perfect height for a toddler to see the most important man in her life — her daddy.

Ana Lu should be able to enjoy seeing a photo of her daddy smiling at her every day during Christmastime. Marriage... divorce... it makes no difference. Her daddy is always with her. She should know it.

~Gretchen Schiller

Thanksgiving Christmas

When you look at your life, the greatest happinesses are family happinesses.
~Joyce Brothers

Christmas in my family was never small. Every year my parents went all out to make sure their kids got the best Christmas money could buy. The result of these grand annual events was usually my father screaming about the Christmas lights.

Every year, Mom would drag Dad to the tree lot next to Walmart and pick the tallest, fattest tree. One year it was actually too fat to fit through the front door, so they had to bring it through the patio door in the kitchen.

When it came time to decorate, the whole family was together. Mom would put in her usual mix of Christmas CDs and we would all work together filling the tree. Once it was complete, a marathon of Christmas movies would begin, accompanied by a glass of eggnog. I cherish those memories.

The holiday season of 1990 started like all the others. It was early November. The family drew names for special Christmas exchanges, wrote out their wish list, and went about their business. I have always been a bigger fan of Thanksgiving, so I procrastinated. Why taint

Thanksgiving with Christmas? It's a sin to put out decorations before Black Friday.

I don't recall exactly when the call came, or how my parents told my older brother, sister, and me. What I do remember is having a Thanksgiving-Christmas to be truly thankful for.

Dad was in the Navy Reserve, and Desert Storm was in full swing. His reserve unit was called into war. Since he was to leave right after Thanksgiving, my family decided we would have Christmas on Thanksgiving.

There was no time to buy a tree, so Mom got creative. She took a half-dead three-foot-tall potted tree in our living room and tossed some tinsel on it. Then we hung as many ornaments as the tree could handle. When we stepped back to marvel at our work, I had to fight off a giggle. Our sad little leafless tree reminded me of the tree in *A Charlie Brown Christmas*.

On Thanksgiving-Christmas morning we woke, ate breakfast together, then turned on the holiday music and began handing out our meager supply of gifts, including a special one I received from my dad. For months I had begged my dad to buy me a stuffed tiger and he refused. Yet that day, my dad extracted a not-so-cleverly hidden large black trash bag from under our Charlie Brown tree.

When he handed me the gift I nearly jumped up and down with glee. I had yet to open the bag but I already knew what was inside. My three-foot-long tiger. More excited than ever before, I tore at the bag and hugged the tiger close.

Shortly before Christmas Mom received a call from Dad saying he was not to be shipped out from North Carolina until after Christmas. So across the Skyway Bridge with a mother terrified of heights, through an Indiana ice storm that froze our car doors shut, and through the Smoky Mountains, my mother drove us to see our father.

Though I have very fond memories of a surprisingly wonderful Christmas in North Carolina, it's the memories of that Thanksgiving-Christmas that stand out. All the months my dad was in Saudi, that special tiger helped me sleep at night. It made me feel like my dad was right there beside me. It was the most precious item I had. I took good care of it, because in my ten-year-old head, I decided that as long as the tiger was unharmed, so would be my father.

I still have that tiger twenty-three years later. She still reminds me how much our family has to be grateful for.

~Star Davies

Joy
in the Shadows

Love is the flower of life, and blossoms unexpectedly and without law,
and must be plucked where it is found,
and enjoyed for the brief hour of its duration.
~D.H. Lawrence

"Everybody come to the living room," my husband invited, "and we'll pass out the gifts." Our grandsons ran from their playroom and plopped down in front of the Christmas tree, waiting for Papa to play Santa Claus.

As the family gathered, my nervousness intensified and I started to get a headache. My son's addiction had reached unparalleled levels, and I never knew how he would respond in family situations. Would he "nod off," feeling the effects of the drugs he was taking, or would he hide out in the bathroom while the family opened presents? Peace, joy, and love didn't enter my mind. I wanted to crawl in bed and avoid the holy day.

Cory, our oldest daughter's boyfriend, had joined us for Christmas. All the presents had been opened when Cory asked Caleb, my daughter's son, to open a gift hidden behind the couch. Caleb ripped off the paper, surprised to find a box of Twix candy bars.

"Pass them out, please," Cory said, taking one for himself. Caleb obeyed.

Cory unwrapped a bar. "Twix bars break apart with a slight amount of pressure." He demonstrated by popping the candy bar in half with a quick snap. "The two halves still taste good, but they are no longer one bar."

"Hmm, this is a strange gift," I thought.

Cory handed Caleb another wrapped box and instructed him to open it; inside he found Snickers bars. "Okay, give one to everybody."

"Now, look at it," Cory said. "The Snickers is thick, solid and harder to break than the Twix bar; it stretches when pulled apart. That's how I feel about Caron and me. We are solid. We may be stretched, but it will be difficult to break us apart." As he uttered those words, he eased off the couch and rested on one knee in front of my daughter.

I thought he slid off because the couch was crowded with grandsons and toys. Then I noticed a diamond engagement ring in his palm. With shaky hands and trembling voice, Robert blurted: "Caron, will you marry me?"

The squeals, screams, and tears started. Finally, when we all had quieted down, she looked him in the eye and said, "Yes." The excitement continued for the afternoon as wedding talk overtook our conversations until everyone left for their homes.

The tree looked naked without its skirt of brightly wrapped gifts. I relaxed in the soft glow of the Christmas lights, replaying the day's events in my mind. I recalled the morning's foreboding thoughts and concerns over my son's behavior, about the hopelessness I felt. But a smile spread across my face as I recalled Cory's surprise marriage proposal. The unique way he "popped the question." It provided a much-needed diversion from the year's agony and sorrow. Now, all I could think was, "Woo hoo! We've got a wedding to plan."

~Sharron K. Cosby

The Glass Hummingbird

When someone you love becomes a memory, the memory becomes a treasure.
~Author Unknown

My wife Julie and I have been collecting Christmas ornaments over the entire course of our thirty-year marriage. Each ornament has a story to tell. The glass hummingbird, for instance, was acquired one October about eighteen years ago, when we were living in Auburn, California. Julie bought it at her favorite little home décor boutique, a place called Serendipity. Its proportions were exactly those of a real hummingbird—which meant that its beak was about an inch and a half long and nearly as thin as a piece of angel hair pasta. As soon as I saw the ornament, I knew it would never last. We have always owned cats—usually no fewer than three or four at a time. And cats love to play with Christmas ornaments. That's why Julie and I normally purchase only ornaments made of wood or fabric or metal or plastic.

"What were you thinking?" I asked Julie when I saw the hummingbird. "That thing will never survive the month of November much less the entire Christmas season."

"I'll put it up high," she said. "The cats won't even notice it."

"They're cats!" I reminded her needlessly. "Height is not a problem for them. They can scale full-sized fir trees. A seven-foot pine tree won't even slow them down."

"I'm not worried," Julie said. "It's clear glass. They won't even notice it. It's the colorful ornaments that catch their attention."

"One swipe at that beak and it will break right off," I said.

"When that happens, we'll pretend it's a sparrow," Julie said. "Or maybe a house finch."

That was eighteen years ago. Two generations of cats have passed through our lives since then, including quite a few rambunctious little troublemakers, but somehow that hummingbird has survived—beak and wings intact—despite numerous feline assaults. It serves as a reminder that, in life, certain things and certain people are much less fragile than they appear.

We have only one ornament that is more precious to us than the hummingbird. It is a small paper tag with the number 50 written on it in thick black felt pen. It's not much to look at, but it means a lot to us. We acquired it about eleven years ago when we were living in Placerville, another small town in northern California. Our house was on two acres and was located just a few parcels away from a Christmas tree lot known as "The Ardencaple Forest," which was owned and operated by a friendly married couple, Norm and Dottie McCally. We saw them now and then at the community mailbox and the local grocery store, but our only regular interaction with the McCallys came every year at Christmas when we drove the few hundred feet from our house to theirs in order to purchase a Christmas tree.

Ardencaple Forest was a cut-it-yourself Christmas tree operation. When you arrived at the farm, Norm McCally would hand you a long-handled saw that looked somewhat like the grim reaper's scythe. After that, you were free to wander through the Ardencaple Forest looking for a tree that suited you. When you found a tree you liked, you would cut it down yourself and then call out for Trevor, the McCally's grandson. He would ride down on a little four-wheel ATV and haul the tree back up to your car.

It was the day after Thanksgiving in 2000 that Julie and I arrived at Ardencaple only to be told by Dottie that her beloved husband Norm had died of a sudden heart attack the previous weekend. This was a shock to us. Norm was an active guy and only about seventy years old. He always looked extremely fit whenever we saw him walking down to fetch the mail. He was one of those people that you expect to live to be 100.

Dottie was so upset by his death that she hadn't planned on opening the Christmas tree farm that year. But the operation of the Ardencaple Forest was a McCally family tradition. Every weekend during the Christmas season, Norm and Dottie's children would show up at Ardencaple with their spouses and their own children and help Norm and Dottie with the work. They helped cut trees for those who didn't want to do it themselves. They wrapped the trees in nets and tied them to the tops of cars. They served cider and other treats to the holiday visitors and performed various other tasks around the place.

The McCally children were not ready to see the family's tree farm shut down for even a single season. And so, just a few days after Norm's funeral, the whole family was at the farm to make sure that Norm's beloved operation was open for business as usual.

After hearing the shocking news about Norm's death, Julie and I grabbed our saw and wandered out to find a Christmas tree. Normally we bought a fairly small tree, but because we thought it might help Dottie financially, we decided that we would buy the biggest tree we could possibly fit into our house. We meandered for nearly an hour before finding a tree that looked like it might fit through our front door. We cut it down and then signaled to Trevor that we were ready for him to haul it up to the car.

When we arrived back at the nerve center of the Ardencaple operation—i.e., the McCally's front yard—Dottie was waiting for us with our tree. We talked a little bit more with her about Norm. After Dottie told us about Norm's life and career, she looked over our tree until she found the price tag. It was a piece of paper about the size and thickness of a business card. On it, written in a firm hand, was the number 50. Dottie looked down at the price tag and said, "See that. Norm went out and put the price tags on the trees just a day before he died. They were probably the last things he ever wrote." We asked her if we could keep the tag and she tearfully complied.

We took the tree home and, though it was massive, we somehow managed to install it in our living room. After decorating the tree with all the usual ornaments we hung Norm's price tag near the top of the tree, where it would be visible for all to see. To others it might have seemed kind of gauche to leave the price tag on a Christmas tree, but for us that tag had become a cherished reminder of a kindly neighbor. It has hung on every Christmas tree we have put up since then.

We haven't been back to Ardencaple Forest since we moved to Sacramento. But every year during the Christmas season, that price tag with the number 50 on it reminds us that life can sometimes be as fragile as... well, the beak of a glass hummingbird.

~Kevin Mims

A Legacy of Love

Although the world is full of suffering, it is also full of the overcoming of it.
~Helen Keller

I was only eleven years old that day I trudged home from school early in December. Snowflakes danced in front of my face. Christmas vacation would soon begin. Yet, at my house, Christmas was just another day. Dad would get a day off from work at the auto parts store. Mom, suffering from schizophrenia, would spend the day at the psychiatric hospital where she resided. Dad and I would go out for a meal at the local diner. But decorations, lights, and cards were things that happened in other homes, not ours.

"Dad, can we get a tree this year?" I had asked the night before.

Now, approaching our small home, built by my father, I sighed and pushed open the door. Inside, a bare pine tree leaned against the living room wall. A few dry pine needles had already fallen to the floor. No freshly baked cookies greeted me. Dad was still at work. Schoolyard friends never came here to visit after school. Never. Not once.

Standing there on the cheap checkerboard patterned floor of the kitchen, I realized that whatever celebration we would experience would have to be of my own making. Alone, I rummaged about in the basement looking for decorations. A cardboard box stuffed in the corner revealed some colored lights and a few dusty ornaments.

I dragged the carton upstairs. Sitting on the floor and pulling the strings of bulbs from the box, I untangled the stiff cords and replaced a bulb here, another there, until at last the whole line worked. Then I set about hanging them on the barren branches.

After supper, I sat down at the kitchen table and began to sort a pile of yellowed Christmas cards bought years earlier by my mother. With my neatest penmanship, I set about addressing the cards to family members. If Dad would not communicate with family members, his eleven-year-old son would take on that responsibility too.

And on the 25th? Each year, I wrote down a wish list of books I wanted for Christmas and my father selected as many of those as he could afford to purchase. No glossy gifts with bright bows appeared. My father, burdened by the load of single parenting, simply handed me a plain brown paper package full of the volumes I had requested.

This was the legacy of holiday memories I brought into my marriage.

My wife knew almost nothing of this history when we walked down the aisle. Emily had come from a home where family traditions abounded. In her parents' home, hundreds of Christmas cards from friends flooded the mailbox each year; her parents hung these cards on long strings that crisscrossed the ceiling in a kaleidoscope of color. Her mother baked bread and cookies. Parties and laughter filled the house. The family gathered guests around the piano to sing as Emily's father played favorite carols. A freshly cut tree glowed with lights, and heaps of wrapped packages from aunts and uncles and grandparents overflowed beneath the branches. Candle-lit services at church marked the true center of the holiday. And early on Christmas morning, stockings stuffed with surprises awaited Emily and her brothers when they awoke.

Thus it happened that, several months after Emily and I moved into our first home, I headed to work one day early in December. While I taught my classes, Emily began decorating the house for the holidays. A fragrant wreath of pinecones and acorns hung on the front door. A manger scene appeared on top of the piano. Cards hung from strings just as they had in her parents' home.

When I walked in the door at the end of the day, a Christmas tree covered with lights and tinsel stood by the front window. My eyes filled with tears as I looked at the homemade stockings, knit by the grandmother of a former student, hanging nearby, awaiting a special midnight visitor. I sniffed the air. Were those freshly baked sweet rolls cooling on the kitchen counter?

After we enjoyed a simple supper of hot soup and homemade bread, Emily turned off all the lights in the house except for those on the branches of the tree. Together, we settled on the couch to enjoy the soft glow. A music box played the soft notes of "Silent Night."

"You have no idea how healing this is for me," I said as I pulled her close. "You see, I was always the one who had to make Christmas happen at my house."

Christmas was still weeks away but my holiday celebration had already begun. My wife's simple gift of lighting candles and hanging red bows marked the start of a new legacy of memories, a family treasure chest of traditions to pass on to our children.

Today, thirty-nine years later, the pattern continues. One morning early in December, I leave for work, and when I return in the evening I discover Emily has decorated for the holidays. When I step into the house at the end of the day, I still gape in wonder to find our house transformed by a legacy of love.

~Gene Barry Chase

The Together Tree

Gifts of time and love are surely the basic ingredients
of a truly merry Christmas.
~Peg Bracken

"But I've never been this far away from home, and it's almost Christmas," I said while fighting back the tears. "And I'm seven months pregnant!"

"I know, baby," he said sitting on the edge of the bed and wrapping his arm around my shoulder. "The NCOIC said we will have base housing by January 10th at the latest."

"That means Christmas in this dark apartment," I whined. "And what is an NCOIC anyway?"

He smiled, shook his head and dropped his arm from my shoulder. "Non-commissioned officer in charge — in this case he's the guy in charge of base housing. Believe me, he outranks every second lieutenant in the Air Force." He walked to the only window in the bedroom and looked out. "Why would anyone build an apartment with only two windows?"

"Can we at least buy a Christmas tree?" I asked.

He turned and faced me. Like so many other college seniors of 1969 he had been transformed into a stand-up-straight, starched-uniform-wearing second lieutenant. At six foot three inches, Mike had always been taller than average, but now his "at attention posture" made him appear much too close to the ceiling. He would surely have hit his head on the light fixture if there had been one.

"If we get a tree, we won't have any decorations. The household goods have to stay in storage until we are assigned to quarters," he said.

Mumbling under my breath about military vocabulary and acronyms, I stood, unplugged the lamp and walked to the living room. Placing the lamp on the small table near the sofa, I lowered my rather large round body to the outlet near the baseboard and plugged it in again. Two windows, no overhead lighting, and only one lamp; this was not exactly home sweet home. It was what the Air Force referred to as "off base contracted temporary quarters." "That's okay," I said. "I just need a little something to get me into the Christmas spirit." This was our second Christmas as a married couple and the first one that either of us had spent away from family.

"We have your grandma's fruit cake," he said with little boy excitement in his voice. Mike always relished every bite of my grandma's sweet and nutty fruitcake.

"You know that has to wait until Christmas Day," I said. "Please, just a small tree."

We drove to a tree lot we had seen near the entrance to Mather Air Force Base. Deciding on a four-foot Douglas fir, and paying our $10, we loaded our little piece of Christmas into the trunk of our car. The top foot of the tree was peeking between the trunk lid and bumper, waving in the now dark streets of Sacramento, California as we drove back to our apartment.

Mike had the early shift for the next two weeks; this meant he had to leave for the base by six a.m.

"Do you have any quarters?" I asked while rolling out of bed, and instinctively cupping my hands under my ever-expanding abdomen.

"Laundromat?" he asked.

"Phone booth." We both smiled. Let's just say being seven months pregnant and trying to fit into an enclosed phone booth made for some very funny images.

By eight o'clock I had collected my quarters and walked the half block to the nearest phone booth. I deposited my first quarter and waited for the operator's instruction. "That will be seventy-five cents for the first three minutes," she said. It was ringing.

"Hello?" I heard a warm familiar Texas accent.

"Grandma, I only have three minutes and I need to ask a favor." I was practically screaming over the sound of the passing cars.

"Are you all right?" she quickly asked.

"Yes ma'am. I need a favor. I need you to send Christmas cards to this address. I need lots of cards, right away. It's the only decoration we will be able to have on our Christmas tree this year. Will you ask everybody you know to send us a card?" I was talking fast. She was quiet. "Are you ready to write down the address?" I continued.

"Is Mike all right? How's that baby?"

"We're all just fine, Grandma. Write down this address," I said again. We exchanged "I love you" just as the operator asked for more quarters. There were quick overlapping goodbyes and then silence.

I had just enough quarters for one more call, this time to my mother-in-law. The conversation played out much the same.

The next day I purchased a roll of red curly ribbon, placed it under the tree and waited for the cards to begin arriving. Three days later, there were five cards in the mailbox. I opened the one from my grandma first. The card was dark blue with golden angels on the front; inside were the words, "peace on earth, goodwill to all men." Best of all it was signed in her familiar handwriting, "Merry Christmas! Love, Grandma and Granddaddy." I poked a hole into the corner of the card, ran a piece of red curly ribbon through the hole and tied it to the tree. I stood back and looked at our tree. It was beautiful!

When Mike came in that afternoon, I met him at the door, babbling with excitement, "Look! Look! We have cards on our tree."

When we awoke on that Christmas morning, we carried our lamp to the living room, placing it so as to "light" our tree, which was now filled with cards. We sat on the floor, eating a breakfast of Grandma's fruitcake, reading the cards, and remembering with joy the people who had sent them. Even though many miles separated us that Christmas morning, it felt as if we were all together around our little tree.

~Melba Payne

A Real Tradition

A mom's hug lasts long after she lets go.
~Author Unknown

For a single mom and two teenage daughters, putting up a real, seven-foot Christmas tree each year was no easy task. An artificial tree would have been much easier, but every time we asked Mom to get one, she acted scandalized by the very suggestion.

"Those things are awful," she said. "It just wouldn't be Christmas without a real tree."

At our house, decorating the tree wasn't just a chore, it was an event. Mom wanted the tree to be perfect, and our pursuit of that perfection usually resulted in some sort of comical disaster.

First, we'd dig up some rusty tools from the basement to try and trim the trunk and bottom branches, but eventually resorted to using a knife from the kitchen drawer. As it turned out, steak knives from the 1970s cut through pine branches fairly well.

The tree was always so heavy and wide that it took the three of us to force it in through the doorway, and in the process we'd gouge the doorframe and carpet the floor with pine needles.

After we heaved the tree into its stand, the ceiling would need to be repainted because the top branch would scratch it after we misjudged the height. Meanwhile, our West Highland Terrier would dive into the fragrant branches to frantically sniff for traces of squirrels and birds. When the tree wasn't balanced just right it toppled over, shattering ornaments and soaking the floor with water.

Next we'd pray that the tree lights still worked. If one bulb blew, the whole string went dark, and you had to test each one to find the culprit. If two bulbs went out, you needed a degree in electrical engineering to light the string again.

Eventually, we'd get to the fun part. It took many trips to the basement to get all the ornaments out of storage. Mom acted perplexed by the growing number of boxes.

"How did we get this many?" she asked. By buying tree decorations in every gift shop between New York and Maine, that's how. Even though we loaded the tree with ornaments until its branches sagged, we never, ever came close to getting all of them on. Yet each year, we bought more.

Wherever we went, we got an ornament to commemorate the trip. If we went to see a Broadway show, we'd check the gift shop for ornaments. Taking ballet classes this year? Get a ballet ornament. Getting married? Having a baby? Great excuses for more tree decorations!

Most of our ornaments were stored wrapped in wads of tissue paper, which forced you to unwrap all of them to find your favorites. Mom supervised and narrated the unwrapping.

"Oooh, I love this one! Remember when we got this on vacation in Maine?" she asked.

I unwrapped an angel. "Aunt Joyce gave you that the year you were born."

Or, "You made that one in fourth grade!"

Once the decorations were on, we'd skirt the tree with a white sheet to reflect the lights and brighten the base of the tree. Next a snowy village was arranged underneath, complete with a mirror for a pond and a pack of old-fashioned ice skaters. Finally, the tissue paper and boxes were packed away, pine needles vacuumed up, and all the lights turned off.

This was the moment that made it all worthwhile. The tree was radiant. The decorations glistened like jewels and there was silence as we gazed at the lights. We'd put our pajamas and robes on, and Mom would have a cup of tea. Many nights we gathered near the tree to admire its beauty and bask in its glow, as if it generated the warmth of a fire.

Each year Mom said, "I just love our Christmas tree. It looks so beautiful this year."

In time, my sister and I moved out, but I always returned to help Mom with the tree. We urged her to at least consider getting an artificial tree; they were becoming more popular and realistic. And even though it was getting more difficult to put up the tree each year, she wouldn't hear of it.

When Mom was diagnosed with advanced cancer at the age of sixty-one, we knew that the next Christmas would be her last. She expressed concern to a friend about how the tree was going to get up that year with her not feeling well, and me with a newborn baby. A few days later that friend arrived at Mom's house, along with her sisters. Energized by our fresh reinforcements, we put up and decorated her tree. Even though we had it done in no time, it was still an event. Mom was so grateful and relieved that she would be able to enjoy the sight and scent of a real tree one final time.

Now that I had my own family, I could fully appreciate how much work a real tree was. When my second daughter was born, I made the momentous decision to break with family tradition, and bought one of those pre-lit artificial trees that comes in a box and smells just awful.

I had to laugh at the things Mom would have said about that. I had become one of "those people" who had fake trees that they put up the day after Thanksgiving. A part of me worried that the experience would feel less special if the tree wasn't real and didn't have that divine evergreen scent.

It didn't take long for me to realize that it wasn't the tree that made the tradition meaningful, it was everything that went on around it. Being together, reflecting on shared memories, and celebrating our holiday spirit were much more important than how perfect the tree was, or where it came from.

And to my relief I found that I looked forward to decorating my artificial tree as much as a real one, especially once my daughters grew old enough to help. The girls get excited to look through their ornaments and admire each one. Somehow, they already have quite a few of them, since we seem to buy a new one everywhere we go. They have some very old ornaments in their collection as well—the ones that once belonged to Grandma.

"That was one of Grandma's favorites," I explain as they unpack the boxes.

My daughter unwraps one decorated in gold-painted macaroni, "You made that during preschool," I tell her.

"This ornament's from the year you started ice skating," I point out.

Each one marks a milestone, and holds a special memory. "Grandma gave this one to you for your first Christmas."

And when the kids have gone to bed, and the house is quiet and dark, I get into my pajamas and make a cup of tea. I sit, and sip, and think of my mother. The stronger the memories flow, the brighter the tree seems to glow.

In that moment I find myself thinking, I just love our Christmas tree. It looks so beautiful this year.

~Amy Travison Jasiewicz

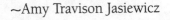

It's Christmas!

Making Memories

*Memory is a way of holding onto the things you love,
the things you are, the things you never want to lose.*

~From the television show The Wonder Years

Every One a Favorite

When you have brought up kids, there are memories you store directly in your tear ducts.

~Robert Brault, www.robertbrault.com

When our girls were in nursery school, my sister Elaine called me a month before Christmas.

"Did you get the notice to send in an empty Jell-O box?" my sister asked me.

"Yes. What's it for?" I asked. My sister had two other children who had already attended First Presbyterian nursery school where Maria, my first child, was now enrolled.

"I'm not telling you, but you'll die when you see it," she promised.

A month later, Maria came home from "The Bucket School," as it's affectionately known, because the children carry a decorated bucket instead of a backpack. She handed me a brown box. It was the Jell-O box. I knew this because it was the correct size and underneath one unevenly painted coat of brown paint I could faintly see the words "Jell-O" in big letters. A ragged rectangle was cut out of one side, a tissue lined the inside where a pack of powdered, cherry gelatin once was, and rolling around inside was a misshapen lump of clay which had hardened with the imprints of my daughter's little fingers still visible.

"Oh, how cute." I exclaimed.

Not wanting to ask what it was for fear her preschool ego would be insulted, I used my tried and true method of getting information. I dance around the issue without asking the real question: "What is it?" After a few questions around the edges, such as "Did you make it?" and "Is this painted with brown paint?" my daughter offered up the desired information. "It's Baby Jesus, Mommy," she squealed as she reached inside, carefully pulled out the lumpy piece of clay and gently placed it in my outstretched hand.

It was the first Christmas decoration made by my first child. At that moment, that lump of clay, that Baby Jesus nestled in Kleenex inside a cardboard dessert box, became my very favorite Christmas decoration.

Years later, I didn't have to ask my sister what the Jell-O box was for. I called Elaine to tell her I had just sent in my empty box and was eagerly awaiting my second lump of clay. Sure enough, a short time later, my son Peter came home with the very same decoration. He proudly held out the brown painted box, trying with little fingers to retrieve the lumpy Baby Jesus from the corner of the box where He had rolled. I exclaimed, "Oh, it's Baby Jesus." The look on my son's face told me how clever he thought I was to have guessed what it was without having to play the twenty questions game.

As I accepted another misshapen lump of clay, and carefully placed it on the tissue in the "manger," I thought of my middle child, Joseph. The child who, because of his severe disability, could not attend the same nursery school as my other two children, and did not get to make a homemade Baby Jesus. I held back my tears, hugged my youngest child, and placed the decoration next to his sister's homemade manger.

My sister and I still put our mini mangers in prominent spots each Christmas, and we still talk about how much we love to bring them out in December. Each year, when I carefully take out and unwrap each box, I have another fleeting moment of sadness that I only have two of them.

I also realize that I have other things, equally as precious: I have a picture of Joe in a homemade frame wearing his Santa Claus tie, looking so handsome seated in his wheelchair next to Santa, or seated at the "North Pole" wearing reindeer antlers and a cute smile. I have hand towels, mugs, and angels made with the imprint of his hands or feet and picture frames with glued-on glitter and sequins. Maybe his little hands couldn't make these decorations on their own, but he was certainly smiling as his aide placed her hand over his hand to help him make these special memories. I can guarantee he felt as proud as my other two children felt when they made their crafts.

I decided years ago not to play favorites. As long as they were made by little hands, whether assisted or unassisted, they are each my very favorite Christmas decoration.

~Laura Guman Fabiani

Made with Loving Hands

The manner of giving is worth more than the gift.
~Pierre Corneille, Le Menteur

It was going to be our leanest Christmas. We had discussed not giving presents at all, but our children were still young. My husband and I remembered the meager years of our childhoods, and we did not want a Christmas without gift giving for our children. So, we got the family together, and we all agreed, that except for the gifts that Santa would bring, we would exchange only gifts that we had made with our own hands.

A hushed peace settled upon us in the month before Christmas. There was no last minute shopping, dashing into a store before it closed and returning with some meaningless, soon-to-be-forgotten gift. This Christmas would require thought and planning.

The house was quiet for weeks as we each ransacked boxes of craft supplies, materials, and ribbons. Bedroom doors closed early, as our daughters giggled and planned all the wonderful surprises that they had in store for each member of the family. I was able to design and make special Christmas ornaments and tiny photo albums telling the story of each child's life. I cannot remember the gift that I made for my husband, but I will never forget the gift that he made for me.

That Christmas he became a man of secrets. Louie, a big man

with large, capable hands, was an electrician in the Navy. I was simply amazed to see the things that he could make work. His powerful hands could pull cables weighing hundreds of pounds with a strength that would bring another man to his knees. However, I had also felt those loving hands gently stroke my headache away, and I'd witnessed the tenderness in those hands as he held a sick child. So, I was curious to see what those hands would create for me for Christmas.

He took over the back bedroom. Sitting at a child's desk, working under the light of a cheap study lamp, he engaged in his mysterious enterprise. He would walk into the house right after work carrying brown paper bags held tightly to his chest. Some of the bags were so tiny, that I couldn't imagine what they contained. I made cookies and cakes and planned the Christmas meal, as I imagined the tantalizing moment when I would unwrap his gift.

As Christmas day neared, I barely saw my husband. I had to insist that he eat something, and even when he did, he was back to work immediately. And no matter how long I stood with my ear to the door, I couldn't hear a sound!

I had never been so excited. I couldn't wait. What was he making? I imagined all sorts of electronic equipment, perhaps a flashing light-board that whistled or clanged. Maybe he was building me some wonderful electronic gizmo! I had a lot of fun trying to guess what the surprise would be. I hadn't a clue.

Christmas day dawned bright and crisp. First came breakfast, and the only things that could be touched before breakfast were the stockings. The girls dove into their stockings, through the nuts and apples, all the way down to the orange that was in the toe. One would think that they had never tasted an orange! They peeled and separated and sucked the juicy fruit, while inhaling a piece of sausage quiche. Breakfast was finished, and we headed for the gifts.

The girls loved every little gift. I had insisted on going last. The girls were so excited, that they wanted me to tear into Louie's gift, but I waited until every gift was opened and "oohed and aahed" over. Then Louie handed me the large, carefully wrapped box.

"Don't shake it," he said, with a mysterious smile.

"Wait until you see it, Momma," smiled Helen.

The girls knew! They had been a part of the conspiracy! Carefully, I unwrapped the box, struggling with the wrapping. Louie flipped his pocketknife out and quickly took care of the tape.

"Afraid someone might break into it?" I asked, with a grin.

"Well, you never know," he answered, with a wink.

Finally, I opened the box. Setting it gently on the floor, I heard a tinkle. What was this? I pulled out miles of tissue paper, and closed my eyes as I reached inside. It was smooth, with tiny parts. Jenny reached over, holding the box, so that I could pull out the gift.

"Gently," she said.

Holding my breath, I pulled it out. Someone pulled an end table close and assisted me in setting my gift down. I opened my eyes, and to my amazement I beheld a lovely porcelain carousel, with tiny horses, a roof, and a music box, beautifully painted, fired, and assembled by my husband. The tears sprung to my eyes. Such delicate beauty, fashioned by big, strong hands.

Louie reached over and lifted the carousel, gently turning the music box key. Lovely tinkling music played, as tears fell from my eyes. It is my most precious Christmas gift, fashioned by loving hands that have taught me that true love is not only sweet, but also surprising.

~Jaye Lewis

92

A Stitch in Time

The best of all gifts around any Christmas tree:
the presence of a happy family all wrapped up in each other.
~Burton Hillis

My seven-year-old daughter wrote, "I was the servant today," on my fine white linen tablecloth. Proud to have carried the delicate serving dishes from the kitchen into the dining room that Christmas Day, Kristin signed her name and wrote the year under her message. I embroidered her message in green.

Some people record their family history in a journal or letters. My family history is recorded on a tablecloth in pencil, then preserved with red and green embroidery over each word—red for odd years and green for even years. We've recorded events momentous and ordinary, such as our exciting family trip to Italy, the year the Red Sox won the World Series, Gary's broken elbow and—four years later—Melissa's broken elbow, new jobs, and adolescent rites of passage including getting braces, pierced ears and driver's licenses. The tablecloth documents several extended family member milestones such as the year my niece Holly survived brain surgery and wrote, "Miracles Happen." Sad events have been noted as well: my mother's passing and when "The world changed on September 11, 2001."

When I reach for the tablecloth in my linen closet the week before Christmas, it's like unwrapping a treasure. I still get a thrill when I gingerly unfold it. Then I set the table in the dining room, creating a festive and nostalgic mood for my family. I spread the ironed cloth over the table pads, running my hands over the words of love while smoothing it out. Then I adorn it with my fine Lenox china and an elegant centerpiece.

With the dining table set, my husband, daughters, and I circle the gathering place to peruse the memories of years past. I particularly enjoy seeing my daughters' handwriting change through the years: Melissa's backward "s" at age five and Kristin's large print, to match her outgoing personality. Kristin and Gary use a lot of space while Melissa and I write smaller. The randomness of the messages in content, shape, penmanship, and placement keeps me interested and feeling renewed every time I scan our humble work of art.

After the dinner plates are cleared away from the table on Christmas night, I lay several pencils in the center of the table, along with homemade biscotti and butter cookies, pies and chocolates. While relaxing with our coffee and dessert, each family member reflects on the year and recalls an event, milestone, or something significant that happened to them during those past twelve months. Then we write our messages on the tablecloth—anywhere we want. Sometimes we write a message of inspiration or wish for the coming year. I treasure the simple prayer "God Bless All My Family" written by my father in 1999.

After the holiday hubbub fades, the gifts are put away, and the needles from the Christmas tree are swept up, I sit down with my tablecloth of memories to begin embroidering. Sometimes I start right at the dining room table. Other times I nestle in a quiet corner chair in my living room with my sewing kit and start by separating the embroidery floss. I work slowly, striving to make each message legible with every stitch. My goal is to complete the embroidery by New Year's Eve. When the final stitch is made, I launder the tablecloth on the gentle cycle, then dry, fold and store it until the following December.

This December will be the seventeenth time I spread my Christmas tablecloth on our dining room table. Sure, there are a couple of faded tea stains, but I simply cover them with a dinner plate or wine glass. Each year, more red and green appear and the white space diminishes. No worry. There's plenty of room for many years of memories to be recorded. What started out as a blank white canvas has been transformed into a cherished family heirloom.

~Joyce Poggi Hager

93

The Train

Just because everything is different doesn't mean anything has changed.

~Irene Peter

As I raced for the Christmas presents under the tree, Dad spun me around and tugged me into the dining room. "Nope. This way, buddy!" On the table a shiny 1957 Santa Fe "O" gauge Lionel train clicked around an oval track. Dad sat close to teach me how to blow the horn, accelerate, stop, uncouple cars, and reverse. A barrel loader vibrated wood barrels up a ramp and dumped them in a gondola car, and a horse car vibrated black rubber horses out a door, down a ramp and into a corral where they moved through chutes, and then back into the horse car. It was the beginning of an empire, one larger and more wonderful than I could possibly have imagined at the time.

With my newspaper delivery earnings, I bought a model of a station and a set of fake trees. For my birthday I asked for a new boxcar and a bag of figurines to inhabit my town. I waited anxiously for Christmas so I could try them out. The second Christmas, Mom had me set up around the tree so she could have the table for holiday dinners. That meant bumping Dad's old train from its place of honor ringing the tree. His was a giant train from the 1930s, each car eight inches high and a foot long, but it showered sparks, and

Dad was afraid they'd set the tree needles on fire, so he retired it to the attic, and gave me his train's oversized metal tunnel, bridge and signal towers.

When we moved, I set my train on an old table in the basement. I painted in roads, lawns, and a lake, and the train stayed up year-round. But when the town was complete, I lost interest. Perhaps, like Christmas or birthdays, once a year is more exciting. I was also a teenager with better things to do—high school girls aren't impressed with Lionel trains. Eventually I packed the set away.

The family changed. My grandparents died, I moved away for a career, married and started a family. Dad died too. But with children, it didn't seem right to have Christmas without the clickety-click and whistle of a train. I dug the set out of Mom's basement closet and set it up around the tree for my daughter. Cindy was only three, but I taught her what my father taught me. Not too fast around the curves, go slow through the tunnel and over the bridge until you're sure nothing hits. As I whispered in her ear, I could hear Dad once again whispering in mine.

But it wasn't the same. For one thing, Cindy didn't want the plastic engineer on the caboose where he'd always ridden. She insisted on having that place taken by a squiggly, rubber crab she'd gotten on a beach vacation. "Crabbie" had to sit with its legs shaking atop the caboose. To her the train was primarily Crabbie's taxi. For another thing, I had cats. Our big orange male, Pow-wow, lay atop my dad's huge tunnel to whack the train as it emerged, the children shrieking with delight. Once he charged into the tunnel as the train entered from the other end and a snarling, thunking rumble ensued. I.Q.-challenged Tulip followed the caboose cautiously, not aware that the engine would sneak up behind her. It goosed her, sending her yowling and clawing up the tree. Eventually these and other cats passed away too, but their stories as well as my own memories of Dad popped out of the train boxes each December.

Our new kittens' characters were judged by how they reacted to the train. And three more children learned to take the throttle.

Each ran the train at least once every Christmas. Even as teenagers, the three girls took a slightly embarrassed turn, but if I suggested not setting it up, there were always groans. "You have to, Dad!" The clickety-click, smell of oil and the nasal horn were as much a part of Christmas as sugar cookies and elves. Over the years our children threw things into the train box—Jeremy's baseball players mingled with my firemen and my dad's old Dick Tracy figurine. Somebody tossed in a few monsters and metal *Monopoly* tokens that had to be set up on the station platform. All the mismatched stuff belonged, and everyone grabbed for special items when the train boxes emerged. To Cindy's disappointment, Crabbie disappeared, but ten years later it was rediscovered inside a boxcar. You'd think the prodigal son had returned.

Four spouses and five grandchildren now swell our holiday gatherings. All—even two-year-old Silas, with his parents whispering instructions—take a turn at the throttle and make the barrels and rubber horses inch along. Everybody learns to fiddle with the horse car door to prevent the horses from jamming up, and everybody learns that tinsel across the track is one of the dozen reasons the train won't run. Lately, we added an electronic crossing gate and threw away a freight station that had been broken, glued, and taped so often it could no longer stand upright, but no matter how the train set grows or crumbles, it's always complete, just like us.

The engine has lost power despite several tune-ups, much as its chief conductor has. The old horn is hoarse, and one coupler doesn't hold the way it should, so the kid driving watches carefully so as not to ram a decoupled car from behind.

There's still magic when the train appears each year. Just as each holiday the family magically assembles from four states to welcome a new baby or measure each other's growth or wrinkles. We pile presents away from the tree now because the train and its village need all the underneath space. We fit the tracks together, add new cars to the old, plug it in and feel that the world is just fine when the old Santa Fe engine pulls the cars around the track and that familiar clickety-click mingles with the adults' talk and children's giggles. It's not just plastic and metal, but the train of our lives that clicks around the track.

~Garrett Bauman

The Doorbell

A grandfather is someone with silver in his hair and gold in his heart.
~Author Unknown

My youngest son, Donald, was always happy to hear that we were going to see my parents. He loved to visit his grandparents in Milwaukee and was always the first one in our station wagon when it was time to leave Chicago, long before his three older siblings were ready. He'd keep urging them on until they hurried just to keep him quiet.

Once we started on our way, it was Don who always asked, "How much longer before we get there?" It didn't matter how many car games we tried to play, how many cows we counted, how many Burma-Shave signs we read, it was always, "Are we almost there?" I didn't realize at the time why he was so eager to visit. After all, once we arrived, he didn't spend a lot of time with either of his grandparents. In fact, he spent more time on the front porch than anywhere else. He loved to ring the doorbell and hear the ding-dong. It got to the point where my father would finally insist that Don stop ringing that bell and come into the house. He always obeyed, of course, after one last push of the button. And it wasn't until we were ready to leave that he begged to ring the bell "just one more time." It got to be a family joke that the only reason Don wanted to go to Milwaukee was to visit the doorbell.

One Christmas, as usual, we drove up to see my parents, laden with pies, cakes, and gifts. This year, Dad met us at the door and, before Don could ring the bell, told him very solemnly that he never wanted to hear him ring that doorbell again, unless it was when we first arrived. Crushed, Don looked at him, on the verge of tears, but he agreed. Then, with Dad's permission, he rang the doorbell one last time. Or so we thought.

After the usual sumptuous dinner was eaten, the leftovers safely stored away and the dishes washed and put into the cupboard, it was time to open gifts. Don was still crestfallen and reluctantly moved into the living room where the fresh fir stood, its branches covered with ornaments collected for over forty years. He had complained of a stomachache soon after we arrived and had eaten very little dinner, so we were all somewhat concerned.

He agreed to hand out the gifts and expressed little interest in most of them. I saw a small flicker of excitement when he looked at the battery-powered car that his older brother, John, unwrapped. Linda's doll didn't interest him at all, nor did Paul's chemistry set. It appeared that all the gifts had been opened before he found one way behind the tree with his name on it. The box was about a foot square and a foot high and was covered with white tissue paper and tied with a red satin ribbon. He tore the box open and pulled out more white tissue paper. There at the bottom of the box was a piece of wood about eight by ten inches in size. Mounted on the front was a doorbell with the push button to ring it. In back was all the wiring connecting the two.

He looked at my father questioningly. "Go ahead," said Dad, "It works. I made it for you." Don gingerly pressed the button to hear the sweet sound he had always loved when he visited Milwaukee. His smile was the biggest ever seen in that house and the hug he lavished upon my father was a wonder to behold. That doorbell became his favorite toy for years.

Don was only six years old the year when Dad made him his very own doorbell. My father has been gone for many years now, but when we visited Don on his farm recently, he took me out to his garage to show me where he had hung the doorbell his grandfather made. It still works.

~Elsie Schmied Knoke

95

Sleeping in Santa's Finest

*When we recall Christmas past, we usually find that the simplest
things — not the great occasions — give off the greatest glow of happiness.*
~Bob Hope

I love Christmas. By late October my thoughts are so con-
sumed by sugar cookies and pine trees that I seem to have
entered my own little Christmas world.

I have always been this way, counting down the days
until Santa would come for weeks. I love the atmosphere, the music
of bells and choir voices that come from every outlet, from churches
to shopping malls, the oversized, gaudy-but-beautiful store decorations, the cheesy specials on TV, my family's traditions.

We have one particularly magical tradition. It all started when I
was around five years old. It was Christmas Eve, and I was downstairs
excitedly playing with my twin brother, Dan, while the adults talked
and laughed upstairs. Dan and I were counting down the minutes
until the night would turn and it would be Christmas Day. It was so
difficult to concentrate on any game!

Then, out of nowhere, our doorbell rang. My brother and I
heard the adults upstairs yell for us to get it, that it must be our aunt,
who was arriving late. Obediently we ran to the door, but we were

confused when we flung the door open and only the yawning black night stared back at us.

My mother stuck her head out the door, murmuring, "That's odd," then gasping with joy as she turned her head to the bench on our front porch. "Dan and Fallon, look over there!"

On that bench was a little Christmas miracle. New pajamas! There was a snowflake-sparkled nightgown for me and red-and-green footie pajamas for Dan. And next to these magical PJs, there was a note! Dan and I squealed and pushed the note into our mother's hands, begging her to read it. With a wide smile, my mother read the note, which said what good kids Dan and I were and how proud our mother must be of us. The note was signed with a cheerful, "See you soon! Santa Claus."

Dan and I were obviously ecstatic. Santa had been at our door! He had left us new pajamas! He wrote us a note! We were so thrilled we could not stop jumping.

After donning the new duds and modeling them for the adults in the house, it was nearly time for bed. But, of course, Dan and I needed to make sure we thanked Santa for such nice pajamas! So, along with the normal cookies and milk (both regular and chocolate, because Dan and I could never decide on which), we dictated a note for Santa to our mother, then in our best five-year-old handwriting, signed our signatures. Dan's was always neater than mine.

That tradition has continued for over a decade. Hearing the doorbell ring and running out to find new pajamas and a note from Santa is as inevitable a part of Christmas as *Rudolph the Red-Nosed Reindeer* appearing on TV.

Luckily, Santa seems to understand how our sense of style has changed as we have grown. Last year, the Christmas when we were seventeen, Dan's pajamas included a comfortable, sporty, long-sleeved cotton shirt with plaid pajama pants. No more footies for him. And Santa ditched the nightgowns for me; this year, I got a baby blue, short-sleeved top that perfectly matched the blue pajama pants covered in smiling reindeer. The fanfare was nearly as great as that first Christmas twelve years ago, with Dan and I modeling the new pajamas for our mother with great excitement.

At this age, even on Christmas Eve, my mother usually heads to bed before Dan and I do. When she kisses us goodnight and crawls into bed, Dan and I quietly sneak into the kitchen. From a stash of Christmas cookies we choose the prettiest ones for a plate. We pour a glass of chocolate milk and regular milk. We write a note telling Santa how much we love and appreciate him. We sign our names. Dan's signature is still far neater than mine.

Before I retire to bed, I sneak a quick peek in my mom's room. She is fast asleep. I smile and gently kiss her forehead, run my fingers over my new pajama pants, then hit the hay.

~Fallon Kane

96

Santa Knows Best

They err who thinks Santa Claus comes down through the chimney;
he really enters through the heart.
~Charles W. Howard

As I flipped the calendar to December that year, I felt sad and inadequate. Photos of my three handsome boys—ages thirteen, ten, and three—were hung throughout my home. Yet, I didn't have a single picture of any of them with Santa Claus! How had this happened?

My oldest, Matthew, was far too shy to sit on Santa's lap when he was small. So I respected his wishes and we waved at Santa from afar. Unfortunately, Daniel followed his older brother's lead. Many Decembers, the kids were too sick or we were too busy and we never stepped into a mall. As I stared at the calendar, I realized my window of opportunity was quickly closing. After all, Michael was already three years old.

So I asked Michael if we should go to the mall and see if Santa Claus was there yet. He thought this was a splendid idea. For months, he had been waiting for Santa to bring him the Thomas & Friends Rescue from Misty Island set. I think he wanted verification that Christmas was finally coming and he would, at long last, get Misty Island.

We arrived at the mall and discovered that Santa was indeed there! Michael even liked the idea of sitting on his lap. However, we decided to return to the mall that weekend with his big brothers. One of the best things about having such a big gap between my older boys and their little brother has been watching the big boys relive the things they loved when they were little. I knew, even though they never actually sat on Santa's lap, they wouldn't want to miss Michael's talk with him.

But then it happened again. As in years past, our few days flew by. Suddenly, it was the week of Christmas and we had not yet made it back to the mall. Also, as in years past, someone was sick. Matthew had been ill during the night. As the morning went on, though, he seemed better. So I casually suggested to all it might be a good day to go to the post office to mail Christmas gifts. After that, we could stop at the mall so Michael could talk to Santa. Everyone agreed this was a superb idea.

We got to the mall around the time Santa was getting back from his lunch and reindeer-feeding break. I brought along our camera because Matthew normally acts as our family photographer. But as I got into line with Michael, I realized I should also buy a photo in case Matthew missed the shot, since he was looking pale and tired. This might be my only chance for one of my kids to have his picture taken with Santa.

Michael covered his mouth shyly as he got onto Santa's lap. Before the photographer took the photo, he asked if my older boys wanted to be in the picture too. I said no. They were excited to watch Michael but they made it clear they would not be photographed with Santa. What if someone they knew was at the mall? The photographer quickly took three photos so I would have my choice of pictures.

After the photos were taken, Santa quickly gave Michael a coloring book and hurried him off his lap. I was a little taken aback by this. I thought Santa would speak to Michael more. I encouraged Michael to go back and tell Santa about Misty Island. But then I realized Santa was out of his chair and moving toward me.

"Are those boys out there with you?" he asked me while pointing to Matthew and Daniel, standing just outside the festive Santa area in the mall.

"Well, yes."

"Then why aren't they up here, too?"

"Well, Santa, to be honest, when they were little they were scared of you. And now they're so big, I can't really carry them up here anymore if they don't want to come."

Santa strode out of his area obviously on a mission. Shoppers gawked. He pointed at my oldest two sons and demanded, "Come here."

If I could go back in time, I would have had the camera at that point. Imagine, if you can, my big boys in the middle of a mall with Santa commanding them to come to him. To put it mildly, my sons were shocked. Daniel quickly realized that saying no to Santa Claus really wasn't an option and he headed toward him. It took a few more seconds for Matthew's feet to start to move.

Santa turned to me and pointed at the camera around Matthew's neck. "Can you use that camera?"

"Yes, sir."

Matthew and Daniel cautiously approached Santa and he carefully arranged all three of my boys on his lap. Michael was overjoyed that his brothers had joined him.

I quickly took three photos. All three reflect the shock on Matthew's face and the joy on Michael's.

As they gathered up their coats and returned to where I was standing, Daniel said to me, "Mom, now Santa wants you."

Thinking something was wrong, I approached his chair. Santa said to Matthew, "Can you work that camera?" and then Santa ordered me to sit on his lap.

A wave of panic crashed over me. There are very few pictures of me in our household because I hate getting my picture taken. My wedding photos were a horrible ordeal for me. Ever since, I have been careful to avoid being photographed. In an attempt to change his mind, I cautioned Santa that I was heavier than I looked. He said it would be fine. I realized then, as the older boys already had, that you can't really say no to Santa Claus. I cautiously sat on his knee and Matthew snapped the picture.

As we left the mall, still in a bit of a daze, I realized what Santa had just done for us. He gave me a photo of all three of my boys, even my teenager, with him. He gave my kids not just a rare picture of me, but a photo of their mom and Santa Claus. He gave us all a memory we will cherish forever. That Christmas will always be the year we all sat on Santa's lap.

Thank you, Santa. You always know just what we really want for Christmas.

~Jill Jackson

97

The Quest for the Perfect Tree

Each day of our lives we make deposits in the memory banks of our children.
~Charles R. Swindoll

"**N**one of them are calling to me yet," I yelled out to my wife Christine and the kids, as we wandered a picturesque Christmas tree farm on the rural east end of Long Island.

"Dad, trees don't talk," my daughter Erin insisted with her glove-covered hands clenched into tight little fists.

"Sure they do, sweetheart. Every year I can hear the right one saying, 'Pick me. Take me home with you,'" I said.

"Dad, just pick one already. It's freezing out, and I'm starving," my son Patrick added.

The children's frustration with my selection methodology had become as much a part of the Christmas tradition as picking out the tree.

"How about this one?" Erin asked.

"That's way too big," Christine replied.

Every year, Christine was adamant that we were going to bring home a smaller tree. But each Christmas we brought one home that scraped the paint off the ceiling when we stood it up in the living room.

"Hey, Dad, what about this one?" Patrick called out from the next row of trees.

"I don't know, Pat. It's kind of thin in the back." I replied.

"We can just put that side up against the wall," Christine suggested.

"There are thousands of trees out here. I don't think we have to settle for one that isn't perfect," I said just before a snowball hit me squarely in the back.

I turned to see Patrick and Erin laughing and high-fiving each other.

"Oh, you better run, Pat!" I shouted as I chased him and his sister through the trees.

Eventually, we all agreed on a tree that would brighten our Christmas. But before we could cut it down, we had to take care of one more annual tradition.

"Okay kids, get in front of the tree and give me a nice smile," Christine said, taking the camera out of her purse.

"Oh, Mom," Patrick and Erin groaned in unison.

"I need this for our Christmas card. It will only take two seconds."

When Christine was done with the picture, it was time to get down to business. I cleared away some snow and lay down on the ground by the base of the tree. But before I started cutting, I stood up and turned to Patrick.

"Why don't you cut it down this year, Pat?"

"Really, Dad?"

"I think you're old enough now," I said, handing him the saw.

When Patrick finished, we waited for the tractor pulling a trailer to bring us to the entrance with other families that had found their perfect trees.

• • •

That's how our Christmas tree selection used to go, but sadly, this Christmas we wouldn't be making our annual trek to the Christmas tree farm. Patrick would not be coming home from his freshman year of college until December 22. Due to other holiday commitments, we could not wait until then to get our tree. We also could not bring ourselves to go to the Christmas tree farm without him.

So Christine and I went to a local retailer with Erin to pick out a tree that someone else had cut down. We found a nice one, but it could not compete with any tree we had brought home from the farm.

"Penny for your thoughts?" Christine asked me as we inched forward in the line at the store.

I did not respond, lost in thought.

"Hello? Anyone in there?" Erin asked, shaking my arm.

"Oh, sorry, I was spacing out there for a minute," I said.

"No kidding. What were you thinking about?" Christine asked.

"The Christmas tree farm—lots of great memories out there."

Turning to my daughter I asked, "What is your favorite memory of the Christmas tree farm?"

"Probably the time we saw the baby deer," she replied. "She was so cute."

"That was very cool," I said. "What do you think your brother's favorite memory was?"

Erin thought about the question for a few moments before replying.

"Well, we all know his favorite part of the trip each year was stopping at the diner for lunch on the way home."

Christine and I laughed and nodded in agreement.

"But the time he nailed you with the snowball was probably his favorite."

"I'm sure it was," I replied, smiling.

As I wrestled with the tree—and my thoughts—while tying it to the roof of the van, a comforting thought occurred to me. It had always been the time we spent together as a family at the Christmas tree farm that was perfect—not the trees.

~Ron Geelan

98

Houston, We Have Lift-Off

It is common sense to take a method and try it. If it fails, admit it frankly and try another. But above all, try something.
~Franklin D. Roosevelt

As soon as my four children were old enough, I began to teach them to bake. Standing on one of the kitchen chairs, the little ones were taught to count four cups of flour or two cups of sugar. With the bigger ones, I tackled fractions: ½ cup of butter or ¼ cup of honey.

As they got older, we tried to expand our expertise to include as many different cookies as possible. Not just chocolate chip, an all time favorite, but pecan sassies, lemon bars, peanut butter blossoms, and raspberry bars. The children were always on the lookout for new cookies. If they were at a friend's house and ran across one they liked, they never hesitated to ask for the recipe.

One year we decided to tackle gingerbread men. I bought an intricate cookie press with lots of details. We planned to hang them on the Christmas tree. Unfortunately, the cookies refused to cooperate and every day a few more would fall off the tree. Of course, my children, Scott, Paula, Melissa, and Glen, had great fun with this.

"Mom, remember. The gingerbread man, he runs away as fast as he can."

"I bet it's peer pressure. Some of them do look a bit chunkier than the others."

"Maybe they're afraid we're going to eat them."

I started getting more creative. I decorated them with Royal Icing, the kind that dries really hard. I painted their faces and clothing. With a garlic press, I made elaborate hairdos; long flowing tresses for the girls and short curly cuts for the boys. The gingerbread people looked great, but they still kept falling off the tree. One year I tried baking them until they were as hard as rocks. I even varnished them, but to no avail. No matter what I did, they wouldn't stay on the tree.

My husband Ed decided they might be too heavy, so he built a small wooden Christmas tree that would hold six boys and six girls. I put the tree on my kitchen counter and hoped for the best.

The next morning, my youngest son Glen came into my bedroom.

"Mom, I have bad news for you. Four of your gingerbread man tried to rappel down the kitchen cabinet and fell to their death. I found them lying on the kitchen floor."

Soon all four of the children began offering suggestions.

"Mom, maybe you haven't told them that you love them as often as you should."

"Have you listened — really listened — to their problems?"

"Since the house is empty all day, we need to play music for them while we're gone. I bet they're lonely."

"Should we ask around school, find a good therapist that they can talk to?"

They began stopping by the tree when they got home from school.

"How was your day?" they'd ask.

"Remember, we really care about you and promise never to eat you."

One night, my oldest son Scott put the tree in the middle of the kitchen table so the gingerbread people would feel like they were part of the family.

I never thought of giving up. I was too determined, or perhaps just too stubborn.

Always searching for the perfect one, I tried more recipes than I can even count. The day I heard Martha Stewart was doing a show on gingerbread, I was so excited that I took half a day off from work. I dutifully copied down every ingredient and all her directions. At the end of the show Martha casually commented, "Of course, if you live in a very humid climate, no matter what you do; they'll never stay on the tree."

I couldn't believe it—there was my answer. I wasn't inadequate and it wasn't a defective recipe. Martha said it wasn't my fault. It was Houston's fault. I was vindicated.

That night, I couldn't wait to tell the children the good news. We all had a good laugh. They said they always had faith in me and knew I would find the answer. They just didn't expect it to take ten years. I finally accepted defeat and bought wooden gingerbread ornaments for my tree.

I guess you never know what will start a family tradition. My fascination with the gingerbread world has become woven into the fabric of our family. Over the years, my children and grandchildren keep buying me gingerbread items for my kitchen. So if you happen to visit my house around the holidays, I'll be happy to show you my extensive gingerbread collection. The day I baked my first gingerbread man, I never dreamed it would take me on such a long journey. I just know that my gingerbread people have provided my family with some very tasty treats and lots of laughs.

~Barbara Ann Carle

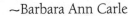

99

Blessing of the Box

Tradition is a guide and not a jailer.
~W. Somerset Maugham

We've had a Christmas box since Linnea was small," my friend Marcia said.

I took a sip of coffee and inquired. "What's a Christmas box?"

"Well, we do a twelve-days-before-Christmas countdown. I choose an activity for each day. I write the activity on decorated index cards. The activities may be something like wrapping gifts, baking cookies, or singing carols for a sick loved one," she said.

I smiled. I liked the idea.

Marcia proceeded to share. She was a four-star mom and I wanted to listen. "Each day, we pull one activity from the box. My girls learn a lot, and it helps to pass those long days before Christmas."

I could tell by the joy in my friend's warm brown eyes that the Christmas box had been a real blessing for her family. I wanted that blessing for my family, too.

The next day, I made a trip to the craft store. I found a beautiful box. Gold. Shiny. Removable lid. Just the right size to sit on our mantle. I also bought a smart pack of dark green index cards. Perfect for the activities. When I got home, I had a personal brainstorm. Read a book about Christmas. Dance to a Christmas CD. Pour hot chocolate in a thermos and take a ride to see Christmas lights. Bake gingerbread men. I printed the activities in bold, clear script and was certain that my five boys would love, love, love the Christmas box. We were all about tradition. This new one would be just right.

"I think it's a great idea," my husband said.

"Me, too." I was fully satisfied and filled with joyful anticipation. I couldn't wait for the twelfth day before Christmas.

December opened like a racehorse at the starting block. Hard. Fast. There were activities. Parties. Programs. Precious times with family and friends. Before I could blink, it was time to begin the Twelve Days of Christmas activities.

I introduced the box and plunked it on the mantle. My five sons, staggered in age from fifteen to one, smiled.

"Tell me what's in the box!" said five-year old Samuel. "What will we do? Where will we go? Will we make crafts?"

"Crafts," three-year-old Gabriel said. "I love crafts. Can we paint?"

"Well, tomorrow will tell, guys," I said. "We'll begin tomorrow. I'm excited, too. This will be fun, fun, fun."

The next day we extracted a crisp, green card from the gold box. "Sing Christmas carols around the Christmas tree." Simple enough. After dinner, my family assembled around the tree. We had a glorious time.

The next day's activity wasn't as serene. The day was already jam-packed full. It was our homeschool co-op gingerbread baking day. Then we had program practice for church. The card we pulled from the box said "Help put stamps on Christmas cards." I hadn't even bought the cards. I jabbed it back into the box and rooted around for something simpler. "Read *'Twas the Night Before Christmas*" was a better fit. Even still, with the busyness of the day, the activity brought me some stress.

The next day's activity was to bake cookies. We squeezed the gingerbread boys between a piano recital and dinner with friends. By the fourth day, I was exhausted, and the box was only adding to my holiday fatigue. It had become one more thing to do. One more December pressure.

"I don't think that it's supposed to be an anxiety filled thing," my husband said. "It's for fun. If you're not having fun, then stop."

"But the boys love the Christmas box. It's special. They look forward to the activities. They count on it."

"Even still," Lonny said. "If you're stressing about having fun, you're not having fun."

I knew that he was right. But I kept seeing the happiness in the green eyes of my sweet band of sons. So what if I wanted to take the box and hide it in the fresh fallen snow? The kids were having a blast.

It was two days before Christmas when I'd just had enough. My shopping wasn't complete. I had to plan the Christmas Eve menu. I needed to bake two-dozen more cookies for a social at church. When little Gabriel tugged on the back of my sweater, I felt my blood pressure rise. One more thing on my list. The blasted blessing of the box.

"Mom," Gabriel said. "There's two more days until Christmas."

"I know sweet boy," I said.

"Well, I was wondering..."

"Gabriel, I love you. But I can't take time for the box just now," I snapped. "I have a long list of things to do. When I'm finished, I'll think about driving to see lights or making snow angels or cutting gift tags from old Christmas cards."

Gabe's round, green eyes filled with tears. "I only wanted," he said, "to know if you could read to me." Then I noticed 'Twas the Night Before Christmas cuffed under his little arm.

"Oh, Gabe," I said. "Please forgive me. I was feeling tired. You only wanted to read."

I scooped my son into my arms. We snuggled deep into our big brown leather chair. I read to him and stroked his hair and enjoyed the sweet, simple moment of just holding my son.

It was all he really wanted. It was what I wanted, too.

The next morning I found myself brainstorming again. I removed the box from the mantle. Shook the activity cards to the table. Then I placed a small notebook and pencil inside the shiny, gold box.

"It's a blessing box," I announced to my five sons. "Instead of trying to create blessings, we're going to sit back and appreciate them. Whenever we see that we've received a Christmas blessing, we'll write it in this little notebook."

It didn't take long for the notebook to fill. Cookies with Mom. Sitting by the fire with Dad. Playing in the snow.

I still loved Marcia's idea. The activity box has been precious to her family, and I hope it will be for years to come. But we've found what works for our family, too. Our tradition. And it's just as sweet.

~Shawnelle Eliasen

100

The Treasure Hunt

*A great spouse loves you exactly as you are. An extraordinary spouse helps
you grow; inspires you to be, do and give your very best.*
~Fawn Weaver

I still went through the motions. Turned on the tree lights and
the Christmas music. Tried to find some of that old Christmas
morning magic. But, of course, it wasn't the same. The kids
and the grandkids were grown and gone, scattered from one
coast to the other. No one made it home for Christmas. Or rather, not
to our home. We'd been invited to join some other family members
but traveling during the holidays was such a bother. So Paul and I
just stayed home.

We slept in on Christmas mornings now. No more getting up at
five a.m. We wandered downstairs a little after nine. He got his coffee,
I got my tea, and we went in to sit by the tree. There were only a few
packages to open. A couple of the kids ordered something online
and had it shipped directly. We opened those as they arrived. Most
just sent gift cards. It was easier and they knew we really didn't need
anything.

I pulled out the boxes one by one and we took turns opening
them. The usual gifts — a sweater I'd admired at the mall, his season
pass to the golf course, the latest book by my favorite author — and
then we were done. I was gathering up the torn wrapping paper when
I caught Paul watching me with an odd expression.

"You missed something," he told me.

"I don't think so." I leaned down and looked under the tree. Nothing but the red plaid tree skirt.

"Not under the tree." He pointed higher, to a branch about half-way up. There was a small white envelope that read "Lin—1 of 5."

A treasure hunt. We used to do them for the kids, clues scattered around the house that would lead them to some gift that was too big to fit under the tree or maybe something extra special, or even just to get them over that "no more presents to open" let-down when they were young.

I stood up and retrieved the envelope. What would have prompted him to do this? I opened it and read the clue.

Seek your second clue under our very first treasure.

Our very first treasure? How am I supposed to remember? Oh. Our first treasure hunt. It was our first year together. Newlyweds and poor as church mice, I had fallen in love with a painting at a local gallery, something we could not afford but my silly husband had bought for me anyway. He'd led me by clues stashed all over our tiny apartment to the back of the closet where he'd hidden it the day before. It had been the showpiece of our living room; now it hung in the unused guest room, pretty much forgotten. I felt a sharp twinge of regret as I eased the second envelope from under its frame.

I was gone so long and how you welcomed me back.

Gone so long? He must mean that year his job took him out of the country. Thirteen months. The kids and I decided to save his separation bonus and add to it all year, sacrificing Friday night pizza and movies and special treats, so we could surprise him when he came home. I remember that weekend, walking him through the showroom, "just to look," coaxing him to tell us the one he liked best. That beautiful full-sized pool table he had always wanted. I'd had it delivered the day before Christmas and charged the kids with making sure he didn't go down to the basement that night.

I made my way downstairs and looked at the pool table. Green vinyl covered the orange felt. I could almost hear the sound of pool balls clacking and the kids yelling, "I call the winner." Now it sat covered with empty boxes that waited for Christmas decorations to be packed away after New Year's. My already sagging spirits drooped lower. What was Paul thinking? Pointing out all the things we had worked so hard for? Things we had once thought so important, that were now unused and collecting dust. I had to force myself to read the next clue.

You were so mad because I was gone on Christmas Eve. And the kids wouldn't tell you why.

The piano. He bought it used and went to pick it up that Christmas Eve. My piano. I'd always played and I was certain I could teach the kids. I did, too. A couple of them still play. But I don't. Not anymore. My fingers are stiff with arthritis and won't dance over the keys like they used to. Just like the pool table, the piano sat idle. Collecting dust. All that money wasted. I felt myself getting angry. What was Paul trying to say here? Okay, so I didn't play the piano any more. He didn't play on his precious pool table anymore either. I picked up the next clue and ripped it open.

We bought six that year. All brand new, in different sizes and colors.

The bicycles. Oh, what a year that was. New bicycles for everyone. No hand-me-downs, with the younger boys forced to ride their older sisters' "girl bikes." We rode together every Sunday, all the way to the state park and back. Even when the older ones were pulling away, starting their own lives, they'd come back for our Sunday rides. I walked into the garage. Only two bikes remained, hanging from the ceiling on large orange hooks. Unused, yes, but loved in their day. And then I got it. I felt my anger slip away. I pulled the last envelope out of the spokes of a wheel.

Two full shelves. I always ask if we need them all.

My photo albums. Filling the shelves Paul built into the spare room closet for me. Our whole lives, captured and laid out, year after year. I hurried upstairs where Paul was waiting for me. I understood now what he'd been trying to show me. Not the forgotten painting or the unused pool table. Not the piano or the bikes, most of which were long gone. They were just things, and it wasn't about things. Not at all. It was about the sacrificing, and the giving, and the sharing, and the memories. I looked at him standing there, a hint of hopefulness in his smile.

"I thought maybe we'd spend the day looking at some of these," he offered.

I returned his smile with one brighter than I'd given him in a long time. "Let's start with the first one," I said. "And look at them all."

~LD Masterson

The Twelve Days of Surprises

Each day comes bearing its own gifts. Untie the ribbons.
~Ruth Ann Schabacker

Our best Christmas ever started with a twig—or a small tree limb leaning against a kitchen cabinet. "Where did that twig come from?" I asked my husband Richard.

We had just said goodbye to our oldest grandson, who often stopped on his way home from high school. Our entire family was still reeling from the news we had received in September that Richard's colon cancer was stage four and he had weeks, maybe a few months to live. Since that traumatic surprise diagnosis, the brightest hours of our day included visits from our children and grandchildren.

Twenty-four hours later, Cole stopped by again and now the twig sat in a coffee can with no explanation. The following day, he casually added a piece of artificial fruit and a pathetic looking bird.

"Do you suppose that has something to do with a partridge in a pear tree?" Richard commented.

The following day, our youngest daughter Beth stopped by with her two daughters, Annabelle, three, and Lily, one. When I opened the door Annabelle handed me a box of chocolate turtles.

"Thanks but I'm just not hungry," Richard said when I showed him our gift.

"Mom! Dad!" Beth said, her voice sounding rather impatient. "Don't you get it? Cole brought the partridge in the pear tree and these are the two turtle doves."

"Well duh! We finally get it," we both answered. "Is there going to be more?"

"You'll just have to wait and see," Beth answered mysteriously.

On Monday afternoon, our older daughter, Richelle called and asked, "What time are you planning dinner? We'd like to visit after the triplets get home from school."

"Great!" I said. "We'll look forward to seeing all of you."

The doorbell rang about five o'clock and in walked three eleven-year-old boys, wearing white shirts, black pants, black berets, and fake mustaches. "Goot eve'ning, Madam, Monsieur," Kit uttered with his best French accent.

"We've brought French bread for your dinner," Nate added as he gave me a basket of croissants.

"Merci," I played along and asked the third boy, "And what is your name, sir?"

"Uh, uh, I ees one of dee three French guys," Riley stammered. We all laughed and thanked them for adding a special remembrance to our day.

Tuesday brought more fun when our "calling bird" arrived. Lily toddled toward her grandfather, covered with feathers taped to her clothes and a plastic telephone snuggled next to her ear. "Hi, Bompa," she said, using the grandchildren's special nickname while holding out her hand for his usual high-five.

"Are you my calling bird?" he tenderly touched her hand and smiled. "You're worth at least four birds," he added.

Part of our week always included a day of chemotherapy treatment and those days were long and unpleasant. On the way home from the doctor's office, Richard wondered aloud, "I can't wait to see what the family has for us tonight." His newfound excitement was catching and I too focused on the evening's rendition of "five golden rings."

This time, the family member responsible for our evening's entertainment was our daughter-in-law, Kristi. "This isn't humorous like the others," she began. "Instead, I've brought five of my high school swimming medals. Each one represents a special gift you've given me."

After she had draped our necks with medals representing acceptance, understanding, caring, forgiveness, and love, all three faces were covered in tears. "You can keep the medals," she added as she was leaving. "May they remind you of how much I love you."

An ongoing discussion regarding the best all-time baseball player was the basis for the next day's Christmas surprise. Richard chose Walter Johnson and ten-year-old grandson Clayton argued that Nolan Ryan was the greatest. Clayton arrived wearing a T-shirt bearing the sign, "Walter Johnson, NO" written on the front, and "Nolan Ryan RULES" decorated with six golden eggs covered the back.

When the doorbell rang the next evening, I found an eight-year-old ballerina on our doorstep carrying a special basket of Beanie Babies—swans, ducks, chickens, and others. "This is my day to visit and I want to share my friends with you," Amanda said as she took each Beanie Baby out and set them on her Bompa's lap.

"Thanks for bringing your swans for us to see," we answered. "However, the best part is that we get to see you," we chorused.

Grandson Brady was known for his love of joke books so it wasn't a surprise when he incorporated jokes on his special day. The surprise was his milking maid costume. With a scarf tied around his head, an apron tied around his waist, and two pails tied to a broom handle laying across his shoulders, this thirteen-year-old boy had us laughing before he ever told us one of the eight jokes he'd written on pieces of paper and placed in his milk pails.

On the ninth evening, the five females in the family plus four giggling males turned on the radio and joined in the twirling and two-step dancing around the room. We all laughed and clapped to the beat of the music.

"What do you think they're going to do tonight?" Richard asked early the next morning. When that evening was over, we both vowed we'd never forget the ten lords-a-leaping. Three adult men and seven boys filed in wearing tights under their swimming trunks, Burger King crowns on their heads and began jumping and leaping until our family room floor vibrated.

On Christmas Eve, our favorite evening of the whole year, all eighteen of us followed our usual schedule of an early Christmas dinner, attending church services, and then heading back to our house for family time together. "Mom and Dad, we want you to sit here in the living room," our son Ryan suggested, "And we'll begin our eleventh day celebration."

Then the music began—"kazoo" music and singers singing, "On the first day of Christmas, our family gave to you..." Each child wore or carried the costume he or she had used for their designated Christmas Surprise Day. They sang the entire song and when they sang, "On the eleventh day of Christmas, our family gave to you," Ryan stepped forward and said, "Eleven plus family members who all love you very, very much."

Once again, they left us wanting more. As they sang, "On the twelfth day of Christmas, my family gave to me," Clayton announced, "You'll just have to wait and see!"

On Christmas morning, the director of the twelve previous events, son-in-law Bob, handed me a copy of *The Real 12 Days of Christmas*, autographed by each member of our family. He asked me to read it out loud. Our group quieted and I began reading how the true love, the giver of the gifts, represents God. God's first gift, the valiant partridge was an ancient symbol for Jesus and the pear tree represents the cross. The fascinating story of the Christmas carol that brought overwhelming joy to our family took on new meaning.

After everyone left and we were settled in our recliners, Richard said, "This was the best Christmas I ever had."

Sometimes God saves the best for last.

~Betty Johnson Dalrymple

It's Christmas!

Meet Our Contributors
Meet Our Authors
Thank You
About Chicken Soup for the Soul

Meet Our
Contributors

Kristina J. Adams has bachelor's and master's degrees in Elementary Education and minored in English as a Second Language. Teaching sixth grade social studies in Middlebury, IN, she enjoys relating stories of growing up overseas when they connect to curriculum. She and her husband Ryan have two children, Mackenzie and Carter.

Deborah Agler received her master's degree from Purdue University. She has a communications consulting firm, teaches communications and journalism at the university level, and writes features, nonfiction, and Christian-themed novels for young people. Spending time with her wonderful family is her great joy! E-mail her at agler.deborah@gmail.com.

Laura Amann is a freelance writer and editor. She lives in the Chicago area with her husband and four children. Her award-winning essays have appeared in *Salon, Brain, Child, Chicago Parent* and Sun-Times Media. E-mail her at laura@laura-amann.com.

Ximena Tagle Ames was born in Chile and came to the United States in 1954. After retiring from a career as a psychotherapist, she began to pursue her love of writing and has won prizes for her poetry. E-mail her at ximena622@hotmail.com.

Andrea B. teaches middle school Language Arts in Oregon. She enjoys going to the beach with her family, baking her grandmother's famous breads, taking Taekwondo classes with her family, and practicing yoga. In her spare time, Annie likes to write about her family memories and classroom experiences.

Jennifer Yardley Barney received her master's degree in psychology from Utah State University. She works as a school psychologist with children from elementary school to high school. Jennifer and her husband, Andrew, love hiking, backpacking, playing board games, and spending time with their families.

Garrett Bauman has written frequently for the *Chicken Soup for the Soul* series, as well as for *Sierra*, *Yankee* and other publications. He retired a few years ago as a professor of English to assume full-time duties as grandpa and chief engineer of the family. E-mail him at garrett.bauman@yahoo.com.

Kara M. Bietz writes young adult fiction from her home in North Georgia, where she lives with her husband Steven and their two children, Ryan and Lauren. Her husband and children are her biggest cheerleaders, as well as an endless source of inspiration and laughter.

Barbara Black is an award-winning writer with thirty years experience, publishing fiction, non-fiction, poetry, articles, and opinion columns, as well as book, theater, and film reviews. She loves adventure travel, the arts, and gardening. She lives in Victoria, BC, with her cat and philosopher. E-mail her at barbaralb@telus.net.

Lil Blosfield is the Chief Financial Officer for Child and Adolescent Behavioral Health. She loves writing and has been published in several *Chicken Soup for the Soul* anthologies. In addition to writing, Lil enjoys family time, warm summer days and cozy winter nights. She always makes sure to take time to laugh! E-mail her at LBlosfield40@msn.com.

Long Beach, Washington author **Jan Bono's** specialty is humorous personal experience. She has published several such collections, two poetry chapbooks, nine one-act plays, and a dinner theater mystery. She's written for *Guideposts*, *Star*, and *Woman's World*, currently writing a mystery series set on the southwest Washington coast. Learn more at www.JanBonoBooks.com.

Debra Ayers Brown is a writer, humorist, blogger, magazine columnist, and award-winning marketing professional. Her stories have appeared in the *Chicken Soup for the Soul* series, *Guideposts*, *Woman's World*, *Liberty Life*, and others. She is a Southeastern Writers Association Board Member. Learn more at www.About.Me/DebraAyersBrown.

Leigh Ann Bryant loves to read, write, travel, and spend time with family. She and her husband Lonnie share three sons and three granddaughters. She is the author of *In My Defense*, a narrative nonfiction about domestic violence and the consequences of taking her abuser's life in self-defense. Learn more at www.leighannbryant.com.

Lori Bryant is an author, speaker, poet and inspirational storyteller. She enjoys working with women and speaks regularly in California women's prisons. She is a frequent contributor to the *Chicken Soup for the Soul* series as well as *Zoe Life* devotionals and *Conversations of Courage*. E-mail her at Lobrya9@aol.com.

John P. Buentello is the author of essays, stories and poetry. He is the co-author of the novel *Reproduction Rights* and the short story collection *Binary Tales*. He is currently at work on a mystery novel and a collection of children's poetry. E-mail him at jakkhakk@yahoo.com.

Dawn Byrne is a married mother of four and a grandmother. She writes full-time from her home in southern New Jersey about fictional and non-fictional families. She is a member of three writers' groups, teaches Sunday school and volunteers for Habitat for Humanity. Reading is her obsession.

Barbara Canale is a Catholic freelance writer. She has been published in twelve books in the *Chicken Soup for the Soul* series. She is the author of *Our Labor of Love: A Romanian Adoption Chronicle*, and *Prayers, Papers & Play: Devotions for Every College Student*, from Liguori Publications. She volunteers in her church and community.

Lorraine Cannistra received her Bachelor of Science degree in English and Master of Science degree in Rehabilitation Counseling from Emporia State University. She enjoys advocating, cooking, reading, writing and motivational speaking. Her passion is wheelchair ballroom dance. Read her blog at healthonwheels.wordpress.com and e-mail her at lcannistra@yahoo.com.

Barbara Ann Carle is a personal essay writer and poet. Her work has been published in various anthologies including *Chicken Soup for the Soul: Grieving and Recovery*. Her poems have been widely published. She is a mother of four, grandmother of six and lives in Friendswood, TX with her husband.

Gene Chase is a retired professor of mathematics and computer science from Messiah College. He teaches History of Mathematics part-time. This autobiographical essay is part of his desire to leave a legacy of family for his children and grandchildren. E-mail him at chase@messiah.edu.

Michele Christian-Oldham has been an established writer for over twenty years. She is a freelance writer for a local newspaper and has a variety of published short stories. Michele is currently working on her first children's book. E-mail her at michelechristian819@yahoo.com or visit her website www.michelechristianoldham.com.

Lisa Ricard Claro is a freelance commercial copywriter and award-winning short story author, nominated in 2012 for the Pushcart Prize. Published across multiple media, Lisa is a member of RWA/GRW and SCBWI. She resides in Georgia with her husband of thirty-three years and believes in love and happy endings.

Liz Cook is a recently retired nurse, pastor's wife, mother, grandmother and foster parent. She loves to spend time with her family, writing, and looking after babies who need special love and attention. She plans to concentrate future writing on children's stories. E-mail her at lizard1203@sbcglobal.net.

Sharron Cosby enjoys reading, writing, and family time. Her first book, a devotional, entitled *Praying for Your Addicted Loved One: 90 in 90* was released in 2013. Follow her blog at www.efamilyrecovery.com and e-mail her at skcosby@aol.com.

Betty Johnson Dalrymple is a freelance writer of inspirational devotions and stories and a contributor to numerous popular devotional books. She enjoys traveling, golfing and spending time with her husband and their large blended family consisting of nineteen grandchildren.

Connie Davidson is a wife, mother and grandma. She received her Social Service Worker diploma with honours from Fanshawe College and lives in Southern Ontario, Canada. This is Connie's first story submitted for publication. Connie enjoys writing poetry as well. E-mail her at cdavidson001@amtelecom.net.

Star Davies received her Associate of Arts degree with high honors and is pursuing her Bachelor of Arts degree in Professional Writing. She works as a freelance fantasy writer and as a writing specialist for the University of Wisconsin. Star lives with her husband and two young children. Learn more at www.stardavies.com.

Linda C. Defew admits that her writing is a blessing. Telling her life experiences, which included a debilitating disease, turned her life around. Now, she writes hoping to inspire other women who face obstacles to follow her lead. E-mail her at oldest@tds.net.

Pam Depoyan holds a B.A. degree in English from Loyola Marymount University, Los Angeles, CA. Her writing has appeared in *Highlights for Children*, *Pray*, and the *Chicken Soup for the Soul* series. She loves crafting "word-photo stories" that draw readers into their own moments of God's wonder. Read more at wordglow.wordpress.com.

Jeannie Dotson teaches middle school in Powell County, Kentucky. She enjoys writing, reading poetry, and teaching kids. This is her third contribution to the *Chicken Soup for the Soul* anthology.

Shawnelle Eliasen and her husband Lonny raise their brood of boys in Illinois. Her stories have been published in *Guideposts*, *MomSense* magazine, *Marriage Partnership*, *Thriving Family*, *Cup of Comfort* books, numerous *Chicken Soup for the Soul* anthologies, and more. Visit her blog, "Family Grace with My Five Sons," at Shawnellewrites. blogspot.com.

Laura Guman Fabiani has always loved the season of Christmas, especially decorating with the homemade gifts from her children. She still believes in the magic of Santa Claus. E-mail Laura at LGF8998@ gmail.com.

RoseAnn Faulkner is a retired elementary school teacher from Yuma, AZ. She credits her writing group, Write on the Edge, for providing inspiration, encouragement and invaluable story critiques. RoseAnn is married and has two sons. E-mail her at roseannfaulkner@gmail. com.

Peggy Frezon is author of the newly released book *The Dieting with my Dog Guide to Weight Loss and Maintenance*, and other books about dogs. She's also editor at Be the Change for Animals. Fetch her free newsletter, *Pawsitively Pets*, at peggyfrezon.blogspot.com/p/pawsitively-pets.html. Connect at her blog www.peggyfrezon.blogspot.com, Facebook www.facebook.com/PeggyFrezonBooks or Twitter @peggyfrezon.

Lynn Gale is a part-time writer who lives in Alberta, Canada, with her husband, JP. She writes short stories, middle grade novels and adult romance. Through Sundowners Toastmasters, she turns her love of storytelling into speeches. She believes in finding and following your passion no matter what your age. Learn more at www.lynngale.ca.

Ron Geelan received his bachelor's degree from Providence College in 1992. After spending fifteen years in financial services, he is now pursuing a career in law enforcement. Ron is a previous contributor to the *Chicken Soup for the Soul* series, and his articles and essays have appeared in numerous regional and national publications.

Joyce Hager writes and is copy editor for *Echoes of LBI*, the arts and lifestyle magazine of Long Beach Island, NJ. She is currently working on a memoir about growing up with her older brother who is intellectually disabled. Read Joyce's blog "Musing Off the Mat" at www.joycehager.com.

Janie Hall has written talks and newsletters for Baptist Marriage Encounter and has been published in *Texas Outdoor Sports News*, *Senior Circle*, *Western Woman* and *Granbury Showcase* magazines. Janie has two published books, *Scooter's Adventures* and *Duty Honor Courage* and is a member of Writers' Bloc of Granbury, Texas where she lives.

Gloria Jean Hansen has been a writer since childhood, mother, grandmother, nurse and bluegrass musician more recently. She enjoys writing, camping with family, and skiing in her spare time. She has written five published books. One day she will live by the river and write full-time. E-mail her at glowin@persona.ca.

Jill Haymaker is a family law attorney in Fort Collins, CO. She received her law degree from the University of Nebraska in 1995. She enjoys outdoor activities and sporting events with her three grown children and three granddaughters. She also writes contemporary romance novels. E-mail her at jillhaymaker@aol.com.

Jamie Henderson is a freelance writer who lives in Maine.

Zach Hively earned degrees at the University of New Mexico and Trinity College Dublin, as well as a Fulbright grant to Germany. He works as a freelance editor, writer, and teacher. He is also an environmental journalist for the *New Mexico Mercury*. E-mail him at znhively@gmail.com.

Jill Jackson earned a Bachelor of Science degree from Eastern Michigan University with majors in Consumer Affairs and Written Communications. She has worked as a manager in health care and human services. She enjoys being a full-time mom to her three wonderful sons and writes in her free time.

M.M. Jarrell received her M.S. degree in Instructional Design from the University of South Alabama. As an academic advisor in higher education, she works with students to accomplish goals. Her philosophy is that challenges make us stronger, so view them as a learning tool. Ballroom dancing is her passion. E-mail her at mmjarrel@gmail.com.

Amy Travison Jasiewicz graduated *summa cum laude* from The College of Saint Rose with a B.A. degree in Public Communications. She is a freelance writer and editor and enjoys photography and volunteering.

Her two daughters are her greatest creation and inspiration. E-mail her at amytjaz@nycap.rr.com.

Ron Kaiser lives in wonder that the most strikingly beautiful and witty woman ever to have lived chose to marry him. Compared to Ron Kaiser's wife, Helen of Troy would look like a poorly embalmed, 2,000-year-old mummy. His wife's hair alone is enough to make men cry.

Fallon Kane is thrilled to appear in her third *Chicken Soup for the Soul* book. She is currently studying psychology and criminal justice at Adelphi University. She would like to thank her mother, brother, Lucille, Kyle, Meredith, Casey, and the Bryants for everything they do for her. E-mail her at fluffyfallon@aol.com.

Jill Kemerer writes inspirational romance novels. Coffee fuels her mornings; chocolate, her afternoons. After graduating *magna cum laude* and working as an electrical engineer, Jill became a stay-at-home mom. When not writing, she adores magazines, fluffy animals, and her hilarious family. Connect with Jill at www.jillkemerer.com.

Vicki Kitchner recently retired after teaching Exceptional Student Education for thirty years. She and her husband divide their time between North Carolina and Florida unless they're off on an adventure such as backpacking around Mont Blanc or floating down the Colorado River in a dory. E-mail her at Vicki@hikersrest.com.

Elsie Schmied Knoke, a retired RN, has been published in *Chicken Soup for the Nurse's Soul* and *Chicken Soup for the Soul: True Love*. She enjoys singing in her church choir and working with their quilting projects. She has five granddaughters and four great-grandchildren. E-mail her at esknoke@bellsouth.net.

Miranda Koerner is a writer living in San Antonio, TX, with her husband and two Chihuahuas, Bitty and Bear. She's been published in *Chicken Soup for the Soul: Food and Love* and several magazines and newspapers. Her YA novel, *Butterfly Dress*, and middle grade novel, *Blue Mermaid*, are available. Visit www.wordsnwhimsy.com.

Joyce Laird is a freelance writer living in Southern California. Her features have been published in magazines including, *Cat Fancy*, *Grit*, *Mature Living*, and *Vibrant Life*. She contributes regularly to *Woman's World* and to the *Chicken Soup for the Soul* anthology. Joyce is also a member of Mystery Writers of America.

Dorothy LaMantia writes stories of everyday redemption and faith. A former English teacher, she has won an award for reporting from the Catholic Press Association. She is married, has three children, and loves being a grandmother. E-mail her at dotelama@aol.com.

Monika LaPlante is a marine biologist and environmental scientist with a Bachelor of Science degree from Northeastern University. She is currently a graduate student at Pace University studying Computer Science. Monika is an avid scuba diver and underwater filmmaker. Check out her films on her website at www.monikalaplante.com.

Rick Lauber is the author of *Caregiver's Guide for Canadians*, a freelance writer (print and online) and graduate of the Professional Writing Program (Grant MacEwan University—Edmonton, AB). E-mail him at lauber.rick@gmail.com.

Lynne Leite has two great loves—faith and family. She is a speaker and author and desires to be a blessing to others by sharing stories of hope and inspiration. You can learn more about Lynne and read her devotional blog by visiting her website at www.CurlyGirl4God.com.

JéAnne Leites received her diploma in freelance journalism in 1997. She has published several magazine articles and currently maintains a Christian poetry website. Ms. Leites lives with her husband, Robert, and her son, Denver, in a small town in North Carolina.

Kathy Levine has been writing about books for the publishing industry since 1986 and her essays have been published in *Newsday* and *The New York Times*. A graduate of Adelphi University, she is a member of the Long Island Writers' Guild and Literacy Volunteers. E-mail her at kathylevine1@optonline.net.

Jaye Lewis is an award-winning inspirational author from the Appalachian Mountains of Virginia. Her constant companion is her doxie Dixie Mae, a rescue from a puppy mill. Jaye celebrates the miracles of every day by keeping her heart open. Visit Jaye's author page on Facebook at www.facebook.com/JayeLewisAuthor?ref=hl.

Jane Lonnqvist is a retired high school special education teacher, married forty-two years with two sons and two grandsons. She has had more than forty short stories published in small and literary magazines and was a columnist for four years with a local newspaper. Jane still submits occasional columns. Contact her at nlonn@yahoo. com.

Ed Marriott once said, "To me, Christmas is about the birth of our Lord and Savior, Christmas carols, family and friends sharing a meal, giving toys to children, food baskets; and maybe, for a few days a year, we treat each other with a little more caring, kindness and respect." Ed passed away on 04/12/2013. He will be missed!

Born in Boston and a die-hard Red Sox fan, **LD Masterson** lives in Ohio where she divides her time between writing and enjoying her grandchildren. She writes mystery and suspense, and recently published a short story in the anthology *Flights of Fiction*. Catch her at ldmasterson-author.blogspot.com or e-mail her at lin@ldmasterson. com.

Louise McConnell is a teacher and pastor. She has enjoyed reading all her life and has recently decided to try her hand at both fiction and non-fiction writing. E-mail her at quileydown@yahoo.com.

Annette McDermott is a freelance writer and children's author whose work has been published in both adult and children's magazines and online. She enjoys writing about a wide variety of subjects but specializes in holistic living topics. When she's not busy writing and raising her family, Annette enjoys singing, gardening, and reading. E-mail her at annette@annettemcdermott.net.

Bridget McNamara-Fenesy is a business consultant when she is not pursuing her passion of writing, and holds a BA degree from the University of Notre Dame, and a JD degree from the University of Denver. She thanks her family for being the source of her muse. E-mail her at bridgetmcnamara@comcast.net.

Jane Miller is the founder of The RUFF Writers, www.theruffwriters.com, an intergenerational writing project that started with visits to a personal care home with her youngest daughter (the baby in the story) and the family dog. Jane is an adjunct journalism instructor at the Penn State Greater Allegheny campus. She and her husband Rick have been married for thirty-four years.

Kevin Mims lives in Sacramento, CA with his wife, Julie. He is a notary public, the operator of a vintage cookbook business, and a freelance writer. His work has appeared in *The New York Times*, *Ellery Queen's Mystery Magazine*, on National Public Radio, and elsewhere.

Katie Mitchell received her Bachelor of Arts degree, with honors, from Missouri State University. Currently, she is Communications Manager for a large outdoor retailer. She enjoys reading, traveling, flea markets, volunteering with non-profits and is a Big Sis in the Big Brothers Big Sisters organization.

Marya Morin is a freelance writer. Her stories and poems have appeared in publications such as *Woman's World* and Hallmark. Marya also penned a weekly humor column for an online newsletter, and writes custom poetry on request. She lives in the country with her husband. E-mail her at Akushla514@hotmail.com.

Nicole L.V. Mullis is a columnist and playwright living in Michigan. Her work has appeared in the *Battle Creek Enquirer* (2006-present), Stage of Life, *Mount Hope* magazine, *The Broken Plate*, and *Epiphany*. Her play, *On Bended Knee*, was the 2013 recipient of the Robert J. Pickering Award for Playwriting Excellence.

Katie O'Connell is a writer, teacher, mother of two, and lover of all things creative and inspiring. She is passionate about observing life's little moments and the lessons they reveal if we give them our attention. Katie is currently completing a children's book about her grandfather.

Mark Parisi's award-winning "off the mark" cartoon appears in newspapers worldwide. You can also find his cartoons on calendars, cards, books, T-shirts and more. Visit www.offthemark.com to view 7000+ cartoons. Mark resides in Massachusetts with his wife and business partner, Lynn, along with their daughter, Jen, three cats and a dog.

Melba Payne is a graduate of Texas Christian University. She is the wife of a retired Air Force Lt. Colonel, mother of two daughters and Nana to five fabulous grandchildren! She is a retired kindergarten teacher who enjoys writing and photography.

Melissa Pearn is currently enrolled in her fourth year at the University of Ontario Institute of Technology working toward her bachelor's degree (honours) in Criminology and Justice Studies. Melissa enjoys reading, writing, and spending time with family. She aspires to become a lawyer and hopes to continue writing in the future.

Stephanie Piro is the Saturday chick of King Features' "Six Chix" team of women cartoonists. She also draws and writes the single panel

"Fair Game." Her cartoons have been published in magazines, books, cards and calendars. She also designs gift items for her Cafepress Shop and Etsy shop. Learn more at www.stephaniepiro.com and stephanie-piro.blogspot.com/.

Winter Prosapio is an award-winning humor columnist, freelance travel writer and media relations expert. Her regular humor column appears in the New Braunfels *Herald-Zeitung*. Her writing has appeared in numerous publications and she's the author of two books.

Susan R. Ray's weekly newspaper column "Where We Are" is available at susanrray.com. A retired teacher, she plays with her six grandchildren, bakes bread, plays *Scrabble*, stitches, reads, and writes—columns, memoirs, and stories for her grands and contributes to the *Chicken Soup for the Soul* series. E-mail her at srray@charter. net.

Dan Reynolds' cartoons are seen in every city in the country via greeting cards (from American Greetings, Papyrus, Nobleworks, and others) and nationally in *Reader's Digest*.

Annie Riess is a freelance writer of stories about faith and family and has had numerous articles published in magazines and periodicals. She also teaches piano and farms with her husband in Western Canada. Annie takes pleasure in spending time with family and friends. E-mail her at writerariess@gmail.com.

Bruce Robinson is an award-winning internationally published cartoonist whose work has appeared in many consumer and trade magazines including the *National Enquirer*, *The Saturday Evening Post* and *Woman's World*. He is also the author of *Good Medicine* and *Bow Wows & Meows* Dog/Cat cartoon books. Visit him at www.BowWowsAndMeows.net or e-mail him at CartoonsByBruceRobinson@hotmail.com.

Nan Rockey graduated from Taylor University in 2012 with a BA degree in Media Communications and a writing emphasis. She married a fellow writer, Jordan Rockey, in February 2013 and enjoys creating stories and spending time with her husband and pet tortoise in Bloomington, IN. E-mail her at nanleajohnson@gmail.com.

Angela Rolleman is a social worker, writer, speaker, trainer, entrepreneur, wife, daughter, aunt, sister and friend. She is founder of Mission: Empowerment, a company that provides personal and professional development seminars and events. Angela loves animals, travelling, reading and spending time in nature. To learn more, visit www.angelarolleman.com or www.missionempowerment.ca.

Mona Rottinghaus has a passion for life, continually seeking new challenges. Her hobbies include sewing, embroidering, writing, music, and gardening. She plans to write an inspirational book documenting her journey into the world of mental illness and the lessons she learned. Learn more at monatheoriginal.blogspot.com or e-mail her at mona@monasoriginals.com.

Gretchen Schiller holds out hope that one day eggnog will be for sale throughout summer. Recently divorced, she's co-parenting with her ex-husband to raise their happy three-year-old daughter, Ana Lucia. Gretchen has started an online community via her website that supports and encourages healthy co-parenting. Visit her website at www.sassysinglemom.com.

After a twenty-five-year career in the communications industry, **Jackie Shelton** still has a hard time focusing on any one area of it, so she's stopped trying. Now she runs a small marketing firm and teaches journalism in Reno. Her most important role, though, is mother to two teen sons. Learn more at www.jax-marketing.com.

Margie Reins Smith is a retired journalist. She now writes for local publications, volunteers as a docent at the Detroit Institute of Arts, tutors Detroit Public School children in reading, maintains a blog (margiereinssmith.weebly.com) and dotes on her four grandchildren. E-mail her at ms0006@comcast.net.

Diane Stark is a former teacher turned stay-at-home mom and freelance writer. She loves to write about the important things in life: her family and her faith. She is a frequent contributor to the *Chicken Soup for the Soul* series. E-mail Diane at DianeStark19@yahoo.com.

L.A. Strucke is a writer, songwriter and producer. A lifelong advocate for the arts, she seeks to inspire others through words and music. She graduated from Rowan University in 2005 and thanks her children, who have encouraged her to make a difference in the world. E-mail her at lastrucke@gmail.com or www.lastrucke.com.

Christmastime reminds us to be grateful. **JC Sullivan's** prized possession is her passport. Having been to more than 100 countries, her goal is to see them all. Not financially rich, she barters, takes odd jobs, and sells inspirational prose. Learn more at www.backpackingpoet.com.

E. Sutton has a Bachelor of Arts degree from the University of North Texas. Her hobbies are writing and art. She belongs to a small writers' group where the members help hone each other's craft. E-mail her at eas.paint@gmail.com.

Writing ever since getting her first rejection at age thirteen, **Nancy Sweetland** has published articles, juvenile poetry, stories, and picture and chapter books. She has published over eighty adult short stories, two romance novels and has won more than forty regional and national awards in short stories and poetry.

Donna Teti loves to write inspirational stories and poems that will lift a person's spirit. She has previously been published in the *Chicken Soup for the Soul* anthology, *Guideposts* magazine, and many compilation books. Enjoy more of Donna's inspirational stories and poems at donnateti.com or on Facebook at Twinpop Inspirations.

Elizabeth Laing Thompson, now the mother of four children, is a young adult novelist, inspirational speaker, laundry slayer, tantrum defeater, and giggle collector. When she is not elbow-deep in diapers and dishes, she writes for moms, for teens, and for her own sanity. Follow her at www.lizzylit.com.

Heather Thompson is a resident in obstetrics and gynecology in Canada. In her free time she enjoys skiing, cycling, hiking, and cooking. She is also passionate about travel and social justice. Heather hopes to work on overseas missions when she is finished with her residency. E-mail her at heather.t@shaw.ca.

Patti Ann Thompson is an award-winning freelance writer, motivational speaker and author of *Seeing God Through New Eyes*. She is a 2001 honors graduate of Emporia State University and currently serves the Community Bible Study organization in Kansas. Patti Ann resides with her husband, Larry, in Shawnee, KS.

Stacy Voss is the founder of Eyes of Your Heart Ministries (EyesOfYourHeart.com), which helps women "See Life Differently. Live Courageously." She loves to run, chase her two young kids and all things chocolate (dark, please!). She is a passionate speaker for women's events, luncheons and retreats. E-mail her at Stacy@eyesofyourheart.com.

Even as a young child, **Sally Walls** loved to write. She has a passion for encouragement and a heart for people. Other short stories she has written have been published in *Chicken Soup for the Soul: O Canada* and in *Chicken Soup for the Soul: Devotional Stories for Tough Times*.

Robert F. Walsh is a syndicated columnist and English teacher in Connecticut. He lives with his incredible wife Kristen, three puppies, and a rickety ten-speed without baseball cards in the spokes. You can read more at RobertFWalsh.net or follow him on Twitter at @ RobertFWalsh.

After many years of being a "struggling" actor in Los Angeles, **Alan Zacher** came back home to St. Louis, MO to write. He has had several stories published at Kalikion, and in 2012 his murder/mystery novel, *I'm No P.I.*, was published by Post Mortem Press.

Sheri Zeck enjoys writing creative nonfiction stories that encourage, inspire and entertain others. She lives in Milan, IL, with her husband and three daughters. She has contributed stories to the *Chicken Soup for the Soul* series, *Guideposts*, *Farm & Ranch Living* and various other magazines. Visit her website at www.sherizeck.com.

Meet Our Authors

Jack Canfield is the co-creator of the *Chicken Soup for the Soul* series, which *Time* magazine has called "the publishing phenomenon of the decade." Jack is also the coauthor of many other bestselling books.

Jack is the CEO of the Canfield Training Group in Santa Barbara, California, and founder of the Foundation for Self-Esteem in Culver City, California. He has conducted intensive personal and professional development seminars on the principles of success for more than a million people in 23 countries, has spoken to hundreds of thousands of people at more than 1,000 corporations, universities, professional conferences and conventions, and has been seen by millions more on national television shows.

Jack has received many awards and honors, including three honorary doctorates and a Guinness World Records Certificate for having seven books from the *Chicken Soup for the Soul* series appearing on the New York Times bestseller list on May 24, 1998.

You can reach Jack at www.jackcanfield.com.

Mark Victor Hansen is the co-founder of Chicken Soup for the Soul, along with Jack Canfield. He is a sought-after keynote speaker, bestselling author, and marketing maven. Mark's powerful messages of possibility, opportunity, and action have created powerful change in thousands of organizations and millions of individuals worldwide.

Mark is a prolific writer with many bestselling books in addition to the *Chicken Soup for the Soul* series. Mark has had a profound influence in the field of human potential through his library of audios, videos, and articles in the areas of big thinking, sales achievement, wealth building, publishing success, and personal and professional development. He is also the founder of the MEGA Seminar Series.

Mark has received numerous awards that honor his entrepreneurial spirit, philanthropic heart, and business acumen. He is a lifetime member of the Horatio Alger Association of Distinguished Americans.

You can reach Mark at www.markvictorhansen.com.

Amy Newmark has been Chicken Soup for the Soul's publisher, coauthor, and editor-in-chief for the last five years, after a 30-year career as a writer, speaker, financial analyst, and business executive in the worlds of finance and telecommunications. Amy is a *magna cum laude* graduate of Harvard College, where she majored in Portuguese, minored in French, and traveled extensively. She and her husband have four grown children.

After a long career writing books on telecommunications, voluminous financial reports, business plans, and corporate press releases, Chicken Soup for the Soul is a breath of fresh air for Amy. She has fallen in love with Chicken Soup for the Soul and its life-changing books, and really enjoys putting these books together for Chicken Soup for the Soul's wonderful readers. She has coauthored more than six dozen *Chicken Soup for the Soul* books and has edited another three dozen.

You can reach Amy with any questions or comments through webmaster@chickensoupforthesoul.com and you can follow her on Twitter @amynewmark or @chickensoupsoul.

Thank You

We want to say a big thank you to everyone who submitted a story for this book. We know that you poured your hearts and souls into the thousands of stories that you shared with us. We appreciate your willingness to open up your lives to other Chicken Soup for the Soul readers and share your own experiences.

Working on this book in the heat of summer was a real treat. We even had Christmas music playing in our office while we read the stories. Our editor Madeline Clapps and I had a great time putting together this collection. We could only choose a small percentage of the stories that were submitted, but every single one was read and even the ones that do not appear in the book had an influence on us and on the final manuscript.

We also want to thank our assistant publisher D'ette Corona for working with all the contributors and for proofreading the manuscript. Editors Kristiana Pastir and Barbara LoMonaco did their normal magic on pre-production and proofreading. Finally, we owe a very special thanks to our creative director and book producer, Brian Taylor at Pneuma Books, for his brilliant vision for our covers and interiors.

~Amy Newmark

Improving Your
Life Every Day

R eal people sharing real stories—for twenty years. Now, Chicken Soup for the Soul has gone beyond the bookstore to become a world leader in life improvement. Through books, movies, DVDs, online resources and other partnerships, we bring hope, courage, inspiration and love to hundreds of millions of people around the world. Chicken Soup for the Soul's writers and readers belong to a one-of-a-kind global community, sharing advice, support, guidance, comfort, and knowledge.

Chicken Soup for the Soul stories have been translated into more than forty languages and can be found in more than one hundred countries. Every day, millions of people experience a Chicken Soup for the Soul story in a book, magazine, newspaper or online. As we share our life experiences through these stories, we offer hope, comfort and inspiration to one another. The stories travel from person to person, and from country to country, helping to improve lives everywhere.

Share with Us

We all have had Chicken Soup for the Soul moments in our lives. If you would like to share your story or poem with millions of people around the world, go to chickensoup.com and click on "Submit Your Story." You may be able to help another reader, and become a published author at the same time. Some of our past contributors have launched writing and speaking careers from the publication of their stories in our books!

Our submission volume has been increasing steadily—the quality and quantity of your submissions has been fabulous. We only accept story submissions via our website. They are no longer accepted via mail or fax.

To contact us regarding other matters, please send us an e-mail through webmaster@chickensoupforthesoul.com, or fax or write us at:

Chicken Soup for the Soul
P.O. Box 700
Cos Cob, CT 06807-0700
Fax: 203-861-7194

One more note from your friends at Chicken Soup for the Soul: Occasionally, we receive an unsolicited book manuscript from one of our readers, and we would like to respectfully inform you that we do not accept unsolicited manuscripts and we must discard the ones that appear.

Share the magic and joy of Christmas. You'll love these heartwarming, inspirational, and fun stories of Christmas miracles, family reunions, charity, the wonder of children, the joy of giving, and family and religious traditions.

978-1-61159-901-5

Holiday

Christmas is a magical time of year—a time of family, friends, and traditions. And all the joys, blessings, and excitement of the season are captured in this book of 101 new holiday stories. With stories about finding the perfect Christmas tree, being with family, and seeing the wonder in a child's eyes, this book will delight every reader, from the young to the young at heart, and bring back the magic of the holiday season. "Santa-safe" for kids!

978-1-935096-54-2

Cheer!

Everyone loves Christmas and the holiday season. We reunite scattered family members, watch the wonder in a child's eyes, and feel the joy of giving gifts. The rituals of the holiday season give a rhythm to the years and create a foundation for our lives, as we gather with family, with our communities at church, at school, and even at the mall, to share the special spirit of the season, brightening those long winter days. "Santa-safe" for kids!

978-1-935096-15-3

Holiday